# THE WORD IN THE DESERT

# THE WORD IN THE DESERT

## Anglican and Roman Catholic Reactions to Liturgical Reform

**Barry Spurr**

The Lutterworth Press
Cambridge

The Lutterworth Press
P.O. Box 60
Cambridge
CB1 2NT

British Library Cataloguing in Publication Data:
A catalogue record is available from the British Library.

ISBN 0 7188 2921 2



Printed in Great Britain by
Redwood Books

# CONTENTS

Words strain,
Crack and sometimes break, under the burden,
Under the tension, slip, slide, perish,
Decay with imprecision, will not stay in place,
Will not stay still. Shrieking voices
Scolding, mocking, or merely chattering,
Always assail them. The Word in the desert
Is most attacked by voices of temptation,
The crying shadow of the funeral dance,
The loud lament of the disconsolate chimera.

T.S. Eliot, 'Burnt Norton', V,
*Four Quartets*

# PREFACE AND ACKNOWLEDGMENTS

From its earliest days, the Christian community has gathered to celebrate the resurrection of Jesus Christ in services of prayer and praise and thanksgiving. This action has always been regarded as an essential activity. Accordingly, it is known as the 'liturgy' – from the Greek for 'people' and 'work'. Although we have no documentary knowledge of the earliest forms of Christian communal prayer, later evidence – such as the first *Apology* and *Dialogue* of Justin Martyr from the second century, and the *Apostolic Tradition* of Hippolytus from the early third – shows that regular forms of words and established procedures of ceremonial characterised the worship of the Christians at Rome from the beginning. This is scarcely surprising. It is in the nature of all community life, sacred or secular, that it should be ordered. Even those Christian Churches which have prided themselves on their freedom from formal liturgical constraints inevitably become accustomed to set forms of spontaneity. We are creatures of habit. And while the history of liturgical observance through the twenty centuries of Christianity reveals a rich diversity, it is also united by fidelity to customs of verbal utterance in which such petitions as the Lord's Prayer are common elements.

While the words of worship, like those of Scripture, have been – and continue to be – subject to divergent interpretations and are uttered in a wide variety of liturgical contexts, most Christians have agreed that the language of prayer, like biblical language, is infused with sacredness. Both in services of word and sacrament, liturgical speech is sanctified by association. The meticulous Tridentine priest, careful to enunciate exactly the Latin formula of consecration over the host to effect the presence of Christ, the quietly kneeling Anglican parishioner divinely warmed by the comfortable words of Cranmer, the enthusiastic Wesleyan preacher whose fervent intonation strikes the hearts of his listeners to awaken them to new life in the Lord, and the ecstatic modern charismatic whose glossolalia is the expression of possession by the Holy Spirit, all testify to the transcendent power of sacred language. And these numinous qualities coexist with the didactic, doctrinal component of liturgy. Worship, properly ordered, is both instructive and inspirational.

The two most influential compendia of public liturgy in the history of Western Christendom have been the Roman Catholic Tridentine Missal and the Anglican Book of Common Prayer. Both demonstrate the ecclesiastical determination for liturgical and theological order. Prior to the Council of Trent, although the Roman rite was ubiquitous in Europe, there were so many variations in the celebration of the mass that it could be said to be different in every diocese. Such variableness was intolerable to the absolutist spirit of the Counter-Reformation. So the Tridentine fathers prepared a new Missal, completed in 1570, to be used (as decreed in the bull *Quo Primum Tempore*) in all churches for all time. Earlier in the same century, in England, Thomas Cranmer, Archbishop of Canterbury, embodied his interpretation of the teaching of the continental Reformation in the first and second Books of Common Prayer in 1549 and 1552, setting in motion a liturgical process which, through the national and ecclesiastical vicissitudes of the next hundred years, culminated in the definitive service book of the Church of England – the Book of Common Prayer, 1662.

After several centuries in service, these books are now disappearing from use. After the Second Vatican Council ended in 1965, the Tridentine rite was modified and the use of English in place of Latin permitted. The new order of mass, promulgated in the 1969 *Missale Romanum*, replaced the Tridentine rite in 1969 and 1970, and though published in Latin, was immediately celebrated in English in most churches in English-speaking countries. In the same period, Anglican experimentation with Prayer Book revision led to the production of several new service books in the Church of England and the other provinces of the Anglican Communion. The English *Alternative Service Book*, for example, appeared in 1980 after a series of experimental rites had been tested over the years.

Today, a generation of Roman Catholics and Anglicans has grown up unfamiliar with the traditional liturgical language of their Churches, while, among the younger clergy, the Tridentine Missal and the Book of Common Prayer are known, if at all, only as subjects of historical study at seminary and theological college. Although the Vatican, in the conservative spirit of the pontificate of John Paul II, gave permission for the traditional mass to be celebrated in strictly controlled circumstances where a pronounced pastoral need was recognised by the bishop, and although the Book of Common Prayer is still heard in many Anglican parish churches and cathedrals – especially in England, but, even there, most usually in combination with modern services and at unpopular times as a temporary concession to the elderly – it seems likely that both books will have disappeared from all but rare use by the end of the century.

This outcome will be far from an expression of the unanimous consent of worshippers. The fundamental changes in Western liturgical celebration over the last twenty-five years – of which the translation of the Roman rite into the vernacular tongues and the replacement of the Cranmerian idiom with services in modern English are the most striking – have been challenged by vociferous protest, especially from the laity, and accompanied by an acceleration of the declining church attendance they were supposed to assist in arresting.

This most recent chapter of the liturgical movement, which has excited a passionate and protracted debate in the Church of Rome and in Anglicanism, engendering at least as much unedifying uncharitableness as sweetness and light, provides instructive insights into the Church of our day. Further, in purporting to enshrine cherished contemporary values – egalitarianism rather than authoritarianism, individuality rather than tradition, relevance instead of detachment and, most recently, feminism – it is sociologically illuminating. But, most momentously, modern liturgical revision is seen by its critics as the ecclesiastical linguistic expression of the humanistic process, initiated at the Renaissance and achieving apotheosis in the twentieth century, 'to naturalise the supernatural [as M.H. Abrams has put it] and humanise the divine'.[1] The influence of the triumph of the scientific and technological interpretation of life and of the post-medieval disenchantment of the world on the liturgy, conservatives argue, both expresses and abets a secularised Christianity.

Secularisation had been strenuously resisted by the Church through the centuries prior to the twentieth – as the combative demeanour of Vatican I strikingly demonstrated: 'if anyone say that the doctrines of the Church can ever receive a sense in accordance with the progress of science, other than that sense which the Church has understood and still understands, let him be anathema'. But a century later, when the terrestrial trinity of materialism, humanism and scientism had attained its apogee in the West, the response of progressive thought in Christendom was for open-minded engagement with the world's priorities rather than outright denunciation. The not unreasonable principle was promoted that if the Church's membership were to be retained and fortified, and the unbaptised majority successfully evangelised, then the powerful seductions of secular culture could not be simply ignored or repudiated, but had to be understood and – to a degree – accommodated. Bishop John

[1] Quoted by Stephen Prickett, *Words and 'The Word'* (Cambridge, 1986), 95.

Robinson's *Honest to God*, published in 1963, is a notable expression of this viewpoint.

As the leaders of the Churches were slowly persuaded by the sociologists and some theologians of the necessity of relevance to the modern world, they began to direct liturgiologists to replace outmoded ceremonial forms and language (which, it had formerly been argued, were expressive of transcendental timelessness by virtue of their antique character) with liturgies affirming the eternal verities of the faith in rituals and through linguistic expression redolent of the present and embodying contemporary theological thought. The preservation of the supernatural, in these circumstances, from contamination by the mutabilities of the moment, while persuasive in theory, has, however, proved to be profoundly problematic in practice.

It is the purpose of this study to trace the history of this liturgical phenomenon, to describe its impact on modern Christianity, and to analyse its conservative critique. My main emphasis is on the experience of the Anglican Church. However – as has already been suggested – the Anglican liturgical revolution cannot be considered without regard to similar developments in Roman Catholicism which have often influenced Anglican reforms. Moreover, conservative Catholic reaction to 'renewal' – usually called by the Italian name, *aggiornamento* – provides an informative contrast with its Anglican counterpart. Further, I have examined characteristics of the conservative reaction in both the 'old world' and the new to indicate its pervasiveness. As a time-frame, I have taken the thirty-three years from the summoning, by Pope John XXIII, of the Second Vatican Council, in 1962, to the present. In the latter half of this period the battles have become most dramatic, leading to significant schism in both Churches.

There is no shortage of material – from a host of monographs and of articles, in a variety of journals which have sprung up in response to liturgical and doctrinal reform, to book-length critiques. As early as 1983, Professor David Martin estimated that the bibliography of writing in favour of the preservation of the Book of Common Prayer alone would fill 200 pages.[2] To have dealt with all of this would have required a gargantuan study. I have aimed to be representative rather than exhaustive.

This work is the fruit of some twenty years' personal observation of liturgical change in the Anglican Church of Australia, and of ten years' research for several public addresses and articles presented to various societies and publications concerned with the liturgical

2 'An Open Letter to Our Patron', *Faith and Worship*, Winter 1983, 17.

movement. I owe thanks to them all for encouraging me to order my thoughts on this subject.

I am also indebted to those who have answered my questions, provided me with information or read drafts of chapters. In particular I would thank the Revd Father Edward Black, Superior of the Society of Saint Pius X (England); Mrs Susan Cooke, Secretary of the Latin Mass Society (England); the Revd John Cowburn, SJ; Mr Christopher Francis, Secretary of the Association for Latin Liturgy (England); Mr Martin Lynch, former Secretary of the Association for Latin Liturgy; the Very Revd Canon John McHugh; Professor Anthony Lo Bello, Chairman of the Latin Liturgy Association (USA); the Very Revd Michael Napier, Provost of the Oratory; the Revd Richard Price; the Revd Christopher Willcock, SJ; Miss Clara Zilahi of Downham Market, Norfolk; the Revd Canon Lawrence Bartlett, sometime Secretary of the Australian Liturgical Commission; the Revd John Beer; Mrs Elaine Bishop, of Women against the Ordination of Women (England); the Revd Dr John Bunyan, Rector of Chester Hill (Australia); the Revd Dr Evan Burge, Warden of Trinity College, University of Melbourne; Mrs Gordon A.T. Heath, Chairman of the International Council for the Apostolic Faith (USA); the Revd Dr Peter Jensen, Principal of Moore Theological College, Sydney; the late Revd Dr William Jobling of the Department of Religious Studies, University of Sydney; Mr C.A. Anthony Kilmister, Chairman of the Prayer Book Society (England); Emeritus Professor the Revd David Martin; the Rt Revd L.E.W. Renfrey; the Revd David Robarts; the Rt Revd Dr Geoffrey Rowell, sometime Fellow and Chaplain of Keble College, Oxford; the Revd Dr Charles Sherlock of the Australian Liturgical Commission; the Rt Hon the Lord Sudeley, patron of the Prayer Book Society (England); Mrs Margot Thompson and Mrs R.J.R. Trefusis of the Prayer Book Society (England); the Revd R.T.A. Waddell, OGS; Professor G.A. Wilkes, Challis Professor of English Literature in the University of Sydney, and Dr L.D. Wheeler of the Prayer Book Society (New South Wales).

Colleen Frith, Joan Harriss, Annette Krausmann, Rosemary Raiche and Patricia Ricketts transferred my manuscript onto the word processor with admirable skill. I thank them all.

# 1
# THE LITURGICAL MOVEMENT

## I

Liturgical change is not merely a modern phenomenon. A survey of the history of Christianity reveals that the liturgy is constantly evolving. Certainly there have been protracted periods of stability in the use of particular rites, but there are equally remarkable epochs of change, such as the continuous development of the Divine Office through the Middle Ages to the Renaissance. Even where liturgical changelessness is cherished as symbolic of eternal truth and ecclesiastical uniformity, as in the case of the Tridentine mass, different styles of celebration – in the use of music, for example, and the type of music used – differentiate century from century in worshipping custom.

A comparison of the pattern and character of Sunday service in a representative Anglican parish church in England at the beginning of the nineteenth century with those of the same church a century later shows how markedly liturgical celebration can vary even though the same service book remains in use. In *One Church, One Lord* – a title not devoid of irony – in which John Whale traces the history of St Mary's Church at Barnes, London, it is shown that although the Book of Common Prayer was the constant standard of worship and doctrine from the Restoration to the present century, it was subject to an abundance of liturgical and doctrinal interpretations as rectors imposed their churchmanship on the parish and broader developments in worshipping style made their mark. With regard to music, Whale notes that 'at the beginning of the nineteenth century most Anglicans sang no hymns at all. . . . By the end of the century they were singing thousands.'[1] This legacy of Methodism and of the subsequent Evangelical revival within the Church of England significantly altered the atmosphere of worship, introducing a congregational enthusiasm upon which the eighteenth century would have frowned.

In the same period, as a result of the Catholic movement within Anglicanism, the preference for the offices of Mattins and Evensong

[1] p.[130].

over Holy Communion began to be reversed – a process which has culminated, in our day, in the virtual disappearance of the offices from parish worship. The Tractarian theologians had rediscovered sacramentalism, and the ritualists who succeeded them expressed their teachings ceremonially. This liturgical development eventually extended even to the most conservative Evangelicals, who were gradually to vary their rule of quarterly celebrations of Holy Communion to the now customary weekly eucharist, while retaining the memorialism of Reformation doctrine.

These changes occurred at the same time as significant and kindred stirrings in the liturgical life of Roman Catholicism. In the 1830s, the very decade of the beginning of the Oxford Movement, the newly created abbot of the French Benedictine community at Solesmes, Dom Prosper Guéranger, set about the restoration of the celebration of the Roman ritual on medieval principles, communicating his research and practice to the wider Church through his influential journal *L'Année Liturgique*. Like the Anglo-Catholics who had been inspired by the Oxford apostles, Dom Prosper was a Romantic who looked back wistfully to the ages of faith. Contradictory as it may seem, these remote beginnings of the modern liturgical movement belong to the story of the Gothic revival. One of the prominent achievements of Solesmes was the recovery of Gregorian chant, which had been increasingly neglected after the rise of polyphony in the Renaissance, the operatic styles of the eighteenth century and the sentimental decadence of much Romantic liturgical music. Yet, today, the plainsong revived in the nineteenth century has again fallen into disuse in favour of contemporary settings of an aesthetic poverty admitted by all but the most zealous proponents of the modern rites (see Chapter 6).

Critics of liturgical innovation in our time often speak and write as though the prevalence of the Missal and the Prayer Book from the sixteenth century to the 1960s guaranteed the immutability of the worship of Rome and Canterbury through that long period. Nothing could be further from the truth. Nonetheless, the liturgical changes of the twentieth century, of which the disposal of these books is the fundamental feature, are the most thoroughgoing in the modern history of the Church and have occurred, like so many of the revolutions of modern life, with unprecedented rapidity.

## II

At the beginning of the twentieth century there was widespread clerical impatience with both the Roman Catholic and the Anglican liturgies, in spite (or because) of the advances of the liturgical movement. The focus of Roman Catholic dissatisfaction was lay inertia. The medieval view of the liturgy as a sacerdotal act performed by the priest on behalf of the people – who were left to pursue their own devotions, such as the rosary – had scarcely been discredited by the medievalising Abbot Guéranger. It was a conception, many were coming to believe, that was theologically erroneous and pastorally unhelpful.

Certainly it was alien to the zeitgeist. This was the great age of humanitarianism, and while the clerical character of the Roman Church had been further emphasised by the definition of papal infallibility in 1870, the seminal encyclical of Leo XIII, *Rerum Novarum* (1891), revealed a new concern for the worldly well-being, in addition to the divine vocation, of the faithful. Then, at Malines in 1909, a liturgical conference was held – now seen as a landmark in the modern reform of the liturgy – where theological analysis was linked with pastoral concern as the delegates expounded their persuasive understanding of the eucharist as 'the common action of the people of the church, an action which involved them all in a sharing in the saving work of Christ in and for the world'.[2] However, their call for the translation of the mass out of Latin into the vernacular tongues with the object of further realising the laity's active and knowledgeable participation in worship fell on deaf ears. In this period also, Pius X was vocal in urging the people's involvement in their mass, advocating, for example, their more frequent communion. Seeds had been sown in the early decades of the new century which would bear fruit, fifty years later, in the resolutions of the Second Vatican Council and in the post-conciliar *aggiornamento*.

The liturgical disquiet of *fin de siècle* Anglicanism was of a different kind. Many of the laity of that Church had already benefited from its liturgical revival. This was true, for example, of the multitude of formerly unchurched working people who came into the care of those Anglo-Catholic clergy who had taken their pastoral and liturgical zeal into the spiritual wastelands of the English industrial parishes. Priests like Charles Lowder of St Peter's, London Docks, combined an heroic effort to improve the mortal lot of their people with a conviction of the necessity for the spiritual nourishment of a beautiful liturgy in the lives of those whose working and living conditions presented vistas of unrelieved squalor and disease.[3]

But their liturgical innovations – eucharistic vestments, altar lights, and so forth – allegedly contravened the law of the Church, while their manner of celebrating the eucharist (in the eastward position, with a 'mixed' chalice, and so on) either contradicted the rubrics

2 H. Ellsworth Chandlee, 'The Liturgical Movement', in J.G. Davies (ed.) *A Dictionary of Liturgy and Worship*, 217.

3 See L.E. Ellsworth, *Charles Lowder and the Ritualist Movement*.

of the Prayer Book or introduced usages, usually of contemporary Roman Catholic origin, that it did not prescribe. While it was conceded that nobody followed the 1662 order *au pied de la lettre*, the Public Worship Regulation Act of 1874 was passed to curb the more eccentric – those seen as Romish – innovations. Everything about this legislation was unpropitious for its success. Erastian in genesis and implementation, it sought to punish precisely those clergy whose sanctity was acknowledged even by those who disagreed with their style of worship. When four priests were actually imprisoned for flouting it, the Act was doomed as martyrdom crowned its rejection. For the rest of the century liturgical anarchy prevailed.

In 1904, a Royal Commission on Ecclesiastical Discipline was established to inquire into the lawlessness of Anglican worship. In 1906 it reported, to nobody's surprise, that

> The law of public worship in the Church of England is too narrow for the religious life of the present generation. . . . It is important that the law should be reformed, that it should admit of reasonable elasticity. . . . Above all it is necessary that it should be obeyed.[4]

In other words, the Book of Common Prayer had to be revised.

The ritual controversies of those days had encouraged the research of several distinguished liturgical scholars, most notably Walter Frere and Percy Dearmer. So the times were right for work to begin on the new Prayer Book that was finally presented to Parliament for approval in 1927.

This book contained the 1662 services, with additional alternative orders which had been framed, using the Cranmerian style, after often bitter debates between the Evangelical, liberal and Anglo-Catholic parties – a protracted controversy arousing national interest on a scale almost impossible to credit today. But Parliament, stirred up by Protestant agitation to the effect that the new book would reintroduce popery into the Established Church – principally by allowing 'reservation' of the sacrament – twice refused to endorse it: in 1927 and again in 1928, to the satisfaction of both the Evangelicals and the Anglo-Catholics, the former wanting no change from 1662, which they regarded as a document of the Reformation, the latter judging the proposed alterations and deviations insufficiently Catholic. Nonetheless, '1928', as it came to be known, was published and widely used in the Anglican Communion for many years.[5]

4 In G.J. Cuming, *A History of Anglican Liturgy*, 2nd edn., 163.

5 Those who plead today for the retention of '1662' are often ridiculed by their modernising critics for confusing the sixteenth and seventeenth century compilation with '1928'. Certainly the services in the two books, particularly the Holy Communion, are different in substance and structure, but they possess unity of language. To this quality, at least, conservatives may validly refer as a common element of the two volumes.

The acrimony associated with the production of the revised Prayer Book, combined with the secular turmoil of the 1930s and the Second World War, discouraged the bishops from substantial liturgical change for a generation. Such developments as occurred, and their temper, are usefully indicated in the career and prolific writing of Eric Milner-White, Dean of King's College, Cambridge, and later of York (though his membership of the Liturgical Commission after the Second World War was an unhappy closing chapter to his life. Milner-White found himself increasingly out of sympathy with the Commission's plans and, in particular, its modernisation of liturgical language.)

In the 1950s and 1960s a combination of events, however, led to a series of revisions of Anglican liturgy which proved to be the most far-reaching since the Reformation.

The first of these was the provision, in 1950, of a liturgy for the Church of South India – a communion uniting Anglicans and non-episcopal bodies. Although ambiguously related to Anglicanism, its worship was mainly inspired by the Book of Common Prayer. But it drew as well on Protestant manuals and from ancient liturgies. Structurally, its eucharist expresses the influence of the most important Anglican liturgical study of the post-war period: *The Shape of the Liturgy*, by Dom Gregory Dix, which emphasised its classical arrangement. With this combination of diverse elements, the South Indian liturgy was the first ecumenical service and has been described as 'one of the most significant liturgical events of this century', marking 'the transition from the rites of the Prayer Book to the new liturgies we now have in Anglicanism', influencing 'almost every form of eucharistic revision that has taken place since its publication'.[6]

The other pertinent event, of course, was the Second Vatican Council, which began meeting in 1962. The Council's liturgical deliberations, often misrepresented today as a sudden disturbance of established custom, were, in fact, the culmination of several decades of liturgical scholarship and experiment.

## III

For Roman Catholicism, the inter-war period had seen the advent of the so-called Dialogue Mass, where the people were permitted to sing or say the Ordinary (such as the *Gloria* and *Credo*) in Latin with the priest. Then lectors were introduced to read the Proper of the mass (the scriptural and other material which varied with the calendar) in the vernacular, while the celebrant satisfied the Tridentine

[6] Alan Dunstan, 'The Eucharist in Anglicanism after 1662', in C. Jones, G. Wainwright and E. Yarnold (eds) *The Study of Liturgy*, 277.

rubrics and tradition by reciting them in Latin. Some radical clergy, such as Louis Evely, Principal of Cardinal Mercier College near Brussels, went even further: he was celebrating entirely in French and from the westward position in the early 1950s.[7] Generally there was increasing desire for fundamental change in the Roman Catholic liturgy, not merely alterations to the Tridentine rite, and an almost Anglican degree of diversity developed as different ideas were tested, especially by progressive clergy in continental Europe and the United States. As at Trent, the Roman authorities determined to impose order on this burgeoning diversity, while they recognised the necessity for reform. In 1947, Pius XII had issued the first papal encyclical to be devoted wholly to the discussion of the Church's worship (*Mediator Dei et Hominum*). Its theory was given practical expression in the revision of the Holy Week observance in 1955 which, by restoring the principal services to the evening hours, enabled the fuller involvement of the laity in the celebration of the Paschal mystery. Here, as throughout these years, the leitmotif of liturgical revision was a pastoral concern for the enhancement of the people's understanding of worship.

This preoccupation achieved its most significant and influential recognition in 1963, at Vatican II, in the Constitution on the Sacred Liturgy. It is most important to note, however, that this decree envisages the perpetuation of Latin as the mode of public prayer:

> The use of the Latin language . . . is to be preserved in the Latin rites.[8]

Certainly, the Constitution foresees the wider application of the vernacular in worship – 'especially in readings, directives and some prayers and chants'[9] – but, as legislation, it is conservative rather than innovative. By preserving Latin while increasing the opportunities for the use of the vernacular, the document envisages only extensions of the linguistic duality that had obtained for generations and which is evident in missals in use much earlier in the century. In a continental layman's missal published in 1921, *'en harmonie avec les récents décrets pontificaux'*, parallel translations are given in French of the entire Latin texts of the Ordinary and Proper of the mass, of the nuptial and requiem masses, along with other devotions such as the Stations of the Cross.[10] The same custom was followed in missals printed for the English-speaking laity.[11] Long before Vatican II, liter-

[7] Neville Cryer, *Louis Evely: Once a Priest*, 37.

[8] 'The Constitution on the Sacred Liturgy', in A. Flannery (ed.) *Vatican Council II: The Conciliar and Post Conciliar Documents*, 13. Hereafter cited as *'Documents'*.

[9] *ibid.*

[10] *Missel des Saints Évangiles.*

[11] See, for example, *The Layman's Missal and Prayer Book.*

ate people were well aware of what was being said at the altar, they heard the epistle and gospel in the vernacular, and they had a measure of spoken participation. Their devotional exercises outside mass were normally in their own tongue – a vernacular, nonetheless, of a stylised religiose kind (as in the English translation of the popular *Salve Regina,* also widely-known in Latin: 'Hail, holy Queen . . .') – and they participated in such services as the now obsolete Benediction 'with great fervour'.[12] So when a typical parish in the Australian city of Melbourne inaugurated a novena to Our Lady of Perpetual Succour in 1960,

> the first night drew a congregation of more than six hundred. In three weeks numbers were up to eight hundred. Friday night, 'novena night', rapidly became a parish high point, attracting families with young children and teenagers about to begin the weekend's social life. But at the end of 1969 the novena was stopped because of lack of support.[13]

It is as erroneous to suggest that Roman Catholic congregations were in linguistic ignorance before the Council as it is to argue that its principal liturgical achievement (or disgrace) was to dispose of Latin as the primary language of worship. The triumph of the vernacular and the annihilation of Latin belong to the decade *after* Vatican II as consequences of 'representations by hierarchies from all over the world'.[14] Indeed, it is more than likely that such post-conciliar developments were not only not intended but would not have been approved by the fathers of the Council itself, as one of them has testified:

> the bishops were under the impression that the liturgy had been fully discussed. In retrospect it is clear that they were given the opportunity of discussing only general principles. Subsequent changes were more radical than those intended by Pope John and the bishops who passed the decree on the liturgy. His sermon at the end of the first session shows that Pope John did not suspect what was being planned by the liturgical experts.[15]

In the several 'instructions' issued after the liturgical Constitution, the gradual acceptance of fully vernacular liturgies may be traced. Coexisting with this, however, is a strain of apprehensiveness on the part of the authorities about the complete disappearance of Latin from worship – not only the Latin of the Tridentine mass, which was

[12] John Ainslie, 'English Liturgical Music before Vatican II', in J.D. Crichton, H.E. Winstone and J.R. Ainslie (eds) *English Catholic Worship*, 48.

[13] Edmund Campion, *Australian Catholics*, 213.

[14] *Documents*, 39.

[15] Cardinal John Heenan, *A Crown of Thorns*, in Michael Davies, 'Changes in the Mass' (privately published monograph), 1.

largely superseded by the vernacular, in stages, from 1964, but that of the *Novus Ordo Missae* as well. In the instruction on liturgical music of 1967, for example, 'pastors of souls' are charged

> to take care that besides the vernacular 'the faithful may be able to say or sing together in Latin those parts of the Ordinary of the mass which pertains to them' [quoting here from the Constitution on the Liturgy].

Recognising that the disappearance of a Latin text would entail the neglect of the great music written to accompany it, the instruction further recommends that 'certain churches, above all in large cities' should preserve at least one Sunday mass in Latin, with the Gregorian chant.[16]

But the most interesting post-conciliar liturgical document is the third instruction on the Constitution, issued in 1970. Repudiating various liturgical novelties introduced during the 1960s, it also expresses considerable reservations about the literary quality of the vernacular texts:

> It would be better not to hurry through the work of translation. With the help of many experts, not only theologians and liturgists, but also writers and poets, the vernacular liturgical texts will be works of real literary merit and of enduring quality, whose harmony of style and expression will reflect the deeper riches of their content.[17]

Unfortunately, the translation of the Roman Missal into English had already been completed before these cautionary directions were issued.

In 1974, the 'Note on the Obligation to use the new Roman Missal' seemed to sound the death-knell of the Tridentine mass, permitting its use only in private by priests 'who, on account of advanced years or infirm health, find it difficult to use the new Order of the Roman Missal or the Mass Lectionary'.[18]

A principal purpose of the reforms – in particular, of vernacularisation – was to focus each parish on its intelligible, communal celebration of the eucharist. Yet the Roman Catholicism emerging from the 'fortress Church' of pre-conciliar days into a pluralistic body – from 'collective-expressive' to 'individual-expressive' – was patient both of individualism and a culture of change. Indeed the desire for, and expectation of, ongoing renewal may have rendered the inevitability of the developing predictability of the new mass insufficiently stimulating for many who had come to expect innovation and novelty as components of their Christian worship.

16 *Documents*, 92-3.
17 *Documents*, 220.
18 *Documents*, 281.

'Paraliturgies' could cater for these expectations. They might not be held in a church or chapel – preferably not, indeed, so that freedom of expression would not be inhibited – and there might not be a priest in charge, nor set prayers or gestures, as in this prayer group's worship organised in Australia in 1972 by the Catholic Enquiry Centre:

> The meeting started without any formality at all. . . . The silence was broken by someone reading a passage from one of St Paul's epistles. Another prayed out loud. . . . It was quite spontaneous, obviously unprepared. The words were faltering and completely unemotional, but there was an obvious deep sincerity in them.[19]

Such style of worship could be assimilated to the charismatic movement in post-conciliar Roman Catholicism, with its varying degrees of detachment from formal liturgical worship, as traditionally defined. But even within the mass, experiment seemingly knew no bounds:

> Some Passionist Fathers, during their Missions, have produced a puppet monkey for Children's Masses which is worn throughout the mass . . . by the celebrant. At specific moments children have been invited to call out 'Bananas'. . . . In 1984 came further creative liturgies at a 'peace and justice' live-in seminar in Adelaide. All masses held throughout the week were conducted in the common room rather than in the Chapel. The rubrics were changed and Tip Top sliced bread was used for the eucharist. The 'altar' consisted of two desk drawers on top of one another, and the priest did not wear any vestments until some commented and he wore a stole as a 'concession'. . . . At the final mass, someone chose John Lennon's *Imagine* as the Entrance Hymn, with the words provided on the overhead projector:
>
> > 'Imagine there's no Heaven, It isn't very hard to try,
> > No Hell below us, Above us only sky'.[20]

For the vast majority of parishes, however, where neither charismatic worship nor bizarre experimentation has been pursued, there is the burgeoning problem that the no longer 'new' liturgy has become so settled in its conduct and circumstances, for both priest and people, that the enlivening spirit of renewal appears to be as absent from the eucharistic celebration as it was from the pre-conciliar liturgies, but with the added disadvantage that the regularly proclaimed expectation of renewal is persistently disappointed.

Addressing the 'unfinished agenda' of the liturgy, Archbishop

19 Quoted in Campion, *Australian Catholics,* 215.

20 Michael Gilchrist, *Rome or the Bush,* 49-50.

Rembert Weakland, OSB, of Milwaukee, recognises 'a discontent among our faithful with regard to liturgical renewal', deriving from the expectations of a secular civilisation attuned to rapid change and instant gratification, the spirit of which the Church had, to a degree, accommodated in its search for 'relevant' worship. But liturgy, by its nature and through its requirement to foster a 'collective memory' of doctrine and devotion, is (he argues) the contradiction of these expectations.[21] So 'young people', for example, 'say that liturgy is boring', and they are correct. In a 'culture that lives by entertainment' and diversion, 'liturgy will always be boring', for, as Cardinal Joseph Ratzinger has contended,

> the liturgy is not a show, a spectacle. . . . The life of the liturgy does not consist in 'pleasant' surprises and attractive 'ideas' but in solemn repetitions. It cannot be an expression of what is current and transitory, for it expresses the mystery of the Holy.[22]

Archbishop Weakland argues further (and unfashionably) that liturgy is not a 'therapeutic exercise' to gratify a person's individual needs:

> This personalistic view of every aspect of life, how it affects me, what do I get out of it, pervades our culture. Liturgy is not a group therapy session.

Consequently, liturgy is not 'a form of intimacy':

> Liturgy joins all gathered into a unity, but that oneness is deeply spiritual and not the kind that would go under the rubric of intimacy in today's world.

Indeed, liturgy that is therapeutic in the sociologico-psychological senses may be inadequate theologically and spiritually: 'a worshipping community where [people] feel totally at home with like-minded people' may confuse 'liturgy' with 'comfort', whereas liturgy should both 'challenge us . . . to look at the darker side of our nature' and encourage us to enter the 'transcendent dimension' in an 'encounter with the all holy, the Sacred'.

This critique brings into focus the tensions between renewal and stability, individual expression and authority, self-fulfilment and submission, celebratory joy and the consciousness of sin, innovation and tradition, relevance to contemporaneity and an emphasis on perennial truths of the faith, accessible comprehensibility and transcendent mystery, plain speaking and numinous language in the liturgical debate in post-conciliar Roman Catholicism.

At its heart, however, is the dispute over the intentions for the liturgy of the decrees of the Vatican Council. Pope John Paul II, a

21 'Song of the Church: One with Christ, One with the World'.

22 The Ratzinger Report, in Gilchrist, *op.cit.*, 41.

proponent of reform at Vatican II, apologised, in *Dominicae Cenae*, to the faithful for the errors of the subsequent implementation of the liturgical decree:

> I would like to ask forgiveness – in my own name and in the name of all of you venerable and dear Brothers in the Episcopate – for everything which, for whatever reason, through whatever human weakness, impatience or negligence, and also through the at times partial, one-sided and erroneous application of the directives of the Second Vatican Council, may have caused scandal and disturbance concerning the doctrine and veneration due to this great Sacrament.[23]

## IV

The process of the disposal of Latin as the language of worship in Roman Catholicism is paralleled by the erosion of Cranmerian English and its derivatives (as used, for example, in '1928') in the experimental rites of the Anglican Communion.

In 1965, in the Church of England, the Prayer Book (Alternative and Other Services) Measure was enacted to give official status to the proposals of the 1920s. The subsequent revision, dismally known as 'Series 1', was essentially conservative, like the liturgical decree of the Vatican Council – affirming what had been accepted for decades. The revolutionary spirit of the early 1960s had yet to make its belated impact on the Churches. The eucharist of this Series is notable for its Catholic structure, incorporating such features of '1928' as the combination of the prayers of consecration and oblation which had been separated by the communion in '1662', but including such innovations as the removal of the *Gloria* from the end of the service, where it had remained in '1928', to its historic place at the beginning. This rite was mainly popular among Anglo-Catholics. Evangelicals, in these years, continued to use the Book of Common Prayer.

Linguistically, Series 1 preserves the Cranmerian style in its Catholic order, but new material in the prayer for 'the whole state of Christ's Church' anticipates more sweeping experiment with liturgical language in Series 2 and 3. In '1662' and '1928', this prayer of intercession has a formal integrity and – apart from the naming of the local bishop – a generality of reference. In Series 1, extempore interpolations are permitted to relate the general petitions to individuals and causes of special interest to the parish. For the first time, spoken contemporary language was officially encouraged within the context of a traditional prayer.

23 In Gilchrist, *op.cit.*, 51-2.

Series 2 was authorised for use from 1967. Its eucharist contains much new material, as in this appealing, scriptural affirmation at the fraction:

> The cup of blessing which we bless,
> is it not a sharing of the Blood of Christ?
> The bread which we break,
> is it not a sharing of the Body of Christ?
> We being many are one bread, one Body,
> for we all partake of the one bread.

Probably because of its poetical qualities – it is rhetorical and incantatory – this was judged to be inappropriate to modern liturgy and did not survive this Series. The Cranmerian style is still dominant in Series 2, though there are several revisions of it: one of the petitions of *Gloria in excelsis* has been omitted – the repetition of 'thou that takest away the sins of the world' – to restore the pre-Nicene form. The *Credo*, however, is still in the first person: 'I believe in one God.'

The intercessory prayer is again a significant focus of change. The prescribed text is now subordinate to the directions which only suggest the substance of extempore petitions. In time, these were often composed and offered by a member of the congregation in their personal versions of what they deemed linguistically and prayerfully appropriate:

> Almighty God, who hast promised to hear the prayers of those who ask in faith:
>
> Here he may pray for the Church throughout the world, and especially for the diocese and its bishop; for any particular need of the Church; and a short period of silence may be kept; after which he may say
>
> Lord, in thy mercy
> Hear our prayer.

Where no particular preparation had been made for this section of the service – as at an early celebration – priests could make it up as they went along or resort to using the directions themselves as the substance of their intercessions. The rubrics became their prayer.

The revision of Series 2 brought about a linguistic duality reminiscent of the use together of Latin and the vernacular in the Roman mass before Vatican II, which was emphasised by the growing popularity of the New English Bible for the lections and complicated further by the persistence of a hymnody largely based on nineteenth-century devotional language. This unsatisfactory confusion of tongues began to be resolved on the appearance of Series 3 in 1971, which provided a eucharist entirely in the ecclesiastical version of modern English and, more recently, by hymnals (such as *Hymns for Today's Church*) updated to achieve the desired monochromism of worshipping language (see Chapter 6).

A comparison of the conclusion to the prayers of intercession in these three experimental rites gives an indication of the intended evolution of liturgical language in the Church of England during these few years:

*Series 1*

Grant this, O Father, for Jesus Christ's sake, our only mediator and advocate; who liveth and reigneth with thee in the unity of the Holy Ghost, one God, world without end.
*Amen.*

*Series 2*

Grant these our prayers, O merciful Father, for the sake of thy Son, our Saviour Jesus Christ.
*Amen.*

*Series 3*

Accept these prayers for the sake of your Son, our Saviour Jesus Christ.
*Amen.*

The conclusions have become shorter, less wordy – that of Series 3 is less than half as long as that of Series 1 – the emotive ejaculation 'O' in Series 1 and 2 disappears in Series 3, which further marks the break with the Cranmerian idiom as 'thy' is superseded by 'your'.[24] There are changes in doctrinal emphasis, too. The description of Christ as 'our only mediator and advocate', pointedly included at the Reformation to exclude the mediation of saints, is justifiably omitted and the assertive Trinitarianism of Series 1 is progressively curtailed in Series 2 and 3. The modulation from 'Grant' to 'Accept' may include a changing perception of God – from a judge or king who condescends to grant a petition, to a father who lovingly accepts a gift.

These, however, were only experimental rites. It was not until 1980 that the Church of England finally issued the first authorised alternative to the Book of Common Prayer in England. Unprepossessingly entitled *The Alternative Service Book (1980)*, this bulky compendium had already been preceded, in other parts of the Anglican world, by such alternatives to '1662' and '1928' as *An Australian Prayer*

[24] The most controversial updating in Series 3 was of the Lord's Prayer:

> Our Father in heaven, holy be your name, your kingdom come, your will be done, on earth as in heaven. Give us today our daily bread. Forgive us our sins as we forgive those who sin against us. Do not bring us to the test but deliver us from evil. For the kingdom, the power and the glory are yours now and for ever. Amen.

These alterations to the vocabulary of the best-known and loved of prayers in English were too radical and failed to gain any currency, yet more recent proposals move in the radical direction of 'inclusive' language.

*Book*, published in 1978, and the new Episcopalian liturgy in the United States which appeared in 1979, and was followed by others such as the Canadian *Book of Alternative Services* (1985).

The proliferation of new Prayer Books in the Churches of the Anglican Communion, which will see, for example, two new books in Australia alone in 1994 and 1995 – *In Living Use* and *A Prayer Book for Australia* – with their distinctive characteristics, shows the mature independence of these Churches from the guidance and leadership of the English body; but it is also representative of the dismemberment of the Anglican Communion – evidenced doctrinally in the long-running controversy over the ordination of women to the priesthood and episcopate. As the links with England become less important, the attachment to historical Anglicanism and especially its 'Englishness' will continue to wane. As the Book of Common Prayer is the quintessential embodiment and expression of these ideas, influences and sentiments, its future as a liturgical and devotional manual is even bleaker outside England than within.

This revolution in liturgical identity is reflected in such a statement as this: 'the Liturgical Movement . . . has given Australian Anglicans their first Prayer Book'[25] – the implication being that the Book of Common Prayer, which they had used for 200 years, was never really their book, but something borrowed from or imposed by England and better discarded now that nothing but a vague, sentimental and minority attachment to the 'Old Country' and the old Church remains.

Commercially speaking, this is just as well. The promotion of the new prayer books, very costly to produce, is as much an expression of economic necessity as of a doctrinal and liturgical need. The reason that the New Zealand Church was slow to provide its own prayer book had nothing to do with theological or ritual conservatism. It was because of the financial risks associated with printing a new book for such a small market.

Yet those at the forefront of the promotion of the new liturgies persistently speak of the primacy of the Book of Common Prayer in Church life. The former Primate of the Australian Church and Archbishop of Brisbane, Sir John Grindrod, begins his introduction to *AAPB* by quoting its full title:

> This book is AN AUSTRALIAN PRAYER BOOK 1978 FOR USE TOGETHER WITH THE BOOK OF COMMON PRAYER 1662,

and asserts

> It is supplementary to *The Book of Common Prayer* and not a replacement of it.[26]

But this is exactly what it became in Australian Anglican worship, in

25 Reg Mills, *Anglicans*, 33.

26 *An Australian Prayer Book*, 7.

less than a decade. In England itself, a similar false prediction is made by the anonymous author of the Preface to the *ASB*:

> The Alternative Service Book (1980), as its name implies, is intended to supplement the Book of Common Prayer, not to supersede it.[27]

Yet, by 1994 only 2 per cent of baptisms in the Church of England were administered according to the Book of Common Prayer, while 75 per cent of clergy reported that they preferred to celebrate the communion using the modern rites.[28] However, both authors of the prefaces make the point that the Book of Common Prayer is (as Archbishop Grindrod puts it) 'our controlling standard of doctrine and worship'. That a prayer book that is no longer in significant liturgical use and which, moreover, has been substantially replaced by books of markedly different linguistic style and doctrinal emphasis and entailing a variety of ceremonial changes and innovations can continue to be regarded by a Church as its abiding worshipping authority is nonsense. Of course, some remnants of '1662' survive in *AAPB* and the *ASB*, but, as Geoffrey Cuming has recognised, 'they have taken on the character of family heirlooms in a not wholly congenial setting'.[29]

*The Alternative Service Book* and *An Australian Prayer Book* are not supplements to the Book of Common Prayer. They have either taken its place or they (or their successors) are bound to do so. At the Lambeth Conference in 1988, 'all of the main services – the opening and closing eucharists in Canterbury Cathedral and the eucharist at St Paul's . . . were modern language liturgies'.[30] The more recent publicity prior to the publication of the *New Zealand Prayer Book (1989)* is more honest – it 'will be the predominant book of worship for the New Zealand Anglican Church in the 1990s and beyond. It is not a new version of the Book of Common Prayer, which still remains authorised for use.'[31]

This book contains three collects which refer to God as 'Mother', a new alternative Lord's Prayer which reads

> Eternal Spirit, Earth-maker, pain-bearer, life-giver . . . Father and mother of us all. . . . Your commonwealth . . . come

– 'Kingdom' being both sexist and elitist – alterations to the Nicene Creed, such as the replacement of 'became man' with 'became fully

27 *The Alternative Service Book*, 9.

28 Ted Harrison, 'The God Club', *The Times Magazine*, 19 March 1994, 16.

29 Cuming, *op.cit.*, 230.

30 'Lambeth at Prayer', *The Christian Challenge*, December 1988, 30.

31 'First Ever Prayer Book for New Zealand, at Last', *Church Scene*, 9 December 1988 [1]. Note, again, the 'first ever' description in the title of this article – as though the Book of Common Prayer, used by New Zealanders for generations, was not really their book, but something foreign that had been borrowed or imposed.

human', and the desexing of the Psalter where male imagery, apart from 'Lord', is disallowed. Also, in the Psalter, 'Zion' and 'Israel' are avoided as offensive to Arabs, though retained when they have negative connotations, and in the Catechism God is again described as 'the Father and Mother of us all'. Assuredly, this is not an updated version of the Book of Common Prayer, but a radical new liturgy to be used in its place.

It can be plainly seen today that the Liturgical Movement which began in the nineteenth century with the enrichment of the appreciation of the Missal of 1570 and the Prayer Book of 1662 is, 150 years later, accomplishing their disposal.

## V

The response of conservative clergy and laity to the suppression of the Tridentine mass and the decline of a Latin liturgy in Roman Catholicism and the more gradual replacement of the Cranmerian Prayer Book with the new rites in modern English in the Anglican Communion is an extraordinarily fervid and sustained phenomenon of modern Christianity, which must be taken into consideration in any assessment of the success of the contemporary liturgical movement.

The changes in the language of worship itself have been central to the debate within the Anglican Church, while in Roman Catholicism argument about the replacement of Latin is usually bound up with larger questions of theology and ecclesiology. The most conservative Roman Catholics are less worried about the disappearance of Latin *per se* than of what they regard as the incursions of Protestant heresy into the new texts and the intrusion of modish doctrinal, ethical and sociological teachings into worship. It is said that if they had to choose, they would prefer the Tridentine mass celebrated in the vernacular to the *Novus Ordo* in Latin. Conservative Anglicans, on the contrary, would retain the sonorous diction of 1662, while many, if not most of them, incline to views and follow ceremonial customs arising from interpretations of the eucharistic sacrifice different from Cranmer's. More often than not, theirs has been a polemic based on aesthetics; however, recently there have been signs of wider concerns of a doctrinal character – as in the various Prayer Book Societies' contributions to the debate over the ordination of women.

Nonetheless, it is best to treat separately the conservative reaction to the liturgical movement in the two Communions.

# 2
# CONSERVATIVE REACTIONS
## The Roman Catholic Church

We must admit it is a masterstroke of Protestantism to have declared war on the sacred language. If it should ever succeed in destroying it, it would be well on the way to victory. Exposed to profane gaze, like a virgin who has been violated, from that moment on the Liturgy has lost much of its sacred character, and very soon people find that it is not worthwhile putting aside one's work or pleasure in order to go and listen to what is being said in the way one speaks in the marketplace.

Prosper Guéranger,
*Liturgical Institutions* (1840), I, iv.

One recent survey has put the decline in mass attendance in France at 66%; in Holland it is 54%; in the USA, 30%; in England and Wales (where the reform has been muted in comparison with most countries), 16% – in comparison with an annual increase before the 'renewal'.

Michael Davies,
*The Roman Rite Destroyed* (1978), 7.

This [*aggiornamento*] is truly the destruction of the ancient mass, of the more than thousand-year-old Roman Rite, the destruction of the entire world of faith that belonged to it and was the source of piety and of the courage to confess the Faith for centuries.

Klaus Gamber
*La Réforme Liturgique en question* (1974-8).

## I

There were significant signs of lay apprehension amongst Catholics about the prospect of ritual reform even before the Second Vatican Council had issued its Constitution on the Liturgy and established a commission for its implementation. The novelist Evelyn Waugh, who had become a Roman Catholic in 1930, was opposed to *aggiornamento* from the outset. In a letter to Daphne Acton, early in 1963, he pretended to accept the idea of a modernised ritual for those who 'like making a row in church', advocating that

> every parish might have one rowdy mass a Sunday for those who like it. But there should be silent ones for those who like quiet.

But he challenges the whole concept of vernacularisation:

> The word 'vernacular' is almost meaningless. If they intend to have versions of the liturgy in the everyday speech of everyone they will have to have hundreds of versions. In civilised countries Norway has 2 languages, Spain 3, Milanese can't understand Sicilian etc. When you get to Africa & Asia it is Babel.[1]

Indeed, the fragmentation by language of the sacrament of unity of the universal people of God in multilingual Western societies has been one of the results of vernacular worship, as Michael Gilchrist observes:

> ethnic minorities . . . must now travel about to special masses in Polish, Vietnamese, Latvian, Hungarian, Italian or Croatian, whereas in pre-*Novus Ordo* times they could worship together in their own parishes in a common Latin tongue.[2]

In 1964, Waugh went to Rome to observe Easter, 'to avoid the horrors of the English liturgy',[3] while in at the end of the year he presented the concerns of the laity about the liturgical innovations to Cardinal Heenan and received a reassuring response:

> He showed himself as deeply conservative and sympathetic to those of us who are scared of the new movement. He thinks that 'the intellectuals' are all against him. 'They regard us as mitred peasants', he said.[4]

Within a year, however, it was apparent that the hopes that Waugh had invested in the hierarchy were groundless:

> Cardinal Heenan has been double-faced in the matter. I had dinner with him *à deux* in which he confessed complete sym-

1 Mark Amory (ed.) *The Letters of Evelyn Waugh*, 602.

2 Gilchrist, *Rome or the Bush.*, 37.

3 To Ann Fleming, *op. cit.*, 618.

4 To Katherine Asquith, *Letters*, 624.

> pathy with the conservatives and, as I understood him, promised resistance to the innovations, which he is now pressing forward.[5]

Yet Heenan was responsible, in 1971, for obtaining an indult from Paul VI for the celebration of the old mass in England. Nonetheless, the charge of episcopal hypocrisy, of bishops defending the old amongst conservatives while promoting the new amongst the modernisers, is one of the leitmotifs of the literature critical of liturgical reform, both Roman Catholic and Anglican – and there is much evidence to support it.

So detrimental was *aggiornamento* to Waugh's faith that it might be cited as one of the causes of his death. In the last letters of his life, in 1966, Waugh comments that 'the buggering up of the Church is a deep sorrow to me and to all I know'.[6]

> 1965 was a bad year for me in a number of ways – dentistry, deaths of friends, the 'aggiornamento'. . . .[7]

Twelve days before he died, on Easter Day 1966, Waugh wrote to Lady Mosley:

> Easter used to mean so much to me. Before Pope John and his Council – they destroyed the beauty of the liturgy. I have not yet soaked myself in petrol and gone up in flames, but I now cling to the Faith doggedly without joy. Churchgoing is a pure duty parade. I shall not live to see it restored.[8]

In the next generation, Waugh's son Auberon has continued his father's acerbic criticism of modernisation – but more satirically, in the columns of *Private Eye* (see Appendix).

Then Alec Guinness, the actor, wrote critically in his autobiography of the language of the new mass:

> The banality and vulgarity of the translations which have ousted the sonorous Latin and little Greek are of a supermarket quality. . . . Hand-shaking and embarrassed smiles or quirks have replaced the older courtesies; kneeling is out, queuing is in, and the general tone is rather like a BBC broadcast for tiny tots.[9]

Malcolm Muggeridge observed that 'the modernists are destroying the Roman Catholic Church'.[10]

It was not only the conservative laity of literary sensitivity, however, who were opposed to the early manifestations of liturgical re-

5 Diary for Easter, 1965, *ibid*, 624, n.2.
6 To Nancy Mitford, *ibid*, 633.
7 To Graham Greene, *ibid*, 635.
8 To Diana Mosley, *ibid*, 639.
9 'Blessings in Disguise', in Gilchrist, *op.cit.*, 59.
10 Back cover blurb for Gilchrist, *op.cit.*

form. A trenchant indictment of the theology and liturgy of the post-conciliar Church was made in 1968 by the distinguished Catholic liturgical and patristic scholar, the Oratorian Louis Bouyer.

In *La Décomposition du Catholicisme*, Bouyer interprets liturgical revision as an expression of fundamental doctrinal change. More subtle (and correct) than Waugh, he draws a distinction between the principles the Council espoused – such as collegiality – and the practical results of its reforms:

> today 'collegiality' seems merely a synonym for anarchy and, incredibly, for individualism.[11]

His presentation of the prevalence of subjectivity is at the heart of Bouyer's thesis. Individualism, he argues, contradicts and undermines respect for tradition and authority, the hallmarks of the Catholic faith which had been liturgically embodied in the historicity and universality of the Latin rite. It was a mode of worship which, free from 'abusive clerical manipulation',

> would safeguard the spiritual freedom of the laity, when faced with the easily invasive and oppressive subjectivity of our clergy. But of this nothing remains. Contemporary Catholics now have the right only to have the religion of their pastor, with all its idiosyncrasies, its limitations, its mannerisms and its futilities.[12]

For Bouyer, the eucharist is no longer 'the prayer of the Church', but

> a ballyhoo meeting where [the faithful] are inculcated with political ideas, moral or amoral divagations, and all the other rubbish that today may fill the milky brains of a part of the clergy and their 'militants'.[13]

The 'hoped-for regeneration of Catholicism', he opines, has produced instead 'its accelerated decomposition'. A 'desacralised Christianity' has left the Church with 'no liturgy worthy of the name'.[14]

Bouyer focuses on two of the seminal paradoxes of the liturgical movement. Intended primarily for the benefit of the laity, it has been almost entirely a clerical invention; and while its leading principle has been the enrichment of their worship, probably the majority of lay men and women who had been nurtured in the old ways consider that their devotion, so far from being improved by its measures, has been hindered. In 1980, 70 per cent of the readers of Britain's most popular Roman Catholic paper, *The Universe*, expressed a first preference for the old mass.[15] Twenty years after the Council, a

11 Translated as *The Decomposition of Catholicism* by C.U. Quinn, 30.
12 *ibid.*, 32-3.
13 *op.cit.*, 52.
14 *ibid.*, 105.
15 In Gilchrist, *op.cit.*, 80.

poll of Roman Catholics in the United States – usually regarded as the most forward-looking branch of the Church – showed that 53 per cent of Church members favoured the celebration of the mass in Latin.[16] Yet those few churches in America that tried to retain a Latin liturgy were rebuked by the bishops – one of them being forbidden to persist on the grounds that 'it was drawing away the faithful from all the neighbouring parishes'.[17]

In the light of this well-documented resistance of the laity to *aggiornamento*, the persistent argument of liturgiologists that modernisation of worship has been motivated by a concern for the participation of the laity needs to be assessed in detailed, factual recollection of the worshipping customs of pre-conciliar Catholicism. The propaganda of the modernisers to the effect that this was a non-participatory religion in which the laity, cowed by clerical authoritarianism, simply went through the motions of rituals which were largely meaningless to them, is contradicted by history. Writing of the 'people's religion' of the earlier twentieth century, Edmund Campion (although a champion of *aggiornamento*) acknowledges the richness and vitality of the laity's worship in a wide range of devotions:

> The rosary, Forty Hours, perpetual adoration, novenas, Stations of the Cross, devotion to the Immaculate Conception of the Blessed Virgin Mary, shrines, processions, Benediction of the Most Blessed Sacrament. . . . Each month had its special focus. May, for instance, was the month of Mary. Each day during the month of May the people could attend a recitation of the rosary and the litany of Loreto in the parish church; on Tuesdays and Fridays, Benediction of the Most Blessed Sacrament was given. Other months had other devotions: March, St. Joseph; June, the Sacred Heart; July, the Precious Blood. . . . The rich diversity of all this allowed for individuals to pick and choose. Just as no-one could possibly belong to all the parish societies, so no-one could comprehend the complete range of popular devotions available in this people's religion.[18]

These extra-eucharistic observances were balanced with similarly popular provisions for the people at mass, in a multiplication of prayer books. In *St. Patrick's Prayer-Book*, for example,

> at the *Nobis quoque peccatoribus*, the faithful are exhorted to 'strike your breast and shed a tear'.

In these ways, they participated personally and actively in the offer-

16 'Latin Mass Favoured', *The Sydney Morning Herald*, 24 January 1985, 5.

17 Michael Davies, *The New Mass*, 9.

18 Edmund Campion, *Rockchoppers: Growing up Catholic in Australia*, 54.

ing of the eucharist, in spite of its detachment from them, both linguistically and in the priest's isolation at the distant altar.

This was a religion, Campion argues, that spoke both to the emotions and the intellect – to the needs of 'children or simple folk', while satisfying the more sophisticated 'in the rhetorical grandeur' of the antique Latin ceremonies.

That it cast a spell over children is indisputable, as the Australian poet Christopher Brennan recalled:

> The church fascinated me from the beginning. . . . On Sunday evenings in summer during Vespers, as the light waned, I used to watch the colours fade out of the window, until the body of the Crucified turned livid grey. . . . Next the blaze of candles lit for the Benediction, and the placing of the burse . . . the cross of the burse and the cape of the cope a deep ruby. I could never gaze on them enough.[19]

The parish priest who wore the cope at such ceremonies is customarily depicted today as an unapproachable patriarch, aloof from his people in hierarchical and sacerdotal elevation and a Latino-linguistic inaccessibility. This modern mythology, as Campion writes, is 'false history', used, amongst other reasons, to justify the westward position at the eucharist, so that the formerly 'distant and isolated' priest might be brought into the midst of his people. But in the pre-conciliar parish, the priest was at the very centre of parish family life (to the degree that his photograph was customarily included in family albums). And, in his sacred functions, his detachment was not regretted as separation from that family, but recognised as his special priestly function in the parish and the universal community of the Church. Some priests undoubtedly abused their elevated position, but such abuse has not been eradicated by the democratising renewal:

> With the introduction of multiple innovations in the liturgy, including the general practice of standing instead of kneeling for Communion, an unfortunate side-effect has been the scope provided for a new clericalism. . . . At one early morning weekday mass attended by a bare half-dozen regulars, an old lady attempted to kneel for Communion as she had done for the past sixty or seventy years. Irritated at this insubordination, the priest snapped several times: 'Stand up, madam!' until she was forced to comply. In another city a woman was refused Communion because she dared to kneel down. . . . It seems that post-conciliar pluralism has its selected limits for certain clerics.[20]

19 In Campion, *ibid*, 58.
20 Gilchrist, *op.cit.*, 64.

Campion, nonetheless, interprets the years of Vatican II as 'a springtime in Catholicism'. There was 'euphoria' at the prospect of a 'new church, tolerant, free, open and energetic'. There was 'a burgeoning of liturgical life in the local church'. Yet, thirty years on, in recollection of the worshipping life that was so swiftly and efficiently eradicated in the 1960s and 1970s and a comparison of that dispensation with the worship in the average Roman Catholic parish today, conservatives would argue that that springtime euphoria has failed to fulfil its promise of regeneration of the faith and worship of the laity.

There has been disquiet, also, since the early days of the renewal, in monastic communities – particularly those devoted to offering the liturgy in its fullness. The religious life, of course, was to be one of the spectacular victims of *aggiornamento* and, indeed, renewal had a devastating effect on vocations in general – as these statistics from France indicate:

> Between 1963 and 1971 the total number of seminarians dropped from 21,713 to 8,391. Over the same period the ordinations fell from 573 to 237. [In 1975] ten French dioceses did not produce a single seminarian.[21]

The famous Trappist monk Thomas Merton, though in many ways a radical thinker, was outspokenly critical of the liturgical innovations as they applied to the cloister, complaining in 1964 about

> the useless and trivial and often incomprehensible changes that have been made one on top of another in the last few years. . . .

With reference to vernacularisation, he comments:

> I think that in the long run there will have to be readings in the vernacular, but I wonder if there are not quite a few complexities to consider. There is first of all the matter of Gregorian chant. . . . I am really deeply in love with the chant. I think it is certainly the greatest religious music we have available to us. I also like the Latin office, myself, and am so far demented as to love the Vulgate Psalter. I know that I may have to give them up for the good of others, eventually. But at the same time I think we ought to recognise that something valuable and great in itself cannot be discarded thoughtlessly. I certainly think that it will not be easy to replace by something objectively half as good.[22]

The conflict in Merton's sensibility between the desire for obedience and the force of his individuality – the source of much suffering in

[21] Pierre Solignac, *The Christian Neurosis*, 159.

[22] In Monica Furlong, *Merton: A Biography*, 278.

his life – is articulated here in his acknowledgment of the inevitability of liturgical change and his poet's appreciation of the aesthetic beauty of the traditional language of worship which, personally, he would prefer to retain.

## II

By the end of the 1970s the novelty and shock of reform was waning. The liturgical spontaneity which had challenged the set forms of worship had been regularised. The congregational kiss of peace (where it had not already fallen into desuetude), liturgical applause, priests' extemporisation and so on were now as predictable as signing with the cross and genuflection had been before. But if the authorities had imagined that their conservative critics would have correspondingly mellowed, even disappeared, in the face of apparent defeat, they were mistaken. The reactionaries showed every sign of becoming more agitated and more numerous. Some of those who had favoured reform in principle changed their minds when they saw it in action. The Australian poet, James McAuley (a convert, from Anglicanism, in the 1950s), regretted

> the passing of the old liturgy – though at the time I supported the change to the vernacular even in the fixed parts of the mass. The *periti* (experts) are good at dismantling things; they are not so good at creating new form and order.

He retained his faith 'in a troublous time', by retreating to 'a minimal position':

> I believe in the resurrection; I believe in the mass, though most parish masses are now unpleasant experiences.[23]

And members were recruited to the conservative ranks who could scarcely recall the old dispensation. The Revd Shane Johnson, ordained for the traditionalist Society of Pius X in 1988 at the age of thirty-three, was only eight years old when the Constitution on the Liturgy was promulgated.[24] And the conservatives have become highly organised: traditionalist societies abound in Catholic Europe, in Britain and the New World, and periodical publications have proliferated.

The French monthly *Itinéraires*, edited by Jean Madiran, is the most prominent of these. In America, there was even competition between conservative journals, *The Maryfaithful* describing itself as 'the fastest-growing Catholic paper in the USA', *The Remnant* claiming to be 'America's outstanding traditionalist journal'. *The Remnant*,

23 'A Small Testament', in Leonie Kramer (ed.) *James McAuley*, 135.

24 'Priest with "Medieval Ideas" ordained by Excommunicated Bishop', *The Sydney Morning Herald*, 12 December 1988, 4.

indeed, was responsible for disseminating a document characteristic of the second phase of Roman Catholic conservative reaction, *Changes in the Mass* (1974), by the prolific Michael Davies (the author of such works as a trilogy on *aggiornamento: Cranmer's Godly Order; Pope John's Council;* and *Pope Paul's New Mass;* of *The Roman Rite Destroyed,* and of pamphlets with such titles as 'Communion Under Both Kinds: An Ecumenical Surrender' and 'Communion in the Hand and Similar Frauds').

An English layman, Davies takes a comparison between the *Novus Ordo* and the Anglican Series 3 eucharist as the focus of his polemic in *Changes in the Mass*. As English Roman Catholics are bound to be, he is preoccupied with the theological distinctions between the Anglican and Roman Catholic Churches. But his study of their new eucharistic rites has led him to the disturbing recognition not of the separateness he values but of 'an accelerating convergence' which he deplores.[25]

This has occurred, he alleges, because of a conspiracy between liberal Roman Catholic theologians and liturgiologists and their Anglican and Protestant associates to bring the mass into line with Reformation teaching about the Lord's Supper and thus devise 'a united Christian rite'.[26] The notion of sacrifice has been compromised by the idea of a memorial fellowship meal.

The root of the evil, he argues, was the promotion of ecumenism at the Second Vatican Council; the forum in which it flourished, the Concilium established to promote the liturgical Constitution. This included six 'observers' from other western churches who were in fact, Davies claims, 'participants'. He points his finger especially at Canon R.C.D. Jasper, who sat both on the Concilium and as Chairman of the Church of England Liturgical Commission, and was prominent in the drafting of Series 3. The desire for 'a sentimental and specious togetherness', James McAuley similarly argued, produced statements of belief which are 'only a game of multiple punning on key-words'.[27]

Davies addresses the issue which concerns most Roman Catholic traditionalists today – whether the theology of the mass has been substantially altered in the new rite – concluding that the 'doctrines of the Real Objective Presence and the True Sacrifice',[28] absorbed by the eucharist over fifteen centuries to attain full and final expression

[25] *Changes in the Mass*, 1. (All references are to the later monograph version published in the 'Approaches' series.)

[26] *ibid.*, 10.

[27] 'A Small Testament', *op.cit.*, 137.

[28] *ibid.*, 2. See also Anthony Cekada, *The Problems with the Prayers of the Modern Mass.*

in the Tridentine rite, have been watered down in order to conciliate not only the Anglicans but western Protestant Churches. He bases this judgement in particular on a discussion of the Tridentine offertory and that of the *novus ordo*, noting how the English translation approximates to the 'ambiguous' wording of Series 3.

To augment his doctrinal exposition, Davies also contends that the 'ethos' of Roman Catholic worship has been undermined by several 'Protestant' practices – communion from the chalice, the westward position and, of course, the use of the vernacular. But he is careful to assert that his reverence for the Latin language is primarily for the doctrine it expressed, is only secondarily concerned with the worshipping cult of Catholicism and is hardly an aesthetic matter at all – a point he stresses in his later monograph, *The New Mass*:

> Opposition to the new mass is not based to any great extent upon suffering caused by cultural deprivation . . . although, clearly, responsible Catholics will also make every effort . . . to preserve the Church's treasury of sacred music and the use of Latin in the Liturgy.[29]

However, for many traditionalists, less theologically and liturgically focused than Davies, these distinctions are too clearly drawn, the priorities too firmly established. He comments that

> I am sure that most traditionalists would prefer to assist at a Low Mass in an accurately translated vernacular text of the mass of St. Pius V rather than a sung Latin version of the new mass, however dignified and beautiful.[30]

But this overstates the case. 'Most traditionalists' are like all conservatives. They would be satisfied with nothing less than the *status quo ante*.

Evelyn Waugh, Louis Bouyer, Thomas Merton, Alec Guinness, Michael Davies and Malcolm Muggeridge are all converts to Ro-

[29] Davies, *The New Mass*, 7.

[30] *ibid.*, 8. The confusion between the primacy of theology and concern about the numinous is revealed in this paragraph in a letter from the Secretary of the Latin Mass Society, Mrs Susan Coote:

*I think that the doctrinal aspect of the difference between Old and New Rites is of great importance, perhaps the greatest.* No-one can ad lib the Old Mass, neither can anyone introduce anything unorthodox into the Old Mass. In some churches the New Mass is celebrated with great reverence and devotion, but they are few and far between. There are a great many people I know from my huge correspondence who have to attend the New Mass to fulfil their obligation and who dread Sundays – the introduction of guitars, hand-clapping, hand-shaking at the most important time in the mass, the priest leaving the Sanctuary where the Body and Blood of Our Blessed Lord is left alone, while he trots off down the aisle, shaking hands with the people is a cause for scandal, as is the standing to receive Holy Communion and in the hand. *I suppose the real problem is the loss of the sense of the sacred and transcendent.* [Author's emphasis – letter to the author, 30 May 1989.]

man Catholicism. It is scarcely surprising that they were amongst the most outspoken of critics of *aggiornamento*. Unlike 'cradle Catholics', they had made a daunting journey from non-committal Protestantism or atheism to the absolutism and authoritarianism of the pre-conciliar Church and the disciplines and solemnity of its ritual, only to find that the very exclusivist and reputedly immutable principles that had attracted them were being discounted and even ridiculed within the Church itself, and its liturgy modernised to a point often less decorous and certainly less spiritually rigorous than those of conservative reformed Christianity. Davies ruefully records the observation of Michael Ramsey, Archbishop of Canterbury:

> 'I have experienced Roman rites which are really very Anglican. If you want to find rites that are really Roman, visit some of our old-fashioned Anglo-Catholic shrines'.[31]

Indeed, long after Vatican II, the liturgies of a large number of Anglo-Catholic churches in many countries continued to observe the ritual of *The English Missal*, that unique combination of the Book of Common Prayer and the Tridentine mass, and the ceremonial compendium *Ritual Notes*. Only in recent times have Anglo-Catholics become reconciled to the innovations of the liturgical movement while still retaining in some places their renowned (or notorious) attention to rubrical detail and that cultivation of the beauty of holiness which, many contend, has all but disappeared from Roman Catholic ceremonial.

## III

In England, organised conservative reaction to the vernacularisation began in September 1964, with a petition to the hierarchy of England and Wales, containing nearly 4,000 signatures, pleading for the defence of the traditional Latin celebration. The establishment at the end of 1964 in Norway of the first society devoted to its preservation with the title *Una Voce*, and of a sister society in France, encouraged English Catholics to form a group with the same object – but with a different name: the Latin Mass Society, inaugurated on 24 April 1965. Four years after its formation, however, the abrogation of the Tridentine rite and its replacement by the *Novus Ordo* meant that the Society had to decide whether it would continue to campaign for the old mass or for celebrations of the new order in Latin. A referendum being held, the overwhelming majority voted for the former course. The minority departed, inaugurating the Association for Latin

31 Davies, *Changes in the Mass.*, 17.

Liturgy on 27 September 1969.

Today, both societies continue their independent campaigns. The Association for Latin Liturgy, with some 400 members, approximately 65 of whom are priests, publishes a *Latin Mass Directory* for England and Wales which lists some 400 regular celebrations of the *novus ordo* in Latin in parish churches throughout the country. Such celebrations depend on the personal inclinations of the incumbent and on the determination of parishioners, the bishops tending to remain aloof, although Cardinal Basil Hume of Westminster has shown some support for the work of the Association. (At his cathedral, in 1994, there was a weekday Latin mass. On the first Saturday of each month, there was a Tridentine low mass celebrated in the Cathedral crypt.)[32]

The Association for Latin Liturgy, indeed, is careful to emphasise its separateness from the principles and spirit of the Tridentinists. It makes its position clear in its published statement of aims:

> There are two attitudes among the supporters of the Latin liturgy:
>
> 1. The dynamic, which recognises that a living liturgy is subject to development, reform and renewal, but at the same time perceives the inestimable value of the Latin liturgy, particularly in solemn celebrations, in emphasizing the transcendental reality of the eucharistic act and in demonstrating the continuity of contemporary liturgical worship with that of the Church throughout the ages.
> 2. The static or traditionalist, which regrets that the Church has instituted any liturgical change, and campaigns for the celebration of mass in the form promulgated by Pope St Pius V.

The Association for Latin Liturgy is inspired by the first view. It is thus more concerned with the present and the future than with the past, yet seeking to preserve those elements of the Church's liturgical heritage which are of enduring worth.

Non-militant, conciliatory and, at least theoretically, progressive, its campaign is largely carried out through well-produced publications on liturgical language and music, and through participation by its members on diocesan liturgical commissions. Notable amongst its many productions is a bilingual Sunday missal, simple organ accompaniments for plainsong masses (both published in 1982) and the monograph *Latin in the Liturgy*, by R.H. Richens, its founding chairman. Richens argues that the concept of a special language of worship, different from contemporary speech, has authority dating

32 For the information in this paragraph the author is indebted to the former Honorary Secretary of the Association for Latin Liturgy, Mr Martin Lynch, and the present Secretary, Mr Christopher Francis.

from pre-Christian antiquity and in the worship of Jesus, who spoke Aramaic but worshipped in Hebrew: 'a special sacred language is a commonplace in all religions'. In contrast to the emphasis on relevance in modern liturgiology, Richens clearly distinguishes between the divine and the mundane:

> The importance of such a language is that it is immediately recognised as dedicated to one single and exalted purpose, the worship of God. By virtue of its unique role and associations, it directs the heart and mind at once towards the divine mysteries. . . . It helps to preserve what is so much at risk today, the sense of the sacred, and it supports the necessary recognition that the Christian mysteries are immeasurably deeper than the words that express them.[33]

He also promotes the familiar argument of conservatives that a traditional sacral language links present worshippers with those of the past – 'the *Deo gratias* of the Christians who suffered martyrdom under the Roman Empire is our *Deo gratias*'[34] – and, indeed, of the future. And he rejects the argument from incomprehensibility, claiming both that bilingual missals solve the problem in an age of almost universal literacy and that

> all liturgical worship uses religious symbols, often of considerable complexity, to designate its mysteries and the worshippers require initiation. This is as true for Catholic worship in English as it is in Latin.[35]

However, the Association for Latin Liturgy has no very optimistic views of the likelihood of its success in converting Roman Catholics *en masse* to its principles:

> Most English Catholics take without demur a liturgy of any poor quality which is offered them, as long as they are convinced that it is valid.[36]

It prefers to concentrate its resources in such conspicuous churches as the London Oratory where the *Novus Ordo* was accepted but where its English translation exists alongside celebrations of that rite in Latin, with ceremonies and music largely unchanged from preconciliar days.

Every Sunday and holy day the solemn mass is sung in Latin at the Oratory, while the daily low mass at 8 a.m. is also in Latin. Tridentine mass is celebrated each Sunday morning in the Little Oratory. Worship there, in other words, is in accord with the letter of

33 R.H. Richens, *Latin in the Liturgy*, 3-4.

34 *ibid.*, 4-5.

35 *ibid.*, 11.

36 Letter to the author from the former Honorary Secretary of the Association for Latin Liturgy, Mr Martin Lynch, 29 January 1989.

the Second Vatican Council, but markedly different from the spirit of the post-conciliar reforms. The preservation by the Oratory of a traditional liturgical language and ceremonial within the context of the new rite has been the result of a deliberate policy, as enunciated by the parish priest in the parish magazine in 1975:

> We at the London Oratory have been fortunate that by a sure instinct, which we could not perhaps express adequately in words, we have preserved that atmosphere of the sacred in our public worship, which in other places has been greatly diminished or even destroyed. Even if we have not experienced it, however, we have probably read about a desacralised liturgy, proclaimed as the logical outcome of the spirit of the Second Vatican Council.[37]

Eschewing the doctrinal arguments of the Tridentine traditionalists about sacrifice and presence, he argues (in a way more familiar in conservative Anglican polemic) that a numinous liturgy conveys the sense of transcendence which is at the heart of all true religion. It is God-centred rather than man-centred. He also rejects the argument for modernity in ceremonial, noting the case of the guru of modernism, Harvey Cox, who, after writing *The Secular City*, discovered 'that what Modern Man needed was fantasy and mysticism' and was found 'celebrating some pseudo-Buddhist ritual in oriental vestments'. He concludes:

> If we can learn a lesson from the sad history of the last ten years, it is that we should look to our roots, to our history, and view with grave suspicion any movement that would detach us from our Catholic past. But tradition is not something dead but living. It binds together the past and the present, and assimilates to itself the best of what is new. So we learn that the sacredness of the liturgy guards and protects . . . the Catholic faith.[38]

A more striking phenomenon, however, has been the campaign of the Latin Mass Society, which has persisted with its demand for the reinstatement of the Tridentine mass as the only valid eucharist of the Church. In England, this agitation had dramatic expression in 1975 in the controversy at St Dominic's Church in the Norfolk town of Downham Market.

The long-serving priest of the parish, the Revd Oswald Baker, was asked by his bishop either to desist from celebrating the

37 'Letter from the Parish Priest', *The Oratory Parish Magazine*, March 1975, 3. Worship at the Oratory continues on the same pattern (letter to the author from the Provost and Parish Priest, the Very Revd Michael Napier, 11 November 1991).

38 *ibid.*, 5.

Tridentine rite and introduce the *Novus Ordo* or resign. 'I will go to my death resisting', was Fr Baker's reply.[39] But the Bishop of Northampton was equally determined to ensure that 'all people in the Diocese . . . had the new form of mass available to them'.[40]

As the result of international publicity, including the televising of a protest mass by American television, the parochial conflict at obscure Downham Market suddenly became the focus of world-wide interest amongst conservative Roman Catholics – a paradox which contributed to the bizarre aspects of this affair. Letters and visitors poured in to support Fr Baker, while videos and long-playing records, arranged by the '1570 Action Committee', were released for the international market. A 'poem' was distributed which captures the extremity of the passions that had been aroused:

'Now Downham Market's Golgotha',
I hear the people say,
As from the towns and villages
They set out on their way.

But there's another victim,
In Christ's own image he,
A loved and faithful Parish Priest
For nailing to a tree.

His crime is that he keeps the Faith
Entrusted to his care
And is prepared to die for it,
To hang and suffer there.

But, if Downham Market's Golgotha,
And Judas walks abroad,
Then what has happened to the Church
And where's Our Blessed Lord?

And where is truth – is it newly-born
In Twentieth Century minds?
And do we discard what we believe
To 'keep up with the times'?

No – we shall keep our ancient Faith,
Preserved by martyrs past,
And, united with all holy souls,
God grant we'll be steadfast.
Man cannot create a modern Christ,

39 'Latin Lovers in Protest', *The Sunday Times*, 31 August 1975, 10.
40 'Bishop's Aim "to Make New Mass Available to All"', *The Times*, 19 September 1975, 11.

For He was, is and will be
There in the hands of the faithful Priest
Reaching out to you and me.

So, when we come to Golgotha,
Praise be to God above,
For Christ lives on in Golgotha
And we can feel his love.

The episcopal authorities were unmoved. By February 1976, Fr Baker had withdrawn from St Dominic's, to be replaced by a priest who would conform to the bishop's directives. A 'mass centre' – now known as 'St Pius V Oratory' (in commemoration of the Tridentine pope) – was purchased in the town from donated money, and the term 'separated brethren', once used to describe Anglicans, was applied anew by the Downham traditionalists in their propaganda to abuse their co-religionists and fellow parishioners who had given in to the bishop's wishes and had begun to worship in the modern way at St Dominic's under the newly appointed Fr Sketch. Twenty years later, Fr Baker continues to celebrate the Tridentine rite for congregations of around fifty worshippers, at the Downham Oratory and, on a rota basis, in hired halls in several other towns in East Anglia. Some of his followers have moved permanently to Downham Market for the benefit of the old mass, one coming from as far away as Australia.[41]

In the country at large, in 1989, the Tridentine mass was being celebrated in some thirty mass centres for 4,000 regular worshippers. The Society of St Pius X publishes a monthly newsletter and *The Catholic Quarterly Review*,[42] and it has established a school. These Tridentinists have a recusant spirit. The language of their polemic reflects the fervour of their convictions:

> May this holy season of Lent be the occasion of drawing ever closer to God by making penance and reparation for our sins and particularly for the outrages which are ever increasing towards Our Blessed Lord in the Most Holy Sacrament.[43]

Further, they argue that 'our position is positive not negative. We seek the free use of the Tridentine Rite'.[44] Most importantly, they are associated with the international repudiation of the reforms of Vat-

41 'A Long Battle to Keep a Church Tradition', *Lynn News and Advertiser*, 23 August 1985, 13; letter to the author from Miss Clara Zilahi of Downham Market, 17 July 1994.

42 Information from the Superior of the Society of St Pius X, the Revd Edward Black, letter to the author, 30 January 1989, and Mrs Susan Coote, Secretary of the Latin Mass Society, letter to the author, 30 May 1989.

43 'Letter from Father Black', *Newsletter*, February 1989, 1.

44 Mrs Susan Coote, Secretary of the Latin Mass Society, London; letter to the author, 30 May 1989.

ican II which was led and dominated by the most extraordinary ecclesiastical conservative of the modern age, the French archbishop Marcel Lefebvre.

Born in 1905 and serving in the mission field for some forty years, Lefebvre was successively Archbishop of Dakar, Superior-General of the Holy Ghost Fathers (the principal missionary congregation) and head of the French seminary at Rome. He began his criticism of the Vatican Council in October 1964 by castigating its ecumenical spirit and modernist heresies, the themes of his subsequent book, *J'accuse le Concile*. In 1969, he established a seminary and religious house of the 'International Priestly Society of Saint Pius X' at Econe, in Switzerland. Its traditionalist curriculum was in pointed contradiction to contemporary theological trends and seminarians were initiated into a spirituality, based on the Tridentine mass, of a type that was being rapidly repudiated in official seminaries. The result was as successful in the attraction and retention of seminarians as the modernising courses elsewhere were proving to be disastrous:

> Lefebvre has succeeded by strict observance where others have failed by gimmicks and compromise.[45]

Such gimmickry, called 'creativity', was seen in action at the Glen Waverley seminary in Melbourne in the early 1970s. There was a growing 'reluctance to be shackled by the rubrics':

> Within the magnificent but impractical chapel the furniture would be rearranged at every community mass, to express, as it were, the psychological drive to be free. . . . A climax to 1971 came with the holding of a 'Religious Happening' or 'Rock Service' . . . . The leather-jacketed (now ex-priest) Fr Paul Bongiorno, who tried (not very successfully) to be heard . . . offered such meaningful thoughts as 'Jesus is the clue. Call Him Soul Man, Superstar, call Him what you like – He preached acceptance and love'.[46]

By 1988, the Lefebvrist Society had four bishops – apart from Lefebvre himself – 211 priests, five seminaries with 252 seminarians, and convents and schools in twenty-eight countries.[47] In those years, the activities of the Lefebvrists achieved greater secular publicity than the Council against which they were revolting.

Every effort by Rome to bring this rebel to heel was a failure. He and his supporters prospered in persecution and ostracism. Reacting to Vatican demands that he update the liturgical observance at

[45] B. McSweeney, 'The New Heresy: how Traditionalists could split the Roman Catholic Church', *The Times*, 7 August 1976, 12.

[46] In Gilchrist, *op.cit.*, 130-1.

[47] 'Far-right Rebel gives the Pope a Problem', *The Sydney Morning Herald*, 6 February 1988, 8.

Econe, Archbishop Lefebvre – who described the new mass as 'a bastard rite' – issued a profession of faith in November 1974 which, while affirming his allegiance to

> Catholic Rome, custodian of the Catholic faith and of the traditions needed to preserve this faith

declared that

> we refuse and have always refused to follow the Rome of neo-modernistic and neo-Protestant tendencies so clearly shown in Vatican Council II.[48]

And in direct defiance of papal orders, in June 1976 he ordained twenty-six priests and deacons – an act for which he was subsequently suspended *a divinis* by Paul VI from saying mass and dispensing the sacraments, a measure just short of excommunication.

Lefebvre's response to such discipline was that it was null and void, being the action of a schismatic pontiff who had endorsed the teachings of the heretical council. Lefebvre reflected, in 1981, that

> the ones who are called 'dissident', 'disobedient' or 'rebels' are the ones who are keeping the Faith; while those who are destroying it are called 'faithful', 'submissive' and 'obedient'. How much longer is this lie, this massive imposture to last? Only God knows.[49]

Although there appeared to be some improvement in his relations with the papacy on the succession of John Paul II – especially when the pope, in a conciliatory gesture, issued an indult in October 1984, permitting limited use of the Tridentine rite – such hopes were dashed four years later. In June 1988, after having ordained another sixteen priests, Lefebvre – now aged eighty-two and concerned to perpetuate the traditionalist succession – proceeded, before a congregation of 8,000 followers, to the consecration of four bishops, rejecting a last-minute appeal from the pope against his action, incurring excommunication for himself and the new bishops as a result, and creating the largest schism in the Roman Catholic Church since the Old Catholics rebelled against the decrees of the First Vatican Council in 1870.

Six months later one of these bishops, Richard Williamson, undeterred by his excommunicate status, travelled to Australia to conduct the first traditionalist ordination to the priesthood on that continent.

The story of the Tridentine movement in Australia, indeed, is worthy of brief attention as an index of the far-flung influence of Archbishop Lefebvre and the depth of discontent with the reforms of the Second Vatican Council. For, in their history, Australian Catho-

48 In McSweeney, *op..cit*.

49 Letter to Friends and Benefactors, no. 21, 21 September 1981.

lics have been notable for their obedience to authority, rather than for independence of thought and action.

In 1966, a Latin Mass Society was formed in Melbourne. Its main concern was with Latin as the language of worship rather than with the doctrinal issues that later came to dominate the controversy. But dissatisfaction among its ranks soon led to the formation of other groups, such as *Domus Dei* in Sydney, and the militant Queensland-based Australian Alliance for Catholic Tradition which has enjoyed extra publicity because of the support given to its principles by Australia's best-known film idol, Mel Gibson, whose father, Hutton Gibson (known as 'Pope Hutton'), is its outspoken leader. The Alliance paper is *The War is Now* and it regarded Archbishop Lefebvre as a weak man, likely to come to a compromise with John Paul II, whom it calls the 'Polish ham'.

Several colourful clerical figures have also added spice to the traditionalist revolt in Australia. A Sydney parish priest, the Revd Patrick Fox, having secured permission on account of his age to celebrate the Tridentine rite in private (that is, for himself alone), became notorious for beginning such masses, before congregations of several hundred, with the solemn declaration that 'this mass is private'. The recommendation of his superiors that he should seek psychiatric counselling was ignored.

The Australian Lefebvrists were inspired by several visits by the redoubtable archbishop. The hierarchy adopted the strategy of ignoring their existence, but they have prospered. In 1983 they purchased a redundant Methodist church in suburban Sydney – dedicating it to 'the Child Jesus and St Joseph' – which from the start proved too small for their congregations. When Bishop Williamson came to ordain Fr Johnson in 1988, the service had to be held in the Great Hall of Sydney University. In contrast, the following year, in the large archdiocese of Sydney, not one man presented himself for ordination to the priesthood, although in 1958, for instance, in what Germaine Greer has facetiously called the 'bad old days' before the Council (when she knew the Latin liturgy she loved by heart), no less than forty ordinands were priested.

Undoubtedly the traditionalists in Australia, as elsewhere, are a small minority of the Catholic population. In Sydney, they are newsworthy when 800 of them gather to welcome Archbishop Lefebvre,[50] but when John Paul II visited the city hundreds of thousands turned out. Nonetheless, they are a growing force in an otherwise numerically declining Church, and, with their surprising success in

[50] '800 Pack Hall to hear Traditional Mass in Latin', *The Sydney Morning Herald*, 9 November 1981, 3.

the recruitment of young people, they obviously will not die out in this generation, as the progressivists had hoped. Archbishop Lefebvre was succeeded at Econe in 1983 by a vigorous thirty-seven year old German priest, the Revd Franz Schmidberger. The archbishop died in March 1991. In July, 1994 Fr Schmidberger was in turn succeeded by Bishop Bernard Fellay, a thirty-six-year-old Swiss, who now presides over a society estimated to be serving one million traditionalists.

There is a sense, however, that – in spite of the agitations of the Lefebvrists – the more serious, though less hysterical, criticism comes from those who have remained loyal to the Church in spite of liturgical renewal and who regard the Lefebvrists as 'ultra traditionalists with a sectarian mentality'.[51] Their critique cannot be so easily dismissed as disobedient and schismatic, eccentric and irrelevant. It could prove, in the end, to be far more significant in future liturgical developments.

In his history of the mass, published in 1978, George Every – a convert from Anglicanism where he was a member of the Society of the Sacred Mission, a community particularly concerned with liturgiology – endorses the principles of liturgical study and revision, but criticises many aspects of contemporary reform. For example, he rejects the argument that the modern use of the westward position for the celebration of the eucharist is based on the ceremonial of the early Church:

> It is . . . natural that those who wished for a greater measure of common participation in the mass should wish to bring the altar down from remote heights and nearer the choir and the people. What is to be deplored is the insistence that celebration toward the people is proper, primitive and original. The tradition that Christians pray toward the east, in expectation of the coming of Christ, is much more clearly established than any idea that the eucharist should be celebrated around a table.[52]

He exposes the misunderstanding behind the argument from the 'basilican' position which is most commonly put in support of the current practice:

> When the Roman Church came to worship in basilicas, with an apse at one end for the altar and throne and seats for the presbyters beside the bishop and behind the altar, either this was at the *west* end, so that the celebrant prayed across it, or if

51 The Very Revd Richard Price, Provost and Parish Priest, the London Oratory, letter to the author, 10 January 1989.

52 George Every, *The Mass* (Gill and Macmillan: Dublin, 1978), 164. This argument is also detailed in J.A. Jungmann, *The Early Liturgy*.

> it was at the east *in the time of prayer he commonly moved to the other side of it,* and prayed for the people as their representative[53] [emphasis added].

Whatever the arguments for westward celebration (which, Every argues later, has produced 'a kind of architectural iconoclasm in the treatment of the reredos and the high altar in churches built before Vatican II'),[54] the appeal to history does not support them: 'that prayer should be made facing the east was a tradition common to East and West'.[55]

Elsewhere, Every undertakes a close examination of the eucharistic prayers of the new Roman Missal and finds some serious deficiencies in their English translation – for instance, in the English version of the new Latin form *agnoscens Hostiam, cuius voluisti immolatione placari,* translated as 'and see the victim whose death has reconciled us to yourself' – not 'yourself to us'. He comments:

> This translation is not satisfactory, either verbally or as theology. We may not eliminate from our theological thinking the mysterious working of the will of God to be moved by the death of Christ.[56]

Yet he closes optimistically, pointing out that it is inevitable that literary inadequacies and doctrinal ambiguities will have arisen when so much has been done in such a short time. For all the shortcomings of Vatican II and its works, 'the achievement can be described as miraculous'.[57] He is especially positive about the enhanced appreciation by Catholics of the Bible:

> As the Scriptures come to be read and understood by the whole congregation in the context of the mass, their original role in Christian tradition begins to be rediscovered.[58]

This is in marked contrast with Fr Bouyer's observation:

> On the whole, Catholics today do not bother with the Bible any more than they did yesterday.[59]

In the following year, 1979, *English Catholic Worship* – a study of the reforms of the liturgy in England since 1900 – was published by three leading figures (clerical and lay) in the Society of St Gregory, a long-established English Roman Catholic liturgical organisation.

After a foreword in which Cardinal Hume promotes the romantic view of *aggiornamento*:

> a ceremonial, strongly rubrical liturgy, celebrated by the priest

53 *ibid.*
54 *ibid.*, 177.
55 *ibid.*, 164.
56 *ibid.*, 186.
57 *ibid.*, 190.
58 *ibid.*, 191.
59 *The Decomposition of Catholicism*, 30.

> on behalf of, and in the presence of, the people, has given way to a participatory liturgy expressing the Church as the pilgrim people of God,[60]

and reveals ingenuous puzzlement about the failure of the new rites to inspire great musicians, the authors set about undermining every official claim of the last twenty years about the post-conciliar reforms.

They reject the notion of the laity's passivity before the Council – 'it is surprising on looking back to see how much was being done by the laity'[61] – and, more subtly, challenge the view that 'participation' in worship entails incessant corporate speech and action:

> The fact that most of the congregation at any mass said their own private prayers during it does not detract from their awareness that here was a particularly sacred moment in which to say them.[62]

Cardinal Ratzinger has similarly rejected the narrowly literalistic interpretation of the *actuosa participatio*:

> The impression arose that there was only 'active participation' when there was discernible external activity – speaking, singing, preaching, reading, shaking hands. It was forgotten that the Council also included silence under *actuosa participatio*, for silence facilitates a really deep, personal participation, allowing us to listen inwardly to the Lord's word. Many liturgies now lack all trace of this silence.[63]

The authors of *English Catholic Worship* scorn the idea that relevance to contemporary secular speech and mores is necessary if the young are to be drawn to worship:

> It has never been persuasively shown that, whatever young people may find attractive to listen to in a disco (and perhaps to participate in by 'dancing'), they will find attractive to sing in church.[64]

They cite a bizarre example of the results of parochial liturgical experimentation, published in 1971 as *A Pilgrim's Mass*:

> Here was adaptability in action; the mass was a genuine product of a community (at least, of that gathered for a weekend course) and all the texts of the Ordinary had been rewritten to fit into metrical frameworks for singing. Some of the results were alarming. The Creed was reduced to such banal declarations as 'I believe the church is holy, I believe the church is

60 J.D. Crichton, N.E. Winstone, J.R. Ainslie, (eds) *English Catholic Wordhip*, vii.
61 J.D. Crichton, '1920-1940: The Dawn of a Liturgical Movement', 31.
62 John Ainslie, 'English Liturgical Music before Vatican II', 47.
63 *The Ratzinger Report*, in Gilchrist, 24.
64 John Ainslie, 'English Liturgical Music and the Council', *op. cit.*, 105.

> true,/ I believe the church was made for all men, not just me and you'. The line 'showed us all the way to heaven' was provided with an alternative in a footnote (presumably for those who didn't like the idea of heaven) 'showed us life goes on forever'; and there was an instruction that Verse 6 which 'is meant to sum up the proper reaction to doubts which assail us' could be prefaced by 'an interlude in which people voice significant dilemmas, such as "Why am I a spastic?" to a quiet musical background'. That left (and leaves) one speechless; nevertheless, here for the first time in published form in this country was an Ordinary in which the texts and their functions had been rethought and rewritten to create a 'local liturgy'.[65]

They further deride the modish vocabulary of liturgical newspeak which, they contend, has produced 'a hiatus amounting in many cases to a chasm of Grand Canyon proportions . . . between language and experience, between description and reality, between ideology and fact':

> Thus: 'families' whose members know nothing of each other, 'communities' which are nothing of the sort, 'songs' which are recited, 'acclamations' which are muttered by one voice, baptisms where people are 'bathed' and 'buried' in Christ under 10 ml of water and 'welcomed into a community' which has not bothered to turn up or even been informed of the event, 'meals' at which no-one drinks and where 'sharing one bread' means simultaneous consumption of five hundred individual breads, 'gifts of the people' which are not theirs and which they did not give, 'celebrations' which are joyless and perfunctory discharge of an obligation.[66]

It is this observation which leads to the most challenging comment in the book: that the attention paid to translation and other modernising reforms of the liturgy has been misdirected, deflecting the Church from the goals of true renewal:

> It is already beginning to look as if far too much attention and energy have been devoted to the words, rubrics and translations of the liturgy, which have been examined, revised, criticised and fought over almost in a vacuum of narcissistic introversion. Joseph Gelineau ends his recent book on the future of the liturgy wondering 'if the liturgy today is not more preoccupied with itself than with the Kingdom it proclaims'.

[65] Nicholas Kenyon, 'Into the Melting Pot: Pointers towards a New Liturgical Music', *ibid.*, 129.

[66] Christopher J. Walsh, 'Task Unfinished', 139-40.

> Reforms and revisions we have had in plenty, but liturgical *renewal* will never be achieved until our texts, rites and affirmations are translated not into this or that sort of English but into reality in the lived experience of the people; and they will rarely be experienced as real until the congregations celebrating them are genuine communities of faith, witness and action.[67]

Their view that the modern liturgy is afflicted with a 'corrupting disease' recalls Louis Bouyer's description of it as a 'cadaver decomposed',[68] while their call for a more radical revival than has been achieved echoes Thomas Merton's observations that *aggiornamento* consists of 'token bows in the direction of a changing church and world, empty gestures because the need for a real change of heart and mind was too terrifying to contemplate'.[69] Where these profound problems existed, 'wide unrest and uncertainty on quite fundamental issues of authority and belief', it was 'imprudent' (James McAuley wrote in 1969) to make changes in liturgy:

> It is like having an army in a confused and partly mutinous state and deciding that this would be a good time to remove officers' insignia, abolish saluting and parade drill, and rewrite the rule book. Please do not tell me how exciting, thrilling, challenging, exhilarating, and so forth, it should be to ride the wave of the future, not knowing whether it is going to be a dumper or not.[70]

## IV

Two book-length studies of the 1980s, assessing the first years of the pontificate of John Paul II, both present the pope as determined to reverse the doctrinal and liturgical trends initiated by the Second Vatican Council (where he was, nonetheless, one of the prominent modernising prelates) in order to recover the universality and authority of the pre-conciliar Church.

In *Roman Catholicism: The Search for Relevance,* Bill McSweeney despairingly judges the quest to be futile. He argues that Roman Catholicism underwent an unprecedented, cataclysmic and irreversible change in character after the death of Pius XII in 1958. From a relationship of contradiction to the world, it came – under John XXIII – to a reconciliation with it. The Council, McSweeney argues, was not the 'remarkable breakthrough of the Spirit' alleged by the propa-

67 *ibid.*
68 *The Decomposition of Catholicism,* 105.
69 In Monica Furlong, *Merton,* 276.
70 In Gilchrist, *op.cit.,* 39.

ganda, but an 'act of resignation to social and political pressures'.[71] A sociologist himself, McSweeney has scant regard for the sociological insights of the post-conciliar liturgiologists who failed to realise that

> the loss of a sense of mystery in ritual might prove to be a greater sociological obstacle to Christian commitment than the intellectual deprivation of not understanding the words.[72]

He acknowledges the efforts of John Paul II to recover the lost prestige of the Church and the papacy, but while recognising the pope's personal charisma, he argues that a different, more important charisma – that of the *office* of the pontiff – had been destroyed by his recent predecessors:

> The traditional power of the pope – and the traditional Catholicism which was organised around it as its core – depended on belief in the continuity of faith. . . . Now the breach of continuity has been displayed and, more important, the disunity of faith also.[73]

Indeed, the personal charisma of John Paul II is the focus of much traditionalist polemic. It is seen as the expression of his idiosyncrasy, hindering the universality of the office he holds. While his theological conservatism is grudgingly admitted, he is reviled for his globe-trotting and for such 'media events' as the prayer meeting over which he presided at Assisi in November 1986, which was attended by representatives of all religions, including animists and Shintoists.

Less pessimistic (as its title indicates) is Paul Johnson's *Pope John Paul II and the Catholic Restoration*. He presents an emotive summary of the liturgical vandalism of the preceding twenty years:

> Many busy and eager hands tore at the ancient fabric. . . . By the time the incense cleared, all that was left of the Tridentine liturgy was a beautiful ruin, amid the scattered stones and charred embers of which there arose the plebeian cacophony of homespun services, to the music of adolescent toys. The object was supposedly to secure greater participation in the services by the laity, and a greater understanding of what was said and done at them. But the result was misunderstanding for the young, confusion for the middle-aged and heartbreak for the old. There was also an increasing fall in attendance. Latin largely disappeared, and with it went what Coleridge called 'the willing suspension of disbelief' which a hieratic or arcane language brings to the contemplation of the necessarily

71 8.
72 *ibid.*, 150.
73 *ibid.*, 259.

mysterious.[74]

Johnson agrees with McSweeney that this damage is irreparable, but he believes that John Paul II has the authority to limit its extent 'by insisting that diocesan bishops enforce the new liturgical rules, such as they are, and unauthorised experiments cease'.[75]

While many writers, such as Johnson, have referred in general terms to the numinous quality of traditional liturgical language, there has been a serious deficiency in conservative Roman Catholic polemic of detailed consideration of this concept and of close comparison of the Latin prayers with their translation into modern liturgical English. One attempt to fill the void appeared in 1983 in the unusual form of an 'open letter' (of some fifty pages) by the Revd John McHugh of the University of Durham to Bishop Gray of Shrewsbury. With the inelegant title *On Englishing the Liturgy*, McHugh, addressing the bishop in his capacity as President of the Liturgical Commission of the Bishops' Conference, devotes most of his attention to questioning the wisdom of seeking an English vernacular translation of the mass that will be suitable wherever English is spoken. He begins, however, by offering some valuable reflections on the distinctive qualities of liturgical language under these headings:

(1) It will be formal not informal.
(2) It will be a text written for speaking aloud.
(3) It will always be the address of an inferior to a superior.
(4) Its purpose is not the communication of information but the vocal expression of the innermost convictions of faith.
(5) It is written not to be read out once for all, but to be spoken many times over.[76]

The consideration of such principles and McHugh's exegesis of them are rare phenomena in Catholic conservative polemic. But his paper is another indication that matters of linguistic style cannot be dismissed as peripheral to this debate.

In an unusual twist, McHugh records that he was one of those who 'longed for the introduction of the vernacular liturgy' so that everyone could come to know the 'extraordinary treasures' of the Roman rite. A classicist comfortable with the Latin texts, he nonetheless wanted them to be available to 'all the people of God'. To do justice to their dignity and beauty, however, they needed to be rendered in a 'truly inspiring version'.[77] His quarrel with the current vernacular translations is that they fail to inspire because translators

74 *Pope John Paul II and the Catholic Restoration*, 137-8.
75 *ibid.*
76 4-8.
77 *ibid.*, 42.

have not appreciated the true character of liturgical language. He shows that inspirational English versions are obtainable and already exist. He takes the example of the collect at Vespers on the first Wednesday of the month –

> Adesto, Domine, precibus nostris,
> et die noctuque nos protege,
> ut vicibus temporum tua gubernatione subiecti,
> tua semper incommutabilitate firmemur –

and cites this 'flawless' version from the Book of Common Prayer as proposed in 1928 as a model of its translation and the fitting conclusion to his letter:

> Be present, O merciful God, and protect us through the silent hours of this night, so that we who are wearied by the changes and chances of this fleeting world, may repose upon thy eternal changelessness; through Jesus Christ our Lord.[78]

It would be remarkable, indeed, if John McHugh's appeals were heeded and Roman Catholic liturgiologists were to be discovered poring over the Book of Common Prayer, discarded by the Anglicans, for inspiration and guidance in their future translations into English! In one quarter, this has already happened. When Professor J.A.W. Bennett prepared a bilingual *Ordo Missae* for the Association for Latin Liturgy, he translated 'in a style conformable to the classical tradition of English liturgical prose' – that is to say, the idiom of Cranmer.[79]

## V

The prospects for Roman Catholic traditionalists today are uncertain. Those who are prepared to go into schism can have their liturgical and spiritual needs amply satisfied by the ministrations of Lefebvrist priests, providing they live in a region where they are active. But they are separating themselves from their Church, in spite of their protestations to the effect that they are its faithful remnant. Their position is steeped in contradiction – they are sectarians professing Catholicism. What is more, there are serious divisions in their ranks – for instance, over the status of the popes who have sanctioned the suppression of the Tridentine rite. Fr Baker of Downham Market, for example, is a 'sedevacantist', holding the view that the See of Peter is, in fact, vacant because of the heresies of the current pontiff – who is not a true pope – and his recent predecessors. Officially, however,

[78] *ibid.*

[79] Association for Latin Liturgy, *Statement of Aims*, 3. Some translations of the Orthodox liturgy into English have also followed this style – 'liturgical English at its noblest' (*The Orthodox Liturgy*, vi).

the Society of Pius X distances itself from this view. Then, since the excommunication of Archbishop Lefebvre, several of the clergy formerly associated with him are rumoured to be seeking reconciliation with the Vatican.[80]

Those conservatives who have stayed within the Church, choosing to endure what they regard as the liturgical deprivation and poverty of the last quarter-century, while working for the enrichment of worship in the future, have surely adopted the wiser course. They can be bitter too, in their denunciations of the Lefebvrists who, they argue, by taking an extreme position, have damaged the conservative cause. They commonly criticise Tridentinists for using the rite of 1570 merely as a liturgical flag to give ecclesiastical status and respectability to their right-wing political convictions. The antecedents of Archbishop Lefebvre, claims John McHugh, are Pétain and Vichy, the *Action française*, opposition to Leo XIII, the monarchy and the *ancien régime*.[81]

Since limited use of the Tridentine mass was officially approved by the Vatican, in the apostolic letter *Ecclesia Dei* of 1988, it is possible that the opportunities for its celebration will be extended. And the offering of the *Novus Ordo* in Latin may become more actively urged to satisfy the craving of many of the faithful who desire a more numinous liturgy – especially in cathedrals and prominent churches which have the resources for such celebrations. The London church of the Jesuits, in Farm Street, having disposed of its choir after Vatican II, has since re-established it and offers a full Latin choral mass each Sunday. In 1994, the Tridentine mass was being celebrated regularly in some 150 churches across the United States. And a most interesting development, which I have witnessed at first hand, is the activities of the *Ecclesia Dei* society, founded in Australia in April 1989, which takes its name from the pope's apostolic letter of 2 July 1988, recognising the legitimacy of those who aspire to restore the Tridentine liturgy, and from the pontifical commission of the same name. In association with such similar bodies as the Foundation for Catholic Reform in the United States (whose bi-monthly publication *The Latin Mass* chronicles a world-wide resurgence of interest in traditional liturgy, theology and spirituality within Roman Catholicism, and notably in such religious communities as the Benedictines of the Abbaye Sainte-Madeleine in France), what is most striking about these organisations is that they are attracting a substantial, if not majority membership from people aged under forty, who yearn to recover the worship, doctrine and piety of which they have heard,

[80] *The Christian Challenge*, December 1988, 28.

[81] Letter to the author, 12 March 1989.

but scarcely have had the chance to know in the reforming Church of the last thirty years.

I have observed several of their liturgies in Sydney, which are celebrated weekly and on holy days, with the approval of the cardinal archbishop, in a beautiful convent chapel which had fallen into disuse after the community it served had disintegrated in the wake of the Council and which, accordingly, is unadulterated by the architectural and decorative innovations of 'renewal'. These masses are offered with meticulousness and reverence, to the accompaniment of painstakingly rehearsed Gregorian chant. They are certainly not antiquarian exercises or ritualistic performances. The congregation, like the *schola cantorum* and the acolytes, has a majority of young people and they participate (if, for the most part, silently) with pious fervour in a numinous atmosphere, free of chatter and bustle, peculiarly conducive to prayer and adoration, the *sine qua non* of worship.[82]

It will be interesting to watch the development of this movement; and more generally, it seems certain that greater attention will be paid both to improving the vernacular liturgies – in England, the bishops have successfully encouraged the Vatican to authorise a revised English missal in which improvements have been made in the translations of collects and prefaces – and, through attention to ceremonial and music, to recover something of the lost atmosphere of mystery, once the hallmark of Roman Catholic worship.

There is every sign that the highest authorities are in sympathy with these objectives. A synod of bishops was held in 1990 to examine further the results of the Vatican Council and the problems it has produced –

> rifts between theologians and bishops, decline in church practices in Western countries, dissent over church doctrine on sexual morality and . . . loss of sacredness and piety.[83]

In the meantime, the liturgical debate continues to flourish in the Roman Catholic Church. The conservative reaction to *aggiornamento*, with all its predictable and extraordinary manifestations, is as controversial as ever. It spans a scale from the wistful expostulations of mild-mannered novelists:

> I'm not a very good Catholic but I used to go to mass fairly regularly. I don't now, because since Vatican II the mass has

[82] The author is grateful to Mr Gerard Calihanna for drawing his attention to *Ecclesia Dei* and to Mr Glen Tattersall, its former chairman, for warmly welcoming me to their worship and providing him with much helpful information.

[83] 'Bishops Resolve to Keep Talks Going', *The Sydney Morning Herald*, 2 December 1985, 11.

> become a very inferior thing. It's very poorly written and Palestrina has been replaced by hillbilly hymns and bad folk music. That may seem a superficial objection, but I don't think irritation is a proper state of mind to be at mass in. So I've been forced into simply reading my New Testament and behaving rather like a Protestant[84]

to the lunacy of homicidal maniacs:

> Three people, including a priest, were shot to death in a Catholic Church in Onalaska, Wisconsin. . . . Police and church officials said the priest, Father John Rossiter, 64, was killed as he knelt at the altar after a mass for schoolchildren. . . . Witnesses said that before the mass a man had approached Father Rossiter and objected to the fact that 'Father was allowing the girls to do the reading at mass'.[85]

A disturbing comment on liturgical renewal comes from Stephen Dean, editor of the progressive *Music and Liturgy* magazine. A proponent of *aggiornamento,* Dean confesses to its failure to date, after thirty years and a generation of liturgical experimentation. He recognises changes in custom, but these have not been accompanied, for most Roman Catholics, by 'advances in understanding'. Those who have been liturgically re-educated – a small minority – are running the risk, he argues, of 'constituting themselves as an élite on the basis of superior knowledge'. A movement which had the ideal of congregational participation as its inspiration, in other words, has in fact only enlarged the problem it was designed to eradicate:

> In spite of the privileged position given, by official liturgical teaching, to the assembly as a whole, there can still be a lack of feeling, among ordinary worshippers, that they have any power or function. There is just a slightly larger quasi-clerical caste in charge.

As the Revd Edward Norman, then Dean of Peterhouse, Cambridge, writing of Western Christendom at large in 1984, observed:

> For the last ten years the agenda of the church has been set, and the atmosphere in which it has undertaken its tasks contrived, by a small body of permanent officials in the central agencies of the ecclesiastical bureaucracies.[86]

Further, although Stephen Dean focuses principally on the dearth of distinguished music to accompany the modern liturgies, he does not

84 'Chris Koch: Author', 'Good Weekend Magazine', *The Sydney Morning Herald,* 16 February 1985, 46.

85 'Three Killed in Church', *The Sydney Morning Herald,* 9 February 1985, 17.

86 In Gilchrist, *op.cit.,* 200.

see this as an isolated problem, but a symptom of a larger 'spiritual crisis, a loss of the sacred'. He concludes: 'The promise of the new liturgy has not yet come to fulfilment, as a visit to an average Catholic parish will show.'[87]

This would be a predictable, even smug, criticism from a cross-grained conservative. From an even-tempered liturgical expert, committed to renewal, it is a serious indictment.

[87] Stephen Dean, 'Roman Catholic Music: The Recent Past and the Future', in Robin Sheldon (ed.) *In Spirit and in Truth*, 31-48.

# 3
# CONSERVATIVE REACTIONS
## The Anglican Communion

> 'When I was young, Mr. Lydgate, there was never any question about right and wrong. We knew our catechism, and that was enough; we learned our creed and our duty. Every respectable Church person had the same opinions. But now, if you speak out of the Prayer-book itself, you are liable to be contradicted'.
>
> Mrs Farebrother, in George Eliot, *Middlemarch* (1874), II, xvii.

> The zeal of liturgical reformers has to be admired, and deplored. They over-value the place of contemporary idiom, plain statement, and relevance to secular concerns in the language and ceremonies of the liturgy; and they undervalue familiarity, consistency, antiquity, and the 'pious resonance' of traditional forms. They also set aside too lightly the devotion with which many who are habituated to the traditional liturgy of their church cherish what has been handed down to them. Not just for the sake of its authenticity, but as a sign that the things of the spirit outlast the hectic changes of the world. In the past few years of licensed experiment the Church of England has been comparatively restrained. But it has before it the cautionary example of the Roman church in the British Isles which now displays the consequences of recent liturgical infidelities.
>
> Editorial, 'Freedom of Worship and Doctrine' *The Times*, 9 November 1974.

### I

By virtue of its decentralised character, the Anglican Communion has not experienced the world-wide liturgical transformation of its Roman sister. Some member churches, notably the Episcopal Church of the United States, have been at the forefront of innovations in worship (as in theology), while the mother Church, in England, has been cautiously conservative. Yet the critique of liturgical reformation throughout Anglicanism – especially of the disposal of the Book of Common Prayer – has been organised with a single-mindedness reminiscent of the Tridentinists. This Anglican reaction, however, emerged more slowly than its Roman counterpart, in response to the more gradual intrusion of the new liturgies into Anglican worship in the later 1970s in comparison with the absolute imposition of the *Novus Ordo* some years before.

A remarkable manifestation of concern about the disposal of the Cranmerian Prayer Book were three petitions, with 600 signatories, to the bishops, clergy and laity of the English General Synod in 1979. These were published in a special number of the bi-monthly literary magazine *PN Review*, which also included several essays and statements by prominent figures expressing dismay at the threat to the historic liturgy of the Church of England.

In the first of the petitions – recalling the earlier 'letters of intellectuals' to the authorities about the disposal of Latin in Roman Catholicism – professors and heads of houses at Oxford and Cambridge, scholars from a range of other tertiary institutions in Britain, members of the theatrical profession and representatives of the arts, novelists and poets, and academics in the field of English literature committed themselves to this statement:

> We, the undersigned, are deeply concerned by the policies and tendencies which decree the loss of both the Authorised Version of the English Bible and the Book of Common Prayer. This great act of forgetting, now under way, is a tragic loss to our historic memory and an impoverishment of present awareness.
>
> For centuries these texts have carried forward the freshness and simplicity of our language in its early modern splendour. Without them the resources of expression are reduced, the stock of shared words depleted, and we ourselves diminished. Moreover, they contain nothing which cannot be easily and profitably explained. We ask for their continued and loving use in churches as part of the mainstream of worship and not as vestiges indulged intermittently. We welcome innovations and experiment, but hope that changes will take place alongside the achievements of the past. The younger generation in particular should be acquainted as far as possible with their inheritance.
>
> Clearly this is not an issue confined only to the churches or communities of faith. Some of us do not claim religious belief. Yet we hope that steps are taken to ensure a lively pleasure in the Authorised Version of the Bible in the nation at large. If humane education means anything it includes access to the

> great renderings of epic and wisdom, prophecy and poetry, epistle and gospel.[1]

In the second petition, further prominent scholars, commanders of the armed forces, members of the judiciary, parliament and the aristocracy, leaders of industry and officials of the Prayer Book Society affirmed that the King James Bible and the Prayer Book

> belong to our continuing history as a people and are powerful reminders of who we are. To neglect them is to lose touch with our language in its first simple and supple splendour. There must, of course, be experiment and scholarly efforts to render texts in various forms of contemporary language. But the Authorised Version and the Book of Common Prayer retain a unique power to inspire and communicate. We therefore ask all those with a care for the churches and indeed all those with a care for the spiritual wealth of the country, in its diverse forms, to think how to ensure the widest possible knowledge and love of these texts, especially amongst the younger generation. Our concern for the whole spectrum of aspiration includes our own birthright and patrimony.[2]

In the third, the 'St Cecilia Petition', famous musicians, directors of several renowned musical academies, masters of choristers and organists in the English cathedrals (including the principal Roman Catholic cathedrals) and choral scholars, such as those of King's College, Cambridge, declared that they

> desire to maintain the musical inheritance associated with the Anglican and Roman traditions. We recognise a positive aspect to changes in the ordering of worship, and would want to encourage fresh and powerful contributions to a developing tradition. Nevertheless there are ominous signs that the repository of past achievement is in danger. The musical wealth of the churches is linked to classic texts, biblical and liturgical, of unique force and numinous power. We believe that texts and music should remain as the living patrimony of Christian communities in this country, shared by all, and that every effort should be made to ensure they are known and loved for generations to come.[3]

The petitions were meant to be representative of English national life and, although limited to 600 names, included 'half the people you've ever heard of', as one newspaper commented.

Yet the clause in the first – that 'some of us do not claim religious belief' – though intended to advance the idea that the Bible and the Prayer Book are not only the Church's possession but the nation's

1 *PN Review*, 13, 1979, 51.
2 *ibid.*, 57.
3 *ibid.*, 60.

treasures and need to be preserved for all, played into the hands of the modernisers in the Synod who could respond that they were concerned with providing meaningful and relevant texts of worship to nurture the living faith of the people of God. It was not their brief to preserve cultural artifacts to massage the nostalgia of agnostics and atheists on their rare visits to churches. Also, the characteristically Anglican moderation of recognising the need for some revision, envisaging a situation – probably impossible to sustain and of dubious pastoral merit – where the old and new texts coexist in each parish's worship, sits oddly with the high claims of the superiority of the traditional texts elsewhere in the petitionary statements and, by being conciliatory in approaching opponents with no corresponding intentions, emasculates the force of these offensives.

Nonetheless, the three documents amount to a noteworthy demonstration of concern across a spectrum of the leadership of social and cultural life in a matter about which people such as these are usually reticent when it comes to public confession of their convictions. Professor David Martin, the sociologist-priest from the London School of Economics who organised the petitions, was undoubtedly justified in speculating also that

> if a national petition were to be launched the depth and breadth of feeling among 'all sorts and conditions of men' would become abundantly manifest.[4]

Yet the General Synod, elected by less than 3 per cent of those on the electoral rolls of the Church but the centre of power in these matters, appears to have been utterly unmoved.

The following year, Martin published his study of contemporary Christian theory and practice, *The Breaking of the Image*, which is itself iconoclastic in disposing of the idea of sociology as a science necessarily supportive of progressive ideals. Like the aesthetic-cultural critique of his petitioners, the sociological view of religion he proposes here is markedly different from the legalistic, doctrinal persuasion of the Lefebvrists. Indeed, it approaches an anthropologico-magical interpretation of Christianity:

> Religion is less a rule book than a set of spells by which people are bound in a certain direction. A community is held spellbound by an image, transfixed by a verbal incantation. The spell contains a strange mixture. Potent spells are never pure.[5]

His position is emotively conservative:

> liturgy is habit tempered by affection. Liturgy is use: what people are used to. It is recollection[6]

4 'A Note on the Petitions', *ibid.*, 63.

5 Martin, *The Breaking of the Image*, 82.

6 *ibid*, 85.

– self-evident declarations which, however, might as easily be used to substantiate his opponents' proposals. The beloved worship that Professor Martin is defending was, in the sixteenth century, a novelty violently introduced and greatly detested, while it is not entirely inconceivable that his sentiment about the Cranmerian liturgy:

> lips move along a familiar groove which contains resonance of home and school as well as church. The act of repetition is a summons to complete attention[7]

could be inspired by *The Alternative Service Book* in the twenty-third century.

Professor Martin is on surer ground when he confronts the cherished principle of the liturgical modernisers, that liturgy should be immediately and completely comprehensible – a questionable axiom and probably an unattainable goal. This is usually supported by the erroneous argument that such was Cranmer's aim (a point based on a misinterpretation of the phrase in the twenty-fourth Article, 'understanded of the people', which is not synonymous with 'used by the people') and the preposterous claim, akin to the Roman Catholic modernisers' falsehood that nobody 'understood' or 'participated' in the Latin liturgy before Vatican II, that post-seventeenth century Anglican congregations have found Cranmer incomprehensible:

> One generation after another of the unlearned has apprehended religious truth through liturgical poetry known by rote. Rote and rite are closely connected. They are the things we have by *heart*. Nor does it matter whether or not the full range of meaning is grasped immediately. The full range of meaning cannot be grasped anyway. A poetic statement is not a fuzzy archaism to be cleared up by a modern translation. It is an induction into an historic world of meanings, an offer of a range of alternative visions.[8]

This point is substantiated by the pervasive influence of the Book of Common Prayer in the history of English literature (see Chapter 4).

The mystery of liturgical language, for Martin, is in fact to be preferred to its clarity:

> there is nothing so fascinating as a glorious nugget of half-appreciated meaning, and the hint of additional sense. It invites enquiry and invites mastery.[9]

However, its contemporary revision has been conducted on principles antithetical to these:

> The reformers have ignored the role of rote and rite in establishing and defining selfhood. They have damaged the rhythm

7 *ibid.*, 86.
8 *ibid.*, 90.
9 *ibid.*, 91.

> of verbal incantation and thereby interfered with the very possibility of attention. They have wrecked the powerful rime. They have closed off historic worlds of feeling and acted as though congregations were incapable of picking up alternative visions and meanings. For adult individuality they have substituted childish communality.[10]

'Nobody doubts the cultural disaster now in train', Professor Martin has written elsewhere:

> Theologically, too, the drift is to close off the horizon of the transcendent in favour of folksy get-togethers. The distinctive nature and potency of the sacred is diminished. In particular, the reality of 'desperate wickedness' is expunged. Yet if sin is not a profound infection it is difficult to see why men should seek a Good Physician.[11]

A third contribution by David Martin to the conservative campaign against the disposal of Cranmer was his edition (in collaboration with Peter Mullen) of a collection of essays with the forthright title, *No Alternative: The Prayer Book Controversy*.[12] It discloses the realignment of the age-old divisions in Anglicanism which the liturgical debate and the larger issues of contemporary theology have wrought in recent years.

Conservative Evangelicals and Anglo-Catholics, formerly scarcely on speaking terms and entirely dissociated in worship, have found common cause against their liberal, modernising brethren – a transformation of the divisions by churchmanship most startlingly demonstrated in the co-chairmanship of the Association for the Apostolic Ministry (AAM) by Bishop Graham Leonard of London (now a Roman Catholic) and Archbishop Donald Robinson of Sydney (now retired), the 'highest' and 'lowest' of Anglican prelates. In 1989, the AAM had some 34,000 members in the United Kingdom and 2,000 members (including fourteen bishops) in Australia. More recently, since the ordination of women to the priesthood in both countries, however, the organisation has been overtaken by events and the leadership of the traditionalist lobby in England has passed to the body known as 'Forward in Faith'. At the time of writing, the Australian branch of the AAM is in the process of 'restructuring and renaming'.[13]

Moreover, conservative Evangelicals themselves are fragmenting liturgically, in a division that is best exemplified in the Diocese of Sydney, the most conservative and one of the largest (numeri-

10 *ibid.*

11 In 'Benchmarks of Devotion for the 1990s', statement of the Prayer Book Society, London.

12 Martin and Mullen, *No Alternative: The Prayer Book Controversy.*

13 Information from the Revd David Robarts, letter to the author, 29 July 1994.

cally) of Anglican dioceses in the world. Radically-minded clergy, in Sydney, have dispensed with prayer-book worship of all kinds, Cranmerian and modern. As Mark Strom argues, in an article in *The Briefing*, the journal of the Reformed Evangelical Protestant Association, the most powerful alliance of Sydney's Anglicans, the rules of the Church lead us 'to exchange our birthright in the gospel for a mess of religion':

> Boredom, special buildings, trying hard to be good, pews. . . . [14]

To be freed from these strictures and structures is to embrace 'liberty, creativity and a striving for relevance' – as David Peterson puts it, in his critique of this view from a traditionalist, conservative Evangelical viewpoint, but the results are 'often doctrinally thin, pastorally superficial'. Its anti-liturgical persuasion produces a worshipping situation where 'everything else seems to be a preparation for the sermon' and where 'it is rare to participate in a service where people seem to be intent on meeting with God'. It also produces a worship that is 'almost entirely focused on the needs of the congregation'. Worshippers thus 'forget about the work of the gospel in a world-wide sense, or about political or social needs'. Theologically, the 'luxury of allowing one another to make up local congregational liturgies' endangers the maintenance of doctrinal standards, which liturgy can only uphold 'if it is employed, week by week':

> we need to be reminded of the teaching and confessional value of an agreed liturgy.[15]

But it seems unlikely that Dr Peterson's warnings will be heeded. The growing tendency in Sydney parishes, the Revd Robert Forsyth has reflected, is to abandon orders of liturgy entirely or 'pick and choose' excerpts from them, and he contends that 'the non-liturgical alternatives are not being done that well at all'. The situation is approaching a 'crisis'.[16]

Secondly, *No Alternative* shows how in Anglicanism, unlike Roman Catholicism, resistance to the liturgical movement has widespread clerical support. Moreover, the essays on the American and Australian prayer books indicate both the international character of the critique and its vigour not only in England, where sentiment for the past and cultural factors would necessarily be strong, but in the 'new world' also.

Also, the essays highlight a distinctive feature of the Anglican debate – the concern about the translation of the Bible to be used in the context of the new services. The critique of scriptural revision, of the replacement of the Authorised Version of 1611 with texts in mod-

14 'Reverting to Religion: Even Evangelicals?' 4 April 1994, 2, 4.
15 'Evangelicals and the Future of Liturgy', in *Pressure Points*, 24-31.
16 'The Coming Prayer Book Crisis', *Southern Cross*, September 1993, 32.

ern English, has in fact a longer history than that of the new liturgies. T.S. Eliot, an uncooperative recruit in the 1950s to the commission for the updating of the Psalter, was outspoken in his rejection of the New English Bible (1961), finding in its translations

> something which astonishes in its combination of the vulgar, the trivial and the pedantic; we ask in alarm: 'What is happening to the English language?'

It exhibited 'frequent errors of taste', 'monotonous inferiority of phrasing', 'Boeotian absurdities' and 'verbal infelicities' which disqualified it from liturgical use:

> the life of the reading of gospel and epistle in the liturgy is in the music of the spoken word.[17]

This 'debasement of the noble prose of the Authorised Version'[18] in the name of a contemporary idiom had produced something that was not only ugly but ephemeral:

> What is likely to be the fate of the New English Bible eighty years hence?[19]

Addressing this matter of linguistic debasement, David Holbrook compares 'one of the most glorious moments in the Authorised Version' (the opening of the Gospel according to John):

> In the beginning was the Word, and the Word was with God, and the Word was God.
> The same was in the beginning with God.
> All things were made by Him; and without Him was not anything made that was made.
> In Him was life; and the life was the light of man.
> And the light shineth in darkness; and the darkness comprehended it not

with the same passage in the New English Bible:

> When all things began, the Word already was. The Word dwelt with God, and what God was, the Word was. The Word, then, was with God from the beginning, and through Him all things came to be; no single thing was created without Him. All that came to be was alive with His life, and that life was the light of man. The light shines on in the dark, and the darkness has never mastered it.

And comments:

> This makes nonsense of a great passage, by being hesitant, uncertain and dithering about metaphor. It won't leave the metaphors as metaphors, because it is assumed the modern congregation must not be faced with any mysteries: every-

17 'T.S. Eliot on the Language of the New English Bible', *The Sunday Telegraph*, 16 December 1962, 7.

18 'New English Bible', *Times Literary Supplement*, 12 May 1961, 293.

19 'T.S. Eliot on the Language of the New English Bible', *op. cit.*

> thing must be explained. They have no metaphorical habit. In the first version, Christ is the Word of God, embodied. . . . In the second, the authors seem unclear what the Word is; it takes resort in uncertainty, like a government circular designed to cloak realities. . . . It is a question of emptying language of its metaphorical power, thus killing it.[20]

An explanation for this emptying of meaning was offered by Helen Gardner, the Donne and Eliot scholar, in a sermon, 'The Mystery of Words', where she points out that

> the translators of the New English Bible had two objectives, one of which was admirable, the other, I think, ill-conceived. They wished to make available the work of modern scholarship on the text of the Bible and to provide a translation which represented the original text more precisely. The first aim was a well-defined, scholarly objective. Their second aim was to translate into a modern idiom. This foundered on the fact that nobody has a clear idea of what a modern idiom is.

Seeking a contemporary style, they produced a version notable for its 'lack of vigour and of memorability':

> It is unsatisfactory for reading aloud and for holding in one's head. The use of it in public worship divides the generations, and prevents the sense that in worship we enter into a communion of the living with the dead and the unborn.

Speaking more personally, and of the liturgies in which the New English Bible is heard, she observes that

> I think if I were in great distress or trouble of mind I should find it difficult to bring my sorrows to the most modern of the rites. There is an absence of silence in which differing joys and needs and griefs can be offered up. The service seems too busy, I feel also a lack of adoration, of the sense of the otherness of God, of heights and depths, of awe at what is beyond comprehension: 'Thou art more inward than my inmost and higher than my highest'.[21]

Such public soul-searching has been a remarkable by-product of the theological and liturgical turmoil of modern Anglicanism. Maurice Wiles, writing as the Regius Professor of Divinity at Oxford in *Faith and the Mystery of God*, also produces a personal testament of his Christian experience in the context of a temperate critique of modern priorities in liturgiology, perhaps surprising from a modernising theologian. The book is a combination of theological argument and spiritual autobiography, including reflection on the character of

[20] 'In the Beginning was the Word: Literature and Language Studies', *Meridian*, vol. 11, no. 1, May 1992, 60-1.

[21] *The Cambridge Review*, 1 June 1981, 219-22.

scriptural and liturgical language.

He argues, in sympathy with Professor Stephen Prickett, that the intention of the translators of the *Good News Bible* 'to use language that is natural, clear, simple and unambiguous' is misguided, as religion is '*not about* things that are natural, clear, simple and unambiguous'. Religious language, for Wiles, although necessarily rooted in human experience, is metaphorical and symbolic:

> It takes hold of certain images that are basic to our experience of life and extends their meaning so that they point to what is ultimate. . . . So religious language may appropriately be described as a form of 'imaginative construction' or of 'symbolization'.[22]

This view is essentially poetic. The language of faith, for Wiles, is

> an imaginative construction, reaching out towards a mystery at the limits of human experience. The *vox orandi* must be true to its imaginative, evocative role.[23]

Hence, he endorses E.C. Ratcliff's opinion that worship, like tragedy, should be cathartic – a 'true adoration', or ecstasy, taking us out of and beyond ourselves.[24] Liturgical writing ought not to be redolent of our workaday world, but suggestive of the 'otherness' of God:

> The primary source for the evocative language of worship cannot be found in the present; it is given in images that have established themselves over a long period of time and have come to fulfil a symbolic role within the life of the worshipping community. So worship has, and must have, a strongly traditional and conservative character about it.[25]

In sympathy with Wiles, but more detailed in analysis and bellicose in manner, is *Prayers for the New Babel* by Ian Robinson. He rejects the accusation of mere aestheticism in his preference for the Cranmerian style rather than that of *The Alternative Service Book*:

> I am not an aesthete responding to fine points of style or reading for the sake of *frisson*. Beauty in worship is more substantial: beauty is a mark, perhaps a necessary mark, of the presence of the divine.[26]

Robinson, that is to say, believes in art for faith's sake:

> The beauty of Gregorian chant, the beauty of the English Bible, marks the presence of a spiritual reality.[27]

He tackles the common misconception that '1662' is written in a language contemporaneous with its age – the use of 'thou', for instance, was already 'a special religious one at the date of the publication of

22 Wiles, *Faith and the Mystery of God*, 18.
23 *ibid.*, 93.
24 *ibid.*, 92.
25 *ibid.*, 93.
26 Robinson, *Prayers for the New Babel*, 19.
27 *ibid.*, 20.

the Book of Common Prayer'.[28] Even if Cranmer's had been an idiomatic language it does not necessarily follow that today's English would be similarly suitable for prophecy, praise and prayer:

> It is at least possible – and the Liturgical Commission ought to have taken the possibility with due seriousness – that commonplace contemporary English has no right style for Bible translation or public worship. If not, one must be developed, or the ambition to have new books and services abandoned.[29]

Thus the ecumenical translations of the International Consultation on English Texts – which have been accepted by everyone from the Roman Catholics to the Methodists – are characterless, the linguistic expression of ecumenical imprecision: 'never was there a plainer example of the logic of the lowest common denominator'.[30] Robinson pours scorn on the prosaic ugliness and grammatical confusion of contemporary translation, such as that of the *Agnus Dei*: 'you take away the sins of the world', where 'the avoidance of the ordinary relative clause. . . produces a run of words so un-English as to raise a doubt in the mind about the meaning':

> We may wonder, it is so odd, whether this is a present indicative at all, and if not what? Is it perhaps an imperative? You better do this, you lamb, or else![31]

The opaqueness of worshipping language is a modern phenomenon, rather than Cranmerian:

> 'Thou knowest, Lord, the secrets of our hearts' – will anyone who can understand English at all fail to understand that?[32]

Yet Robinson concluded hopefully, if – from today's perspective – over-optimistically:

> The Prayer Book remains a possible centre to which we can turn to seek a pure and intelligible expression of the Christian way in the 'own tongue' of this nation. It can be used – lived with, lived into. If we do that the other book . . . must meet the fate reserved for failed poems, lies, half-truths and vaguenesses. Its nature is a nothingness and it is not unreasonable to hope that the need to let it take its ordained path to oblivion may soon be commonly recognised. On the expiry of ASB's licence in 1990 a conservatively reformed Book of Common Prayer could imaginably reunite the Church of England.[33]

28 *ibid.*, 22.
29 *ibid.*, 21.
30 *ibid.*, 14.
31 *ibid.*, 15.
32 *ibid.*, 22.
33 *ibid.*, 102.

## II

The matter of liturgical reform and its critique has had implications beyond linguistic and ceremonial styles of worship. Reflecting new theological insights and different doctrinal emphases, it has caused Anglican clergy and laity to ponder the character and substance of their faith in relation to what some have perceived as a new religion. This has inevitably led to crises of commitment. The matter was publicly addressed in a collection of essays, *Why I am Still an Anglican*, published in 1986 – a companion to an earlier volume with the similar, rather desperate title, *Why I am Still a Catholic* and to be contrasted with *They Became Anglicans* of a generation before.

Among the essayists, the prolific author A.N. Wilson, one of the so-called 'young fogeys' and now a declared non-believer, gave as one of his excuses 'the noise' of the Church of England:

> I am glad to belong to a church with a magnificent musical and choral tradition and a liturgy, still used in some places, which is incomparably euphonious, endlessly repeatable. Recently I decided that I should not get stuck in my ways so I started to read the psalms in the modern Roman Catholic version. Within three weeks I was happily back with Coverdale [in '1662'].[34]

Another 'literary child', John Whale, though of distinguished non-conformist stock, similarly portrays himself as an 'addict of words' for whom the Anglican Church is the inevitable denomination:

> Anglicanism remains the literary man's denomination. Of course countless good writers have been members, and a few have been ministers, of either the Free Church or the Roman Catholic tradition in England. But when they have prayed in public, they have used either words composed for the occasion and of uneven merit; or Latin; or – if they are late-twentieth-century Roman Catholics – a leaden English translation from the Latin. Anglicans have had Cranmer. . . . So far from being embarrassed by infelicity, or left unengaged by a foreign tongue, Anglicans have been offered – as long as the minister kept to the words set down for him – prose to charm the most fastidious ear.[35]

He substantiates by some detailed paragraphs in the mode of literary criticism, closing optimistically:

> It may be that those lovers of the Book of Common Prayer who gave it up for lost have been too quick despairers: my impression, from encounters with one or two clerics who had

[34] Toby Churton (ed.) *Why I am Still an Anglican*, 38. A.N. Wilson has a later essay on the same topic, 'Why I Shall Stay an Anglican', in *The Spectator*, July 1985.
[35] *ibid.*, 63.

> dropped it and have taken it up again, is that it is regaining at least a part of the ground it had been driven from.[36]

A different approach is taken by the Labour politician, Frank Field, who had been one of the speakers in the House of Commons debate on the 'Prayer Book (Protection) Bill' which received affirmative votes in both Houses in April 1981. He emphasises the national character of the Church of England, a quality he sees to be threatened by the emphasis on the eucharist in the liturgical reforms. This has accelerated the decline of Anglicanism into sectarianism, serving to 'disenfranchise, or at least put a hurdle before, the three-quarters of the baptised membership of the national Church who were not confirmed'.

It is unlikely, however, that very many of those 'excluded' by the eucharist today would attend Morning Prayer if it were regularly offered. The national phenomenon of secularisation has had a much greater influence than that of the development of the parish communion, and church membership that does not lead to communicant status is not a situation that the Church can very well be expected to tolerate, let alone encourage. But Frank Field states that he will remain an Anglican so long as he perceives 'the Church's intimacy with the culture of the nation'.[37]

With only 2 per cent of English people worshipping regularly as Anglicans, that intimate relationship seems to have dissolved. In numerical terms, commitment to the Church of England is at its lowest ebb and it has been suggested that if Prince Charles were to become king, he would renounce the title of Defender of the Faith and advocate the disestablishment of Anglicanism, thus repudiating the 450-year commitment of the monarchy to the Church of England.[38]

Amongst those who have retained their commitment to Anglicanism however, the principal theme in the conservative defence of the Book of Common Prayer is the appreciation of the numinous qualities of Cranmerian language. The title and substance of Edward Robinson's *The Language of Mystery* (1987) supports this dominant strain. He recognises the gulf that is fixed between 'those who find security in a language sanctified by long usage' and 'those for whom the immediacy of personal experience demands unending experimentation with new forms of expression'.[39] He can be critical of what he terms the 'spirit of antiquarianism' –

> that is simply not open to the possibility that the language of contemporary imagination may carry a revelation for the twentieth century that the language of earlier centuries does not.[40]

36 *ibid.*, 64-5.

37 *ibid.*, 97.

38 'Defender of the Faith Not for Me: Charles', *The Australian*, 27 June 1994, 1.

39 Robinson, *The Language of Mystery*, 3.

40 *ibid.*, 31.

But the operative word here, of course, is 'possibility'. It is not impossible that a worshipping language might be evolved, in our time, that is redolent of mystery. But modern liturgical writing, in his view, has failed in this regard because the priorities of its authors are wrong:

> The desire to put everything into familiar, no-nonsense language is a clear indication of a movement away from the rich complexity of symbolism towards a supposedly easier but certainly a more impoverished form of communication.[41]

Constructively, Robinson provides a theoretical definition of the style of utterance proper to religious ritual:

> First of all . . . it will not be the language of the everyday exchange of information. That kind of language is too direct, too specific, like that realistic pseudo-art that allows of only one possible interpretation, demanding nothing of the imagination and not giving the individual freedom to relate it to his or her own experience or needs. In other words, the language of ritual must not, on the surface at least, too easily make sense.[42]

It must partake of the condition of poetry:

> As each of us may find in a single poetic image some resonance with our own condition, something that touches on our own immediate personal situation, so the language of the rite can bring together in an unspoken unity individuals who at the moment become aware of having each drawn insight from a common source.[43]

From this position, the focus of modern liturgical revision, the goal of immediate and universal meaningfulness, is seen as a futility depriving worshippers of liberty of imagination and producing texts of 'embarrassing banality':

> It is nothing less than tragic that those who have stood for renewal appear to have taken as their highest priority the literal intelligibility of all forms of worship. The resulting product, by freeing the worshipper from the need for any creative effort, is predictably lacking in the power either to express or to evoke an awareness of mystery.[44]

This neatly summarises both the emotive character and the principal objection of mainstream conservative Anglican polemic about the disposal of the Book of Common Prayer.

41 *ibid.*, 59.
42 *ibid.*, 67.
43 *ibid.*, 68.
44 *ibid.*, 69.

### III

Organised conservative protest against liturgical revision in the world-wide Anglican Communion has had its principal focus in the activities and publications of the Prayer Book Societies. The first of these bodies was established in the United States, by Episcopalians, in 1971, and by 1989 it had 800,000 laity on its mailing list, while the English Society had its genesis in an Action Group for the defence of the Book of Common Prayer, founded in 1972 by Mr Anthony Kilmister and other enthusiasts. In 1975, this became the Prayer Book Society, with branches throughout the British Isles. Later, 'sister societies' were established in Australia, Canada and elsewhere.[45]

The official position of the Society is reminiscent of that of the Association for Latin Liturgy. It points out that it

> does NOT propagate Prayer Book fundamentalism but believes a modest amount of flexibility in usage is both sensible and to be desired.

More specifically, it

> does NOT seek to suppress the Alternative Service Book but is, however, concerned at the extent to which the Alternative Services have displaced the Prayer Book and is alarmed by the extensive pastoral problems which often result from an unfeeling implementation of liturgical change.

It accurately indicates that its membership embraces 'churchmen of widely differing forms of churchmanship'. Yet there is a marked tension, in its manifesto, between these tolerant principles and its other pledges:

> to uphold the worship and doctrine of the Church of England as enshrined [*sic*] in the Book of Common Prayer

and

> to encourage the use of the Book of Common Prayer as a major element in the worshipping life of the Church of England.[46]

This tension becomes acute when some of the polemic of the Society's members, an element of which is devoted to furious, and often unreasoned, denunciations of *The Alternative Service Book* and equally emotive and impassioned defences of the Book of Common Prayer, is encountered. In this mode, the Prayer Book organisations are reminiscent of the Society of St Pius X.

To modernising Anglican theologians and liturgiologists, these bodies are to be ignored or dismissed with contempt as merely collections of geriatric ecclesiastical Luddites. The progressives would

45 For a detailed personal account of the first decade of the English Society, see Ian Thompson, 'Down Memory Lane', *Faith and Heritage*, Spring 1994, 18-25.

46 These aims of the Society are printed on the back of every issue of its periodical publications, *Faith and Worship* and *Faith and Heritage*.

regard the fact that the former chairman of the English Prayer Book Society, R.J.R. Trefusis, is also chairman of an action group in Devon to fight the construction of a new section of the A30 road as characteristic of the stonewalling mentality of the Society's members.[47] But such a caricature, while justified to a point, is as unrepresentative of the breadth and magnitude of support for the Book of Common Prayer as the conservatives' denunciation of all modernisers as heretical iconoclasts – Bishop Jenkins of Durham having been a favourite target for this species of abuse.

Devotion to Cranmerian liturgy is not only the minority taste of precious antiquarians, over-educated aesthetes and lachrymose reactionaries. It has a wider range – as evidenced, for example, by the petitions I have described, by a Gallup poll commissioned in England in 1980 which showed the majority of church-goers to be in favour of traditional texts, and by Dr Roger Homan's 'Chichester Survey', of the same year, which demonstrated that Series 3, so far from attracting people to church or keeping them there, had been a major factor in their declining attendance. Even the Royal Family, usually reticent about partisanship in ecclesiastical affairs, has publicly identified itself with the defence of the Prayer Book, Prince Charles, Princess Margaret and Princess Alexandra speaking strongly, at Prayer Book Society functions, in defence of the Cranmerian liturgy.

And while the majority of Prayer Book supporters are elderly, many are not. Charles Moore, editor of *The Sunday Telegraph*, was born in 1956 and was a trustee of the English Society before his conversion to Roman Catholicism. Indeed, the liturgical revolutionaries, most of whom were nurtured by the radical movements of the 1960s, are now themselves middle-aged. It might not be long before they and their productions will appear outmoded and old-fashioned.

Over the years since its foundation, there has been a widening of the Society's concerns. While it is focused principally on linguistic issues, there has also developed a degree of commentary on theological matters, on the argument that the defence of the Book of Common Prayer is not merely the statement of a preference for a style of language, but for the theology contained therein. Comparing the theology of that liturgy with those produced in accordance with the English Liturgical Commission's declared principle of 'studied ambiguity', for example, Dr Roger Beckwith criticises *The Alternative Service Book* in the Prayer Book Society's *Newsletter* of October 1993: 'a book which aims to teach nothing in particular can, of course, easily end up teaching nothing whatever'.

Disagreements about the limits that should be set on the Society's polemic erupted in December 1992 with the public resignation of

[47] Winter 1981, 2.

Professor David Martin both from a vice-presidency and membership on the grounds that the Society he wanted to belong to should have been concerned with the single issue of the survival of the Prayer Book and not with making pronouncements (about which there was not a consensus amongst its members) about the ordination of women. Yet it seems inevitable that the Society will address these other matters and do so conservatively. Whether this will be its death, as Professor Martin prophesied in a *Church Times* article in May 1993 ('The Logic of Sticking to a Single Issue') remains to be seen.

The most important evidence for the depth and range of appreciation of the Book of Common Prayer and its persisting attraction for worshippers, as well as the most informative sources for the evaluation of the conservative critique, are the periodical publications of the Prayer Book Societies and kindred journals produced by associations which have the maintenance or restoration of traditional Anglican liturgy as one of their objectives.

Almost from the start, the English Prayer Book Society has produced, in addition to its regular *Newsletter*, two periodicals, *Faith and Heritage* and *Faith and Worship* – both appearing twice yearly.

*Faith and Heritage* is the more populist, less scholarly production. Although possessing the appearance of English and Anglican restraint, it is more vitriolic, less reasoned in much of its polemic, than *Faith and Worship*. It customarily sets the disposal of the Book of Common Prayer in the context of the decline of the influence of the Church of England in English culture and civilisation – England's 'heritage' – and explains the erosion of moral values in personal and national life in terms of that decline. Much of its polemic has an Erastian tincture.

The combative demeanour of *Faith and Heritage* is captured in an editorial by the Revd Peter Mullen in 1981, where the newly produced *Alternative Service Book* is denounced as

> a book full of nasty, terse remarks to God. 'You are this. . . .' 'You are that. . . .' BCP *addresses* God as 'Thou' and then adds a subordinate clause; . . . 'Thou that takest away the sins of the world, etc'. No doubt the revisers could have done something similar. Only, watch, they could not; for they became prisoners of their own structures. They would have had to say 'You who', and that expression stuck in the throat of even the most enthusiastic moderniser. So we are left with these nasty little left jabs at the Almighty; single short sharp shocks of sentences, the syntax of the computer.

The Church of England

> has pawned its inheritance and gone cheap as an auxiliary ministry armed with an alternative book which imposes on

> us the graceless, costless vapidity and trendy presidential-candidate-type cheeriness of fake ritual.

This editorial closes with a call to arms:

> Prayer Book Society members must resist this decline with all the strength they can gather after an exhausting campaign. Take comfort in the fact that *genuine* modern literature, as well as the classical stuff [*sic*], is on our side in this struggle. Also because the words of the BCP cannot ever be silenced by the bare incantations of the alternative. ASB? What is it? Another Silly Book.[48]

But this no-holds-barred approach is offset by a letter from the Patron of the Society, the late Bishop Victor Whitsey, a couple of pages later, who addresses the membership in contrastingly restrained, if over-optimistic tones:

> I wish you all to take heart that your work is not in vain. There are already signs that the popularities of the moment are waning in acceptance, and your steady and sober adherence to our own heritage will eventually secure a return to the vehicle of worship of our nation.[49]

Steadiness and sobriety, however, are not in the ascendant in *Faith and Heritage*. Although contributors such as Dr John Lane, begin in the mode of reasoned argument, they usually become intoxicated by their emotions. There is no question that the decline in Prayer Book worship has been heartbreaking for countless Anglicans. Lane puts the case that 'great truths require great language', but his frustrations with the idiom of the new liturgies get the better of him and he emotively describes such statements as 'You take away the sin of the world' as being 'as abhorrent as daubing graffiti on the Cenotaph'.[50] This analogy could not fail of its effect on the many retired servicemen amongst his readership, but it inevitably weakens his argument, and is a gift to his opponents.

*Faith and Heritage*, too is outspokenly anti-clerical. Lord Sudeley, formerly vice-president of the Prayer Book Society, now its patron, gives advice in its pages as to how parochial church councils can retain the Book of Common Prayer in the face of their modernising vicars; Roger Homan reports on the persecution of conservative laity in his parish:

> in my own church there operates a kind of blacklist of traditionalists who are not allowed by the vicar to serve at the altar, read lessons, serve on committees or even design covers for booklets;[51]

48 Winter 1981, 2.
49 *ibid.*, 4.
50 'Liturgy, Language and Legacies', Winter 1981, 8-9.
51 'King Robert of Sicily', Winter 1981, 15.

and even a priest, true to the old ways, turns on the bishop and his brother clergy in an account of his ostracism nonetheless plaintive for being couched in the third person:

> [it is asserted that] the new services are always imposed on unwilling parishioners by scheming parsons. This is all too often true, but can a thought be spared for the parson who is faithful to his ordination vows and still continues to use the old services in the sincerity and truth for which they call?
>
> His is a sorry plight. The hierarchy of his diocese by now entirely consists of those dedicated to innovation and change; he becomes more and more isolated. His benefice house remains mysteriously unrepaired. Tremendous bills for church restoration are imposed upon him from above.
>
> The air is thick with rumours of church closures and the abolition of his benefice at the next vacancy. His schools have been gone for years. His young people and their baptisms, confirmations and weddings are consistently and efficiently poached. He is excluded from diocesan synods and committees (for who among his fellow clergy would dare to nominate or vote for him in the open elections for synods diocesan and national which are still the norm?). His ministry is universally decried and stigmatised as out of date, uncaring and unsuited to the modern world. He ploughs a lonely furrow.[52]

One might have supposed that Dr Runcie, the former Archbishop of Canterbury, would have been spared these attacks as he had been vocal in his support of the traditional texts:

> I will do everything in my power to see that the Prayer Book continues to be, in the words of the pastoral letter issued by my brother archbishop [of York] and me in 1980, 'a living element in the tradition of the Church'. . . . We dare not casually abandon our living link with the past of the Church and nation which is given to us in the Prayer Book.

But such protestations, frequently heard from the episcopate throughout the Anglican world, have done little to arrest the decline in the use of Cranmer, particularly amongst confirmands and ordinands, to whom the future directions of the Church's worship belong – in spite of Dr Runcie's affirmation:

> I am sure that no-one ought to leave a theological college without demonstrating a knowledge of the Prayer Book and having experienced it in living worship. . . . Young people, particularly those training for confirmation, should be as familiar with the Prayer Book and the Authorised Version as they are with *The Alternative Service Book* and modern

52 The Revd Robert Bland, Autumn 1985, 30.

> translations of the Bible.[53]

And the Archbishop is duly censured, in the following number of *Faith and Heritage*, for offering 'merely bland expressions of concern' where 'a clear directive that the promises frequently officially given are, in fact, honoured' is required.[54]

It is certainly the case that the Prayer Book is all but a lost cause in the worship of seminaries. The Principal of Moore Theological College in Sydney, a conservative Evangelical institution which might be supposed to be more reluctant than most to abandon Cranmer, informed me that, in 1989, the majority of his students had been familiar, from confirmation onwards, only with *An Australian Prayer Book*; that apart from occasional services in the parishes to which they are attached and a weekly voluntary BCP service in the college, his students use *AAPB* exclusively – and, as we have seen, once they leave the college, many of them use no liturgy. However, the Cranmerian volume is the subject of 'intensive historical and theological study in the third year', though Dr Jensen specifically rejected Archbishop Runcie's suggestion that ordinands should experience the Book of Common Prayer in 'living worship':

> whereas the doctrinal and historical knowledge of the BCP remains essential for today's ordinands, it is unrealistic to insist that the book remain in liturgical use. . . . The idea that young people should be thoroughly familiar with AV and BCP is also unrealistic and would not help the ministry of the church. It cuts across the principle of both volumes that people should understand what they are doing.[55]

Once again, the ideas that the Authorised Version and Cranmer are beyond the understanding of the people, and that modern translations are comprehensible, and must be preferred, are taken to be self-evident.

Other colleges have some provision for traditional worship – for example, Ridley College in Melbourne, in the liberal Evangelical tradition, has a six-week 'block' of services from the Book of Common Prayer each academic year, including carefully prepared-for celebrations of the communion rites of 1549, 1552 and 1662. Most of the students, encountering Prayer Book worship for the first time, are struck by its 'dignified' and 'solid' character – by the 'density of the wording' and the 'solemnity' that this brings to the celebration. But few, if any of them, while appreciating the opportunity to enter actively into the worshipping heritage of their Church, would envisage conducting such liturgies in the parishes to which they will go

53 'Reflections on the Prayer Book', Spring 1984, 30-2.

54 Letter from Thomas Walter, Autumn 1984, 31.

55 Letter to the author, 14 June 1989.

after ordination.[56] Yet, at Ridley Hall, Cambridge, in 1992, in the

> weekly College Communion, one Service in four is according to the Book of Common Prayer. . . . Most people who leave here are willing and certainly able to lead worship according to the Book of Common Prayer[57]

and at Huron College, in London, Ontario,

> the Book of Common Prayer or the Book of Alternative Services are given equal time in the daily worship in the chapel. In the compulsory course in Pastoral Theology . . . one of the announced goals is 'to help increase students' familiarity with the Book of Common Prayer'.[58]

However, traditionalist colleges of Anglo-Catholic and Evangelical persuasion and worship in England, such as Mirfield and Oak Hill, are under threat of closure – allegedly, in both of these cases, because of their attitudes to women's ministry.

Subjectivity prevails in *Faith and Heritage*:

> I find the whole exercise of these 'modern' forms, in the barrenness and flaccidity of their language, and in their grotesque abandonment of the glories bequeathed to us, too painful to enable me to focus my mind on what I am in Church for at all,[59]

though such articles by clerics as 'Reflections on the Alternative Service Book' by the Revd J.H.B. Andrews and 'The Magnificence of Matins' by Canon Burgess, both in the Autumn 1984 number, offer detailed scriptural, theological and linguistic discussions in the context of reasoned and reasonable debate. The sentiment is not without muscle. As Burgess argues, criticism of the modern services and defence of traditional rites 'does not come only from those who resist change, or regret (with some justification) the passing of memorable phrases'. It also comes from those 'who are fearful for its effect upon the understanding of the Christian faith'.[60] From the polemic in *Faith and Heritage*, it appears that the most important theological misunderstanding fostered by the new liturgies is a diminished emphasis on sin. The revisions present

> a succession of inadequate abbreviations [of Cranmer's General Confession], each more feeble than the last . . . bald and inadequate statements of . . . modern English, which attempt

[56] Information from the Revd Dr Charles Sherlock, visiting lecturer in liturgy at Ridley College; interview with the author, 28 June 1994.

[57] Letter from Canon Hugo de Waal, the then Principal, *Faith and Heritage*, Spring 1992, 25.

[58] George Black, 'Prayer Book Usage at Huron College', Prayer Book Society of Canada *Newsletter*, October 1992, 2.

[59] John Papworth, 'Needless Confusion and Disarray', Autumn 1984, 89.

[60] Autumn 1984, 14.

neither to express nor inspire anything but the most perfunctory contrition.[61]

The more eccentric instances of liturgical experimentation are detailed to draw revulsion from subscribers – such as these versicles and responses and creed, used with the approval of the Bishop of Dover at a youth eucharist in Kent:

L. Become as free as that man called Jesus the Christ
R. Play football with cripples in the park
L. Sing for their supper in asylums
R. Sink their teeth into politics for peace
L. Airlift food and life to the starving
R. Have senses in their souls as sharp as radar
L. Love a man because he is a man
R. Grow flowers in their dustbins
L. Cover their cars with foam rubber
R. Turn all bombs into boomerangs
L. All bullets into blanks
R. And flick-knives into tubes of finger paint
L. Slow down and wait for God
R. Run through 10 Downing Street with muddy feet
L. Laugh with falling spring leaves
R. Dance in the falling summer snow
L. Baptise their babies with love before birth
R. Celebrate Easter as angels down below
AND
L. Hang Christmas banners from the moon
R. Yes, someday soon people will live like that but we plan to start right now
L. Right now Lord. Right now.
R. AMEN. LORD, RIGHT NOW.

*I BELIEVE* in a just and liberating God in whom I live
and who created the world and my neighbours
and in Christ of Nazareth, His only son and my only head
who was born of a woman like my mother
and who suffered under the power of the oppressor;
He was despised, cast out and crucified,
He descended into the mechanisms of power
brought off the coup d'etat took control and reigns with the just and liberating God.
Soon, when everything blows up He will come to judge the rich, poor and indifferent.
I believe in the Church which lives in and for the world,

61 Adrian Leak, Spring 1985, 10.

in the liberation from alienation,
in the equality of men,
in the uprising of the peasants
in the Prince of Peace
and in the new life which appears. AMEN.[62]

The Rector of a Midlands church is also quoted as stating on the Easter Day 1992 BBC TV programme 'Heart of the Matter' that he recites the traditional creeds 'as one would an epic poem'.[63] Yet the defenders of Cranmer are not too refined to use their own versions of debased language in defence of his glories – as in these doggerel verses:

*FLOREAT* CRANMER

O worship the Lord in the beauty of dignity,
Beloved the words if archaic in form;
Don't be seduced by the wiles of modernity
Concocted by clergy who cannot conform!

Everyday language for everyday business,
Everyday thinking in everyday ways.
Here in His Temple the language of holiness
Rises to Heaven in holy-day praise.

Pop groups and tunes which will soon be forgotten –
Musical symbols of present-day strife;
Better the tunes of Hymns Ancient and Modern,
Sung at our christening and loved throughout life.

Mellow and measured the Psalms, newly pointed,
Rhythmic in metre and flowing in phrase.
But worship by numbers, mundane and disjointed –
Uninspired music makes uninspired praise.

Pundits in love with their own erudition,
Prelates who prance to the popular pipe –
*Folie de grandeur* and sins of commission.
Children cry 'Bread', and they offer them tripe.

O worship the Lord in the beauty of dignity.
Great men chose màrtyrdom rather than bend.
*Floreat* Cranmer! Maintain your integrity,
Worship with dignity, world without end![64]

In its Spring number of 1989, *Faith and Heritage* celebrated the

62 Spring 1986, 6-7.
63 'The Wages of Unbelief', The Prayer Book Society *Newsletter*, Summer 1992, [1].
64 By Ben Bolton, Autumn 1987, 22.

quincentenary of Thomas Cranmer's birth. The articles and correspondence reflected the propaganda that the magazine had established through a decade. In the editorial there was the concern for the quality of the nation's life, endangered by the decline in the use of the Book of Common Prayer and exemplified in the impoverishment of modern architecture:

> A walk from Victoria Station to Great Smith Street takes one past rank upon rank of buildings too featureless even to be called hideous; blank, soulless products of a moronic architectural gigantism, void of interest or of the least capacity to inspire. The Prince of Wales could have been describing any one of them when . . . he said: 'Here was the symbol of the whole sad legacy of the 1960s – an up-to-date dinosaur that was born extinct'. How easily his words about the architecture of two decades ago could be applied to its liturgy as well.[65]

Akin to this is an article by the prominent Methodist Lord Soper on 'Why I Value the Prayer Book', showing that it is not only Anglicans, and certainly not only Anglican church-goers, who have strong feelings about the retrenchment of Cranmer.

The covers of *Faith and Worship* immediately indicate its different function and audience. Where *Faith and Heritage* is glossy, with (for several years) the cover illustration, of doubtful choice, of an ancient crumbling church, *Faith and Worship* has a plain finish and sober colours, listing its contents on the front in the manner of mainstream scholarly journals. Professors and Doctors of Philosophy abound among its contributors – Professor David Martin was prominent and was indeed the guest editor (with his fellow-sociologist, Dr Roger Homan) of the special number of the magazine, 'Dialogue with Tradition' (Summer 1984), which included contributions from several academics and the former Archbishop of Canterbury. In other numbers, Bishop Graham Leonard and Mr Enoch Powell are contributors, writing on women's ordination and authority (Leonard), the Reformation Settlement, King Charles, and Cranmer's Relative Pronoun (Powell). In 1994, it had a circulation in excess of 6,000 amongst a membership of the Society, in England, of some 17,000.

*Faith and Worship* aspires to offer an intellectual platform for the conservative or traditionalist viewpoint in the Church of England. Nonetheless, in a publication of the Prayer Book Society, liturgical issues properly prevail. But in this matter, at times, the substance and standard of the writing is indistinguishable from that of *Faith and Heritage* – for example, in 'Crooning in the Crematorium' (Winter

[65] Spring 1989, 5.

1981-2), written by the Revd Peter Mullen, an editor of *Faith and Heritage*.

At its best *Faith and Worship* locates the liturgical debate in the wider contexts of theology and sociology. The lay editor of several of its numbers, I.R. Thompson, commendably exemplifies the need to understand and interpret liturgical reform as a reflection of wider theological change and development, not only in the Anglican Church but in Christendom at large. His editorial of Summer 1980, for instance, deals with the condemnation of the radical Roman Catholic theologian Hans Küng. In the same number, Professor G.R. Dunstan's Maynard Chapman Divinity Lecture at London University offers a trenchant conspectus of the decline of Western Christianity over the half-century 1929-79. Then Ann Bond, in 'Music and Church Worship', presents detailed technical criticism of the difficulties posed by the new liturgies for composers and performers – as in the modern translation of the *Gloria*: 'the words being quite unable to call forth anything but pathetic dactyls or skittish triple rhythms'. While Roger Homan shows how the New English Bible, which allegedly clarifies the scriptural texts for contemporary readers, frequently resorts to vague and circumlocutory vocabulary in dealing with sin and the condemnation of it, while the Authorised Version is plain, frank and forceful – adultery, listed there as one of the sins of the flesh, 'does not get included in the NEB, unless it is covered by the doubtful connotations of 'impurity' and 'uncleanness'.

The articles in *Faith and Worship* are generally more closely and objectively argued than the often impressionistic and emotive fare in *Faith and Heritage*. When *Faith and Worship* does decline to subjectivity it is usually careful to alert its readers, as in Mary Hopson's 'Personal View of the New Marriage Service' (Winter 1981–2). Yet it shares with *Faith and Heritage* a penchant for the scandalous:

> Readers may like to know that on the ASB publication day in November 1980 forty theological students at St John's College, Nottingham, dressed in surplices (or in some cases sheets) and led by a cross bearer, presented themselves to their Principal (the Revd Colin Buchanan) [later Bishop, and editor of the modernising *News of Liturgy*] and one of them, as precentor, proclaimed the words [mimicking the BCP Burial Service]:
>
> > Forasmuch as it has pleased General Synod to take from us our dear Book here departed, we therefore commit the last copy to our Principal, in sure and certain hope that it will not be used again.
>
> The students then presented Colin Buchanan with a battered copy of the BCP (labelled: 'With Love: +Thomas Cantuar')

> and a trumpet sounded the Last Post. The Revd Colin Buchanan thereupon pronounced '*Requiescat in pace*'.[66]

Yet the character of *Faith and Worship* is generally neither sensational nor parochial. It aims to address the Anglican Communion, not only the English Church, and has an international circulation. The leading article in Summer 1982 was devoted to the imposition of the 1979 Book of Common Prayer on the Episcopal Church in the United States, which, the author contends, was

> 'sold a bill of goods' in getting General Convention to approve the new book as a mere updating of its liturgy, only to find that it now had a new theology.[67]

'Is it any wonder', Canon Read concludes, 'that there are so many disaffected, disenchanted, and disaffiliated Episcopalians?' And the same number includes an informed and detailed essay, 'Worship in the Church of Ireland', by Alan Robinson, which traces a century of liturgical revision but explains that the Cranmerian liturgy has survived in that country largely because of the sensitivity of Irish Anglicans to similarities between their Church and the Roman Church and their perception that the modern revisions of Anglican worship have the *Missale Romanum* as their inspiration:

> For those who cherish the services of the Prayer Book, Ireland still provides a relatively safe haven. It is still possible to worship at a Choral Eucharist strictly according to the Stainer Cathedral Prayer Book, celebrated at the North End in surplice and black stole [*sic* – the author means 'scarf']. For the admirer of the new liturgical revolution it is far more difficult to find congenial Churches. For how long this will continue I am unable to judge; but the old ways die hard in Ireland and Prayer Book worship may remain for many years.[68]

Apparently old *Roman* ways do not die hard in Ireland, however. Martin Lynch, of the Association for Latin Liturgy, comments that 'the Latin liturgy in the Republic of Ireland is as dead as British sovereignty there'.[69]

For all its concern with the theological implications of liturgy, including the theology of the aesthetic, and historical, cultural and sociological analyses, *Faith and Worship* wisely does not ignore the most important consideration of liturgical study – the role of worship in nurturing the faith of congregations. In 'The Negation of Holy Charity: A Parochial Case Study', the experience of a parish (the identity of which is kept anonymous) over five years is recounted

66 Letter from C.A.A. Kilmister, Winter 1981-2, 30.
67 'How Episcopalians Were Deceived', Summer 1982, 6.
68 *ibid.*, 27.
69 Letter to the author, 29 January 1989.

and the acrimony generated by liturgical change – enforced by the clergy on a substantially reluctant congregation – is amply conveyed.[70]

More happily, the combination of old and new services, sensitive to different worshipping needs, at St Mary and St Nicholas, Spalding, is recounted by the Revd Christopher Lewis:

> The pattern of sung services is
>
> | | | |
> |---|---|---|
> | First Sunday: | 9.30 a.m. | Morning Service |
> | | 6.30 p.m. | Sung Eucharist (Prayer Book) |
> | Other Sundays: | 9.30 a.m. | Sung Eucharist (ASB Rite A) |
> | | 11.00 a.m. | Sung Eucharist (Prayer Book) |
> | | 6.30 p.m. | Evensong |

The *ASB* eucharist 'deliberately sets out to be "modern", with new hymns, exchanging of the peace, and an informal style', while

> the later Prayer Book service emphasises transcendence and reverent ritual in worship. It is less participatory and is an easier service for a stranger to join without feeling that he has been grasped and included against his will. It could be said that the ASB service focuses on brotherhood in Christ and in the Spirit, whereas the Prayer Book service concentrates more on God the Father.

Lewis acknowledges that his parish's liturgical variety is a luxury only a large church can indulge. Further, the clergy there are flexible and sympathetic to conflicting viewpoints. However, he recognises that the congregation has been split in two and that one set of worshippers tends to be critical of the other: 'the 9.30 service is often labelled casual and superficial, whereas the 11.00 service may be seen as dull and idolatrous'. Yet the advantages outweigh the drawbacks:

> The two main traditions of worship in the Church of England are used and there is a sustained attempt to be faithful to the spirit of each. People can and do go to one service on one Sunday and to the other the next . . . and many people value both traditions.[71]

In the same number, the Rector of St Stephen's, Pimlico, the Revd Richard Chartres, shortly to become Bishop of Stepney, argues that Prayer Book worship is especially to be cherished in a parish all but suffocated by the surrounding secularism of the inner-city – 'amidst the hubbub of traffic and the rectangularity of our office blocks' – where, that is to say, the modern liturgy is usually supposed to be the only option. So far from being 'constitutional escapists', the wor-

70 Spring 1985, 8-16.

71 'A Church for all People', Summer 1984, 8-9.

shippers at his Prayer Book services 'could hardly be more diverse in background and age':

> Two senior politicians and a judge kneel side by side with someone who has spent her life caring for homeless women. There is a university lecturer and the chairman of a major company as well as a soldier's wife, a dressmaker and one retired guardian of some now demolished slipper baths.

Yet these are people who have been 'nurtured in the bosom of the Church of England', and Chartres asks the pertinent evangelical question: 'Does the Prayer Book now have any missionary value?' And contrary to received wisdom on the matter, his experience shows that it is possible for Cranmer to make a more profound impact on the unchurched than that of modern rites:

> There had been no weddings from the parish for eighteen months before Sean and Maureen came to have their banns read. . . . Sean had been baptised a Roman Catholic and Maureen's links with the church were tenuous . . . but she had experienced much illness in her life and knew the meaning of 'affliction', so in consequence she had a natural wisdom beyond her age. They were both very serious about the marriage contract and the depth of the commitment required from both parties. They both felt more deeply than eloquently that only the church had words and ritual powerful enough to do justice to the seriousness of the occasion. I gave them both the Prayer Book service and the newer rite. Studiously refraining from further comment, I left them for a week to make their choice. In the end they reported that the newer one was 'very nice but too ordinary' – they 'wouldn't feel it had been done properly'.
>
> Gently, at several meetings, I tried to understand what was being said. Partly it was a question of using the words that Maureen's parents had used, but there was also power in their strangeness. Just as the bard, at the beginning of the poem Beowulf, opens up his 'word hoard' to find words high and rare enough to fit his theme, so, in a small council flat, the strangeness of archaic words and the rhythms of Tudor English which we savoured aloud helped the three of us to enter into the mystery of marriage. Our very struggle with the language took us deeper into a way of seeing things, the way of self-sacrificial love which does not come naturally to those who have been brought up with the picture of romantic love purveyed by the glossies. By the time we had delved and discussed and rehearsed the words of the vows, they had been committed to memory and, on the wedding day, the couple

> hardly needed any prompting.[72]

The assumptions of the liturgical theorists – that the secular young will only be receptive to a liturgy which speaks their language (which, in any case, modern liturgies fail to do) and is immediately relevant to what are assumed, often cynically and condescendingly, to be their concerns and aspirations – was disproved in a practical pastoral situation.

Professor Owen Chadwick, in a letter to *Faith and Worship*, recounted his similar experience of a young couple's desire for traditional language at their wedding:

> The bride and bridegroom, though young (why do I say *though young*?), wanted St Paul's hymn to charity/love read in the Authorised Version and her father wished to read it in that version. Vicar and family hunted together through the church and the vestry in search of an Authorised Version and at last gave up in despair; so the father brought his own Bible and we all heard the most glorious of religious poems, and sat in that ecstasy which the Anglican tradition tries to keep sober. . . . I am against some of the manifestations of the Prayer Book Society. But when I meet such an experience I am suddenly glad that someone is being a bit militant.[73]

On the other side of the world, at Trinity College in the University of Melbourne, the Warden, Dr Evan Burge, has told me that some 80 per cent of former students returning to the college chapel for their weddings opt for the '1928' service as more 'poetic', more 'evocative'. These people, invariably, have not been brought up with the Book of Common Prayer, but they have heard its language at other weddings and they are also influenced by the fact that it was used at their parents' weddings.

That the views of contributors to *Faith and Worship* and its readers are by no means monochrome, however, is nicely demonstrated in the correspondence section of the Summer 1984 edition, where several writers responded to an article by the Revd Keith Ward on one of the most disputed ceremonial innovations of modern times – the congregational kiss of peace, now used (a survey of clergy in 1994 in England has indicated) at more than 80 per cent of services of Holy Communion.[74] Ward's attitude to it was plainly revealed in his title, 'Leave us in Peace', and several readers concurred with his attitude to this 'great modern liturgical shibboleth':

> The giving of the Peace is ineffective – an unacceptable shortcut to true fellowship; it is introverted – creating a closed-in group which excludes outsiders, without even realising it; and it is

72 'Soberly and in Fear of God', *ibid.*, 13-14.

73 Advent 1993, 28-9.

74 'The God Club', *The Times Magazine*, 19 March 1994, 16.

offensive – intruding on people's lives at their most sensitive point by compelled sociability.

Kathleen Blayney preferred 'the old "Pax" ceremony as performed by the sacred ministers and servers at High Mass'. This was 'dignified and unobtrusive, but the present-day practice of romping about in the aisles, kissing and reaching across the seats with outstretched arms is unseemly and distracting, especially when it occurs just before Communion'. Lawrence Richardson argues that instead of relaxing into love, many experience 'an uncomfortable tension' as the so-called Peace approaches – 'the Peace becomes divisive and defeats its own object'; while M.H.N. Swinburne makes a similar point, showing once again how a practice assumed to be particularly appealing to the young can in fact be repellent to them:

> The compulsory mateyness can . . . upset them or alienate both those with personal anxieties and troubles and the uncommitted or agnostic, as well as those who are simply by temperament reserved and undemonstrative. I know from experience with one of my own daughters that it can be the 'last straw' for a teenager. The Church is not just for extroverts. I would suggest that the new conformity is at least as embarrassing to the uncommitted or unsure as the esoteric genuflections of a previous generation. These were at least optional.

On the other hand, Doreen Grainger testifies to the value of the Peace in her worshipping experience:

> Having recently moved to a new district and looking for a place to worship, I went to the Parish Communion. Greeted by the strong smell of incense and sitting in the back-breaking pews, I felt that this was not for me. But the 'giving of the Peace' was so genuinely welcoming that I wanted to stay and worship with these people. In the psychiatric hospital ward service . . . the Peace is a valuable and valued part.

So, too, does Angela Ashwin:

> On holiday, our family went to the main Sunday Eucharist at Hexham Abbey. We had our three small children with us, all under five. During the first half of the service, we felt embarrassed at the noise and shuffling of our children, and wondered what expression was on the face of the people sitting around us.
>
> At the Peace, we turned round to find friendly faces and a warm welcome. It did not matter that we did not know those people by name, and that we would never see them again. We now felt that we belonged, both here and in the whole family of the Church, and we were able to relax into the second part of the worship. Without the Peace this would not have happened.[75]

[75] Summer 1984, 61-6.

Contrary to the ideas of their opponents, as these letters testify and the range of articles and points of view in *Faith and Worship* also abundantly reveal, members of the Prayer Book Society and contributors to its journals and their readers (many of whom, of course, are not members) do not represent hard and fast agreement on every aspect of liturgical life. Where they are at one, however – as both *Faith and Heritage* and *Faith and Worship* demonstrate – is in their conviction that 'flexibility in usage is both sensible and to be desired'. Those who would argue for the absolute reinstatement of the Book of Common Prayer and the suppression of *The Alternative Service Book* – as their opponents argue for the opposite regime, in a way foreign to the traditions and history of Anglicanism – are a minority. The burden of the polemic – in the words of the Society's principles, printed in every number of these journals – is

> a concern at the extent to which the Alternative Services have displaced the Prayer Book

and alarm at

> the extensive pastoral problems which often result from an unfeeling implementation of liturgical change.

These anxieties are coupled with a plea, addressed especially to the clergy, to be sensitive to the spiritual distress of many churchpeople who are suffering in the wake of the liturgical revolution and to consider whether, in so confidently – and often arrogantly – deriding the Book of Common Prayer, which shaped the faith and vocation of countless Christians for four centuries, they might be destroying the very Church they profess to be reviving.

## IV

The journal literature of conservative liturgical criticism in North America is more varied than its English counterpart, generally more sophisticated in presentation, and often more outspoken and vigorous in reaction to the policies and practices of the Episcopal Church (ECUSA), the most radical member of the Anglican Communion. Of four representative periodicals in the United States, *Lex Orandi, The Seabury Journal, The Christian Challenge* and *The Evangelical Catholic*, and two in Canada, *The Anglican Free Press* and *The Machray Review*, only the first (closely modelled on *Faith and Worship*) and last are organs of the Prayer Book Society.

*The Seabury Journal*, named after the first bishop of ECUSA, was published monthly, over several years, by the Foundation for Anglican Tradition, and sought (as its blurb advertises) 'to stimulate serious theological reflection on the issues facing the church today'. The bias of the journal is clearly summarised in the principles of the Foundation which sponsored it, published in each number:

> to restore, defend and promote the understanding and practice of traditional Christianity as that has been received by the Anglican Church. . . . It will support, defend and maintain traditional Anglicanism wherever it is found and by whatever name it calls itself. It holds the essential elements of traditional Anglicanism to be the Apostolic Succession of Bishops, an all-male priesthood and traditional worship.

To give the Foundation a measure of standing, an 'International Advisory Council' was formed, whose members' names are printed in each number of the Journal, which included such prominent intellectuals as Cleanth Brooks and David Martin, traditionalist bishops such as the Australian Lionel Renfrey and – with a characteristically Episcopalian and Yankee touch – several wealthy laity, including the chairman, Mrs Peggy Heath, of Greenwich, Connecticut. After 1986, when the association between *The Seabury Journal* and the Foundation was disbanded, the Council adopted the new title of the 'International Council for the Apostolic Faith'.

Because of the brief of *The Seabury Journal*, liturgical language is but one of a range of interests addressed by contributors, yet the replacement by ECUSA of the 1928 Book of Common Prayer (deriving from the 1549 original) with the new Book of 1979 is a focus of much of the commentary which generally preserves a scholarly and reasoned demeanour, seasoned with the occasional *cri de coeur*, as in this familiar complaint about a modern ecclesiastical paradox:

> The majority of Episcopal clergy appear to be so caught up in their pursuit of ecumenism and consorting with Liberal Protestants and Romanists in advancing their ideas of social justice, peace and outreach that they have no compassion or sensitivity for their own unhappy people. . . . They preach love for all humankind and rejoice in their 'ecumenical eucharists'. . . . The only people for whom they have no kind word are their fellow Anglicans who are loyal to the traditional worship, sacraments and faith.[76]

The emphasis again, as in England, is on the liturgical movement as the brainchild of bishops and parish priests prepared even to persecute their congregations to enforce their will and who are contemptuous of traditionalist laity. Yet many of the contributors to *The Seabury Journal* are clerics, most of them identified with the 'Continuing Church' movement in North America, which, during the 1980s, spawned a confusingly numerous variety of Churches as refuges for

[76] Dorothy Sutherland Melville, 'Keep Us in the Same', December 1984, 25.

conservatives – both Episcopalians and Canadian Anglicans.

In 1986, the Continuing Church accounted for 380 congregations and two seminaries, affiliated with six 'jurisdictions': the American Episcopal Church, Anglican Catholic Church, Anglican Catholic Church of Canada, Anglican Rite Jurisdiction of the Americas, Diocese of Christ the King and the United Episcopal Church of North America – all of them faithful, in the United States, to the Prayer Book of 1928 and, in Canada, to the Book of Common Prayer. Of the fifty states in the Union, forty-four possessed at least one traditional Anglican congregation, the largest concentration of these being in the north-east, a conservative heartland.[77] By 1987, the Anglican Catholic Church had spread to seven countries, including Australia and New Zealand.

A leading bishop of the Continuing Church, the Most Revd Anthony F.M. Clavier, Primus of the Anglican Episcopal Church, describes the distinction between traditionalists and progressives in antithetical and bellicose terms which, however, with regard to theological subtleties, beg many more questions than they appear to settle:

> We are in the midst of an upheaval in the Church no less serious than that experienced in the 16th, 18th and 19th centuries. The lines are drawn between what I shall term revelationists and what I shall term modernists. Revelationists believe that God has revealed Himself in Jesus Christ. They therefore believe in the essential reliability of the Christian Faith as contained in Holy Scripture and in the Tradition. They logically expect the Church to express such a faith in its teachings and liturgy, that is in the beliefs expressed and in the worship offered.

A modernist, on the other hand,

> rejects such an approach to faith, or rather is prepared to allow simple folk to retain such a faith as long as they don't try and impose such 'dead tradition' on a modern church. Modernists reject the reliability of Scripture. . . . Similarly they reject the doctrinal statements of Creeds, Fathers and Councils as adequate expressions of faith for today.

They are under the spell of relevance:

> Such an approach is marvellously seductive to a society much more keen on what is and shall be than what has gone before. Everyone wants to be special. We don't want to be told that our problems are merely the same boring old sins, our doubts, the same old heresies. The theologians, as isolated from the

[77] A thorough statistical analysis of these Churches is to be found in *The Christian Challenge*, June 1986.

> common man as pre-revolutionary aristocrats in France and Russia, assume that the objections to faith posed by their co-intellectuals are in fact those shared by the man in the pew.

And the focus of his polemic is, again, the liturgical controversy – 'a symbol of our division':

> we are divided by use of different languages of worship. . . . We do not speak the same language, and the tragic result is that the watching world, speaking neither language, is treated to the unedifying spectacle of Christians and Anglicans battling like fish wives in the columns of the local newspaper.[78]

Whether the decision of such as Bishop Clavier to go into schism rather than remain within the official Church and try to find a Christian compromise with its radical members has exacerbated the very situation he criticises is a moot point. There is an obvious analogy to be drawn between the Continuing Church movement and the Tridentinists in Roman Catholicism. Those 2,000 Episcopalians (including six diocesan bishops) who gathered at the 'Episcopal Synod of America' at Fort Worth, in June 1989, and pledged themselves to maintain and restore biblical and traditional standards of belief, morality, worship and church order, while remaining *within* ECUSA, may have chosen the wiser course.

Because of the history of the United States and the non-established minority status of ECUSA, the vexed issue of authority in Anglicanism, always and everywhere enigmatic, is being sorely tested in that liberalising and iconoclastic climate of North American religious life which has prevailed since the 1960s. Without the safeguards and restraints of a dominantly conservative and cautious temperament, of cultural importance, and the oversight of Parliament – as in Britain – and with exceptional powers vested in diocesan bishops, the practical influence of such as Bishop John Spong of Newark, New Jersey (a self-styled 'believing doubter') in the American Church is far stronger than that of such as Dr Jenkins of Durham, who, in spite of all the brouhaha, was little more than an academic gadfly in the well-established English tradition of episcopal rebels, of whom Bishop Barnes of Birmingham is an earlier example.

Moreover, the propensity in the ecclesiastical life of the United States for sectarianism and schism has made the Episcopal Church, with its formularies in the tradition of Anglican comprehensiveness and tolerance, peculiarly vulnerable to anti-authoritarianism and has, accordingly, placed the onus on conservatives to discern where the true authority in Anglicanism might abide and to indicate how it might prevail.

[78] 'Speaking in Tongues', April 1985, 3-5.

In a temperate article in *The Seabury Journal*, 'The Prayer Book and the Authority of Tradition', Robert D. Crouse affirms the necessity for the preservation of traditional liturgy as a focus of authority in ECUSA. He does not contend that authority in Christianity in general is primarily liturgical, or even ecclesiastical or scriptural. Ultimate authority comes from God alone:

> authority must be theologically understood as belonging . . . to God himself, *in* himself, and secondly in the expression of the Word and the bestowal of the Spirit in creation and redemption. In both these senses – in the eternal life of God himself, and in his creative and salvific works – the divine authority is absolute.

Human authority, on the other hand, is limited. So while the Church 'has been commissioned with divine authority', this is exercised 'under conditions of human limitations'. The gifts of God are variously disposed amongst church members – there is no 'specific human locus of authority':

> what we must look for, rather, is the Church's common mind, the *consensus fidelium*.

This, Crouse reminds us,

> established the canon of Holy Scripture . . . promulgated credal affirmations and conciliar formulations . . . defined the forms of apostolic ministry, and sacramental practice, and established the norms of moral and ascetic life.

It is his high appreciation of the *consensus fidelium* which underpins Crouse's conservatism. It is the guarantee against heresy and error, but it is not to be confused with majority rule:

> By 'common mind' . . . we do *not* mean current popular Christian opinion. It is not a matter of counting heads or taking plebiscites. Truth is not established by vote. If you had tried that method in the middle of the fourth century, for instance, the result would probably have been Arian. If you tried it in any later century, the result would almost certainly be unwittingly Pelagian.

And with an eye implicitly turned on the breach with male traditions of apostolic ministry in the ordination of women by ECUSA, he further argues that

> by *consensus fidelium*, we do not mean the common opinion in one diocese or one province of the church, but the mind of the universal Church

– an interpretation, however, that raises difficulties of reconciliation with even more momentous breaches: that with Rome and the papacy at the Reformation and the gradual but radical alteration, through the nineteenth century, in attitudes towards the literal truth of the Bible.

Crouse argues that bishops, acting unilaterally, contrary to tradition, violate their commission:

> Bishops in their *magisterium* (their teaching office) have authority only as they are faithful guardians and interpreters of that traditional *consensus*; they have the particular duties of discerning and defending it.

But while he acknowledges that tradition is a vital and developing phenomenon, his conservatism will not allow developments in doctrine which he perceives to be radical departures from canonical interpretations of the *consensus fidelium*. The problem, indeed, with his article and this approach as a whole is to discover how the common mind of Christians is to be discerned today, and by whom, if not through the procedures (in the Anglican Communion) of General Synods and Conventions. Yet, in Crouse's favour, it must be said that there is a growing conviction amongst all Anglicans that these bodies (largely made up, it is alleged, of professional synod-goers and stooges for various pressure groups) are unrepresentative of their common mind. Nonetheless, the onus is on those who are sceptical about the idea of the Holy Spirit working through such apparently fallible assemblies, to suggest alternative processes where His influence might certainly prevail.

Crouse's solution is to direct his co-religionists, and especially Episcopalians, to the historical Books of Common Prayer where, he argues, the identity, the authority and the unity of Anglicanism abide. The traditional Prayer Book is the Church's interpretation of the common mind of its members, while its modern replacement is the misinterpretation of the *consensus fidelium* by an heretical (albeit clerical, episcopal and synodical) coterie:

> For Anglicans of all persuasions, the Prayer Book has served as the common authority in matters of doctrine, worship and pastoral practice . . . fashioning Anglican unity, shaping our religious outlook, and giving us a *lex orandi* wherein our *lex credendi* has been defined and expressed.

For Crouse, 'everything distinctively Anglican' is embodied in the Prayer Book tradition, and the extent to which that is sustained will determine the survival of Anglicanism:

> the integrity and authority of Anglican tradition, already showing signs of fragmentation, will not well sustain a too radical revision or rejection of the Prayer Book.[79]

An objection to this kind of fear, of course, is that if the Anglican tradition of scriptural discipline and Catholic order is as well-founded and noble as conservatives insist, then the gates of Hell, let

[79] June 1986, 9-13.

alone liturgical renewal, will not prevail against it.

But if Crouse's argument is valid, the evidence of parochial worship in ECUSA in the 1980s seems to suggest that Episcopalians will have forsaken their Anglican birthright by the turn of the century, for the Cranmerian liturgy is decidedly in decline. An order of service from a 'mainstream' parish, St Paul's in Windsor, Vermont, on the feast of Pentecost, 1985, indicates something of how, in the matter not only of rite (liturgical form) but of cult (the 'atmosphere' of worship), some Episcopal parishes have already moved so decidedly beyond the constraints and style of the Cranmerian liturgy as to worship in a manner that challenges the leading principles of Anglican parish services, whether of Evangelical or Catholic conviction, as they have been historically exemplified.

At St Paul's, there were two eucharists celebrated at Pentecost. The first, at 8 a.m., was in accordance with Rite I, the traditionalist order. The second, the main service at 10 a.m., was the modern Rite II. In the pew-sheet for the day, one line is devoted to the 8 a.m. service – baldly announcing its existence – while fifty lines (plus inserts for the collect and psalm) are devoted to a spirited commentary on each stage of an inventive adaptation of the Rite II service.

The feast of Pentecost is described as 'the birthday of the Church' and, accordingly, the service to commemorate it is here interpreted in terms of a party. Every Sunday 'we have a Sunday party (eucharist)', the commentary explains, but on Pentecost we especially celebrate the 'big human family of mutual care and love to which we all belong!' The Spirit, whose festival it is, is subordinate in this polemic, and the idea that Christians are members of a divine family, as well as a human one, is overlooked. Exclamation marks figure prominently in the prose (attached even to statements that are not exclamations), revealing an apprehension, on the part of the writer, about the force of his vocabulary and sentiments.

The order of the service has been lightheartedly transposed from the traditional nomenclature into the metaphor of a party:

> The party-goers gather
> And sing a song
> And greet their host
> A story is told ·
> Let's sing again
> How about a game? . . .

The climax of this procedure is not, as might be expected at a eucharist, the communion of the Body and Blood of Christ, but the 'game' which occurs at the congregational kiss of peace. This game is the 'Parable of the Balloon' which is given priority in the service by the concentration in the pew-sheet on 'acting out' this novelty.

Balloons are to be distributed and tapped around the church by the people.

> As you tap the balloons to one another, say a blessing – 'God loves you', 'Have a joyful day', 'God goes with you'. And see the wind take the balloon in directions you never intended, just as God takes our blessings to others on the wind of the Spirit.

After this excitement, the act of communion – here parodied, in the party metaphor, as 'Refreshments are served' – would be anticlimactic. And the service closes with the exclamatory rubric: 'just one more song!' – 'hymn' is *passé* – which is the pop lyric, 'We are the World' (which, in any case, is not a hymn, containing not a single phrase of explicit Christian doctrine).

This is a variety of radical liturgical renewal in action, but what is most disturbing about it, from the conservative viewpoint, is its infantilism. Indeed, ECUSA and its proposed associates in the North American COCU (the Consultation on Church Union, a pan-Protestant association) seem to be prone to the equation of Christian life with naivety. That this conception is pervasive in North America, Lionel Dakers has argued, is due to the influence of the 'televangelists' and their simplistic appeals to the emotions, as evident in the music used as in prayers and sermons. Mr Dakers, the Director of the Royal School of Church Music, has argued that

> it is surely the trivial and repetitive nature of the words and music of many choruses . . . which seem to have an almost hypnotic and mesmerising effect on those subjected to them.

This 'all but infantile approach would seem to assume that people have little intelligence or the ability to take in anything more extended'.[80]

In the brochure of the (non-denominational) Union Theological Seminary, in New York, for 1985-6, one of the instructors and a student are shown at the commencement ceremonies blowing soap bubbles into the air – 'Ruth Fowler and Prof. Driver float an idea', reads the caption.[81] No doubt they would be equally at home tapping balloons around St Paul's, Windsor. The symbolic conception of Christians as little children has warrant in Scripture, but perhaps it needs to be balanced with the realistic testimony of St Paul: 'when I became a man, I put away childish things'.

The persistent and relentless emphasis, in the Vermont service, on the jocular, on novelty, on the intellectually undemanding banal-

[80] 'The Establishment and the Need for Change', in Robin Sheldon, (ed.) *In Spirit and in Truth*, 83.

[81] I am grateful to Mrs Peggy Heath, Chairman of the International Council for the Apostolic Faith, for a copy of the pew-sheet of St Paul's, Windsor, Vermont and the Prospectus of the Union Theological Seminary.

ity of the ludic conception and – most markedly – the evasion of concentration on the mature realities of the spiritual life, of sin and redemption (the Collect for Purity is traduced as a greeting of party-goers to the host, and there is no sign of any recognition that 'host', in eucharistic parlance, derives from *hostia*, a victim) consigns the worship of the Church of God and 'the memory of that his precious death' to the fanciful sensibility of a five-year-old. Yet, curiously, the pew-sheet advises that this eucharist was intended chiefly for adults – 'child care is available in the undercroft during the service'. The distorted impression that such a ritual, with its trappings of the escapist activity of a holy club and regressive inclinations to puerility, might give of the Christian religion to the inquiring stranger, the earnest searcher or the troubled spirit who may have stumbled upon it, seeking the wisdom of the ages or Charles Wesley's 'antepast of Heaven', is not edifying to contemplate. Yet radical modernisers would reject this analysis as reactionary, arguing that such a liturgy is 'alive' and, in its festive happiness, welcoming.

Even in the comparative sobriety of Britain such puerility is finding official approval. At a conference of diocesan clergy,

> priest-clown Roly Bain enthralled [the audience] with his outrageously funny and moving presentation of the Gospel message. . . .
>
> He walked the slack rope of Faith, clung to the Cross, juggled the Holy Family's haloes, and tried to make his stuffed dog ('He's so backward I sometimes call him God') jump through a hoop. He failed, which only goes to prove you cannot make God jump through a hoop.

And a Methodist minister in Edinburgh, Tommy Thomson,

> paints his face, puts on a big red nose and a red wig, pulls on a baggy costume and becomes Clownbo, as in Rambo. 'There's a lot of Christ in a clown', said Thomson, 'his innocence, his friendliness, the way he reaches out to people. Too many services get into a rigid pattern in which everyone knows what's coming next. A clown in the pulpit can bring the unexpectedness that enables people to meet God in a fresh way'.

The secular press delighted in the Church-as-circus, in articles with such titles as 'The clown princes of the pulpit'.[82]

However these services are assessed, one point is indisputable: in their liturgical style and doctrinal emphasis, they are a clear departure from the Cranmerian tradition as embodied in the Book of Common Prayer and drawn upon in Methodist service books. The hallmarks of this, in its cultic dimension, are rational order, awful

[82] *The Sun-Herald*, 29 August 1993, 30.

sobriety and mature discipline, ameliorated by celebrated aesthetic components – as in the English cathedral music tradition. In doctrine, its notes are humility in the conviction of sinfulness, comfort in the assurance of redemption, and a pervasive transcendental theocentricity in the substance of the prayers and petitions. These cultic and doctrinal features are expressed in the spirituality and writings of countless Anglicans whose faith, in very different ages and circumstances, was nurtured by those attributes. One thinks, for example, of George Herbert (in the seventeenth century) and John Keble (in the nineteenth).

Meantime, the departure of traditionalist parishes from ECUSA continues apace. Two large communities, St Mark's in Portland, Oregon (with 300 parishioners) and St John's in Quincy, Illinois (with 235 parishioners), both voted to leave in January 1993.[83]

Of the journals I have mentioned, *The Christian Challenge* – 'an independent witness in the Anglican/Episcopal tradition' – is the best produced. It has a long history, having been established in 1962 and usually appearing monthly. Claiming devotion 'to the defence and proclamation of the Faith and Order of the Church as grounded in Scripture and the 1549-1928 Book of Common Prayer', it is the organ of the Foundation for Christian Theology.

Because of this, articles and news items in *The Christian Challenge* are by no means confined to liturgical matters, nor is it parochial – of all conservative journals, it is the most international and ecumenical in flavour – yet opposition to the new Episcopalian prayer book of 1979 and subsequent liturgical proposals is a recurring topic in its editorials, reports and correspondence.

The campaign in ECUSA to eradicate the Book of Common Prayer (1928) from worship and impose the new book of 1979 has been more vigorous and effective than that for *The Alternative Service Book* in England, for all its success, largely because the 1979 *BCP*, unlike *ASB*, which (officially) is only an alternative to '1662', is now the official liturgy of ECUSA. In several dioceses in the United States, indeed, the old liturgy has been banned, the use of the new book being enforced by the bishops in the interests not only of liturgical renewal, but also of theological revision. Although the Book of Common Prayer (1979) contains a 'Rite I' eucharist of traditionalist persuasion, this was included, conservatives argue, as 'a sop, a mere bribe, a ruse'[84] to ensure easy authorisation of the new volume, with the knowledge that most of the clergy, being the supporters or products of the momentous liberalisation and radicalisation of ECUSA in the 1960s, would

[83] 'More US Parishes Leave "Official" Church', *The Messenger*, Eastertide, 1993, 8.
[84] The Revd James W. Law, 'Revision of 1979 BCP Ahead', *The Christian Challenge*, November 1987, 17.

celebrate only its modern services.

A comparison of the baptismal rites of 1928 and 1979 shows how change and omissions in language have a theological significance beyond merely linguistic updating. Whereas the former liturgy made four references to the doctrine of baptismal regeneration, this teaching has been entirely removed from the new rite and replaced by reference to the concept of Christian 'initiation'. To be made regenerate is different from being initiated. One entails a rebirth from a sinful will and so an explicit judgement of the candidate's former state; the other may imply only a non-absolutist improvement of status as one mode of life (humanistic) is discarded for the better way (Christian). By this alteration in language, ECUSA has jettisoned the unfashionable doctrine of original sin. The irony of this process is that the modernising theologians are quick to espouse radical sociological positions. However, in Christian theology, they can eschew the radicalism of orthodox theology for a liberal relativism.

The response of *The Christian Challenge* to this and other tactics of liturgical revision takes the varied forms of articles in defence of the historic Anglican worshipping heritage such as '*Adorare et testari* – Thomas Cranmer: To Worship and to Witness', by Duane Arnold and George Fry (November/December 1986), and reports of the meetings of the American Prayer Book Society, such as that of September 1987 when the following resolutions were passed, indicating (in contrast to the principles and non-combative demeanour of the English Society) the wide conservative interests of the American body and the sense of clearly-drawn battle-lines:

> 1. The assurance of Freedom of Choice by individual parishes in matters of Prayer Book usage and other issues deemed crucial by individual parishes.
>
> 2. Stern and severe disciplining of Bishop Spong for the 11 charges listed in the presentment made by the Committee of Concerned Episcopalians of Red Bank, New Jersey.
>
> 3. The House of Bishops must publicly proclaim the Church's stand on matters pertaining to Christian morality, disassociating itself from positions offensive to holy Scripture.
>
> 4. Decision-making and policy development for the Church must provide the meaningful input and involvement by the laity.
>
> 5. The House of Bishops must recognise the severity of the opposition to the consecration of women as Bishops and refrain from any action on this unconstitutional issue.
>
> 6. The Presiding Bishop must appoint a formal commission, fairly constituted, and honestly representative of all elements of the Church, to deal with those unpopular actions by

the Church Hierarchy that have led to the loss of membership throughout the Church.

7. Finally, the House of Bishops must abandon its commitment to secular political lobbying for radical issues and causes, which may be at variance with the views of many of its members, as improper, and a violation of the basic principles of separation of church and state.[85]

The most extraordinary single event to date in the history of conservative/radical warfare in ECUSA – the controversy at Broken Arrow, Oklahoma – inevitably received detailed coverage in *The Christian Challenge*, which gave its support to the beleaguered priest and his congregation on their resistance to the demand of their bishop, Gerald McAllister, a prominent moderniser, that they use the new prayer book or leave the Church.

This prolonged and tortuous controversy, which came to a head in 1984 with the deposition of the rector, the Revd John Pasco, presents an Anglican parallel to that at Downham Market, in the Roman Catholic Church, several years before (see Chapter 2).[86] As obscure a parish as one could imagine, but possessing a history as a haven for traditionalists since 1969, St Michael and All Angels, Broken Arrow, became the focus of international attention as an example of the persecution of traditionalists by modernisers and, more specifically, of laity and inferior clergy of conservative principles by authoritarian and punitive prelates whose modernising theology purports to be inspired by tolerance, conciliation, liberalism and forgiveness. But these Christian gifts, it is alleged, are extended only so far as the bishops' fellow-Christians agree with their own theological and liturgical viewpoint. Episcopalian prelates such as Presiding Bishop Edmund Browning talk about bearing the 'pain' of the oppressed, such as women and homosexuals. But they may be impatient with the 'pain' of their own churchpeople. The Broken Arrow affair had the added spice (as so often in American church life) of legal wrangling over allegations of financial impropriety. All that was lacking was the sexual scandal commonplace in Episcopalian parochial controversy.

Having been abandoned by their bishop, and because it was not their wish at the time to join one of the continuing bodies (to which many other traditionalists had gone), the people of St Michael's approached Bishop Graham Leonard of London, who, in 1986, declared himself to be in communion with Fr Pasco and his congregation, being 'faithful Anglicans', and promised them 'such spiritual and

[85] 'Prayer Book Society Holds National Conference', November 1987, 16-17.

[86] A detailed history of the Oklahoma controversy is given in John Peart-Binns, *Graham Leonard: Bishop of London*, Chapter 13.

pastoral assistance as is within our power to give'.[87]

The result was almost universal condemnation of Dr Leonard for interfering in a situation beyond his jurisdiction and authority – such an opinion being expressed even by Dr Gareth Bennett, who was soon to commit suicide because of the reaction to his own defence of conservative views in the Preface to *Crockford's Clerical Directory* (1987-8), and by those who had applauded the similarly illegal ordination of women as priests in Philadelphia in 1974. Leonard's response to the furore was that as a Catholic bishop it was his responsibility to give spiritual care to any and all who were faithful to the teachings of Christ's Church and who were bereft of episcopal oversight, and that this pastoral responsibility outweighed considerations of ecclesiastical jurisdiction and diocesan boundaries.

Whatever the validity of his reply, Bishop Leonard's intervention in Oklahoma will stand as one of the signs of the dissolution of worldwide Anglicanism in the later twentieth century, as its new and more extreme bifurcation into conservative and liberal factions takes the Church into a state of an apparently irreconcilable disunity that is a contradiction of the claim even to federation, let alone communion, on which its Catholic integrity and Evangelical outreach are based.

*The Christian Challenge* has continued to monitor liturgical renewal, or 'liturgi-calamity' as it calls it, in ECUSA. It reviewed the so-called Black Book (because of its black cover), *Liturgical Texts for Evaluation* – one of the more recent contributions to thirty years of trial services and worshipping instability, which has cost some $37 million.[88] Sixteen selected congregations and all Episcopal seminaries were chosen as 'evaluation centres' to test the new rites, the Anglo-Catholic Nashotah House in Wisconsin and the Evangelical Trinity Episcopal School in Pennsylvania refusing to use them.

The most important characteristic of the Black Book, showing the increased radicalisation of ECUSA over the decade since the production of the 1979 liturgies, is the use of inclusive language texts, or 'neutered worship', as *The Christian Challenge* calls it. These are provided for both the office and the eucharist, while a musical supplement of psalms and hymns is similarly desexed.

The disposal of patriarchal and masculinist terms and the democratisation of deity indicate the political agenda of the liturgical reformers in ECUSA. The *Gloria Patri* of the old liturgy becomes

> Honour and Glory to God, and God's eternal Word, and to God's Holy Spirit

– where not only is 'Son' deleted, but the proscribed possessive case of 'he' (also proscribed) is replaced by a banal repetitiveness ('God's'),

87 Letter of Bishop Leonard to the priest and people of St Michael's Church, 1 June 1986, in *The Christian Challenge*, September 1986, 29.

88 'A Look at *Liturgical Texts for Evaluation*', January/February 1988, 24-6.

indicating a preoccupation with the eradication of alleged 'sexism'.

In addition to avoiding 'he', 'his', 'man' and so forth, Anglo-Saxon terms such as 'king' and 'kingdom' are replaced by Latinisms, 'royal', 'reign', and so on, as the professed commitment of modern liturgiologists to simpler, vernacular speech is overwhelmed by their duty to feminism. The vigorous active voice – as in 'He that is mighty hath done great things' – is disposed of, in a preference for the flaccidity of the passive – 'for great things have been done for me by the Almighty' – for the same feminist reason, and a term is introduced in English, in order to avoid the dreaded 'he', that is not to be found in the Greek. However, as Christian feminists have argued, they will not allow the obstacles of Scripture to stand in the way of their revolution (see Chapter 5).

The following extended blessing (again contradicting a principle of modern liturgiology – brevity in preference to verbosity) aims to redress what some feminists call the phallogocentric bias of scriptural and liturgical discourse through the ages:

> May the blessing of the God of Abraham and Sarah, and of Jesus Christ born of our sister Mary, and of the Holy Spirit, who broods over the world as a mother over her children, be upon you and remain with you always. . . .

'Almighty' is stripped from 'God' here, as elsewhere, to accommodate the Deity to egalitarianism.

So extreme are the changes of what has come to be known as 'The Black Mass Book' that even women in the ministry of ECUSA have taken exception to it. In *The Christian Challenge* account, it is reported that at the liberal Virginia Theological Seminary, some of the students, including several women, boycotted the use of the Black Book in their chapel and the Episcopalian deacon, the Revd Emily Neal, has rejected it out of hand:

> As a writer, a reader of good literature, as one who loves the English language, I believe in most cases inclusive language tends to degrade, bastardise and desecrate our language. When applied to holy Scripture, which in my opinion should be both as accurate and beautiful as possible, I consider the movement to be incredibly presumptuous, and indeed blasphemous.

Unlike Bishop Jenkins, who claims that opposition to feminism in the Church derives from male neuroses about the female sex, Emily Neal locates the origin of radical Christian feminism in 'the terrible insecurity of women'.

*The Christian Challenge*, closing its report, endorses the view of the Evangelical theologian Professor Patrick Reardon that 'these current experiments in syncretism and cultural idolatry' will bring about the 'very death' of the Christian religion in ECUSA.

*The Evangelical Catholic*, the monthly newsletter of the Evangelical and Catholic Mission, the largest and arguably the most important traditionalist organisation within ECUSA, is the periodical most representative of the new alliance in Anglicanism between the formerly separated brethren of Evangelicalism and Anglo-Catholicism – as its charter proclaims:

> It is Evangelical in affirming the faith grounded in the authority of Holy Scripture. It is Catholic in adhering to the faith and practice of the ancient, undivided and Apostolic Church. Its Mission is to proclaim the Gospel of Jesus Christ and to teach the whole faith to all peoples.

More specifically, it sees its 'mission' to be the reconversion of ECUSA to Christianity.

A valuable section of several numbers of the newsletter, edited by the Anglo-Catholic layman, David Peter Mills, is the column 'Read, Marked, Learned and Inwardly Digested', which is easily overlooked amongst the more customary polemical articles and forecasts of doom (such as William Oddie's contribution of February 1988 – 'Anglicanism at the Eleventh Hour'). In this section, a guest contributor lists several favourite texts expounding classical Anglican divinity – the works of Evelyn Underhill, for example, being often cited. These are suggestions for reading and reflection to assist and encourage the learning and spirituality of conservatives, and this novel emphasis on prayer and thought, based on the neglected tradition of historical Anglican scholarship and devotion, an element usually notable only for its absence in the propaganda from both sides of the conservative/liberal controversy, indicates, by its very novelty, why so much liturgical and theological polemic is intellectually and spiritually impoverished.

*Lex Orandi*, a half-yearly review published by the US Prayer Book Society and edited by its former president, the Revd Jerome Politzer, takes the adage about the relationship of liturgy and theology, *lex orandi lex credendi*, for its inspiration and promotes a scholarly approach to this inter-relationship, along the lines of the English Society's *Faith and Worship*.

In one of Fr Politzer's own articles, 'The Gnostic Book of Common Prayer', the several rites of the 1979 BCP are examined, and he concludes that the volume is heretical:

> The results of recent historical research into the teachings of the Christian Gnostics of the first three centuries has shown the relationship between ancient and modern Gnostic teachings. A theological analysis of the 1979 Book of Common Prayer clearly reveals the penetration of Gnostic doctrines into the contemporary rites and practices of the Episcopal Church.

> The rejection of the doctrine of Original Sin, the dualism implicit in the teaching that the world is controlled by evil powers, doubt concerning the divinity of Christ, the minimizing of the doctrine of Atonement, and blurring of the distinction between the ordained and lay ministry, the relativising of ethical norms, the ordination of women to the sacred ministry, and the elevation of 'knowledge' to the level of dogma are all major Gnostic innovations refuted by Orthodox Christians in the early Church. These teachings are all resurrected and advocated in the 1979 Book of Common Prayer.[89]

The debate over the theology of the new baptismal and confirmation rites is more closely examined in *Lex Orandi* of Winter 1985, by the Revd Christopher Kelley, who perceives errors in biblical analysis, misreadings of patristic evidence and ignorance of Eastern Orthodox practice in the documents supporting these new rites of initiation.[90]

Like all the journals of conservative stamp in ECUSA, *Lex Orandi* extends its commentary well beyond liturgiology – as such articles of the Winter 1986 number reveal: 'Holy Order of Women – the Bishop of London Makes his Position Clear', 'The Bible and AIDS' and so on. As the divisions between the parties widen and become clearer, the view that liturgical matters cannot be discussed in isolation from theology, that such issues as the ordination of women are properly within the province of the Prayer Book Societies, is becoming more prevalent.

In Canada, the story of the advance of modernism is similar to, if somewhat slower than, that in ECUSA. Overtures, modifying orthodox doctrine, have been made to the Protestant Churches, women are being ordained to the priesthood (but not yet to the episcopate) and a new prayer book, misleadingly entitled (like *The Alternative Service Book*) *The Book of Alternative Services*, has been introduced. But the *BAS* has already been superseded in the more advanced parishes. Recalling his period of attachment to the faculty of Regent College in Vancouver, the Rt Revd Michael Green (now the Archbishop of Canterbury's Missionary Extraordinary to England), by his own account,

> helped to found a thoroughly contemporary service at Holy Trinity Church which operates without robes, with very limited and partial use of the Book of Alternative Services, with extempore prayer, with drama, with modern music, with choruses and with an overhead projector.

[89] *Lex Orandi*, Spring 1984, 34.

[90] 'Charles P. Price, *Rites of Initiation*: A Critique', 64-72.

Paradoxically, for all his innovativeness, Bishop Green prefers the Book of Common Prayer to *The Book of Alternative Services* wherein the 'recognition of human wickedness is clipped and manicured' in 'a concession to the spirit of the age. . . . Three cheers for the Book of Common Prayer which doesn't compromise on painful truths!' The *BAS*, he argues – as defective in eucharistic teaching as it is in the matter of sin – is 'a betrayal . . . of New Testament Christianity' which, contrariwise, is 'reflected courageously in the Book of Common Prayer'. Yet he ends his address with a lengthy extempore petition not to be found in any prayer book.[91]

As in the United States, a 'Continuing Church' movement was established in opposition to reform, the former Anglican Bishop of Matabeleland, Robert Mercer, of the Community of the Resurrection, being enthroned as the third Bishop of the Anglican Church (Canada) and Metropolitan of All Canada, in Ottawa on 4 November 1989.

Again, as in ECUSA, some conservatives have elected to remain within the mainstream Anglican Church and fight for the recovery of traditional worship and teaching. A voice for their viewpoint has been found in *The Anglican Free Press*.

In the article, 'Staying and Building', which urges traditionalists not to abandon the Anglican Church of Canada, Canon Tom Smith makes the connection too often overlooked between the Roman Catholic *aggiornamento* and Anglican revisions:

> in great part the problems we are confronted with today in our own church . . . are a spillover from the Second Vatican Council and its aftermath.[92]

In the same number, the best-known of Canadian conservative theological scholars, Wayne Hankey, now a Roman Catholic layman, reviews the Revd Michael Ingham's *Rites for a New Age*, a companion to the new *Book of Alternative Services*. His review is a condemnation of Fr Ingham's account for its 'gross factual errors and self-contradictions'. Dr Hankey repudiates the contention that the modern rites are communal, arguing that they are the expression of

> the private opinions and interests of contemporary existentialist individuals and the sectarian huddles they mistake for communities.

On the sexist-language issue, Hankey rejects Ingham's charge that the Cranmerian liturgy did not provide 'feminine attributes expressing nurture, compassion, gentleness, and life-giving nature', citing phrases redolent of femininity from the Book of Common Prayer:

91 'New Testament Christianity is Reflected Courageously in the Book of Common Prayer', *The Machray Review*, no. 4, February 1994, 1, 5, 6.

92 *The Anglican Free Press*, Michaelmas 1987, 12.

> We are the people of his pasture and the sheep of his hand . . . who of thy tender mercy didst give thine only Son . . . the tender mercy of our God . . . the Lord and giver of life. . . .

Hankey, however, does not consider whether these are exceptional images and that a case can indeed be made for the prevalence of masculine references. The point in this matter is whether or not the 'phallogocentric' bias is justifiable, God-given.

The critique of Ingham's analysis focuses on his ignorance of Anglican tradition, of ecclesiastical architecture, of patristics, of Reformation theology and of history. 'Is this the level of scholarship and reasoning determining the new public liturgy of our church?' Hankey asks:

> What is troubling, and makes all of this serious, is that much in *Rites for a New Age* is elaboration of the introductions in the *BAS* itself. . . . Do not our bishops regard how we worship and what we believe as important? or have they too accepted the 'marginalisation' of the church? Is the church merely a realm of private opinion, experience, enjoyment which makes no difference for the real life of individuals and society?[93]

And the terms of this condemnation are echoed in a letter from the retired bishop of Georgia in ECUSA, the Rt Revd Paul Reeves, who argues that the modern services, that are 'supposed to be *common* prayer', are

> so confused, so subjective, so eccentric, so individualistic, as to produce beliefs that are confused, subjective, eccentric, individualistic.[94]

As elsewhere in the Anglican Communion, in Canada the so-called 'alternative' liturgy is replacing the Book of Common Prayer. 'Without canvassing the congregations', a correspondent of *The Anglican Free Press* alleges, 'the Diocese of Ottawa has placed the *BAS* in all churches'.[95] That this would be the outcome of a determined policy of the bishops was indicated even before the *BAS* appeared. Bishop Lackey wrote in his New Year's message for 1984:

> I now state publicly that when I go to a Parish and celebrate the eucharist at a major service, I hope it will be according to the Third Canadian Order until the Book of Alternative Services is available. This means that adequate preparation of the parish will be required before my visit.[96]

By 1987, the new bishop, John Baycroft, had taken this prelatical directive for the enforcement of the use of the new liturgies a step

93 'The Misunderstanding in the BAS', 5, 13-15.

94 'An Open Letter: To the Many Whom it May Concern', Michaelmas 1987, 17.

95 Letter from W.J. Ellis, Michaelmas 1987, 16.

96 Quoted in Michaelmas 1987, 18.

further by refusing to officiate at confirmations where the Book of Common Prayer was to be used and denouncing any parish persisting in its use as 'disloyal'.[97]

Meantime, at one of the major 'downtown' parishes in Ottawa, the following creed is used officially in place of the Nicene Creed:

> I believe in a God of creation
> who paints our earth with the colours of the rainbow,
> who thunders in a cloudburst and whispers in a breeze,
> who springs forth in the dawn and shines glorious in a sunset,
> who dances at a baby's birth and rejoices in all things new.
>
> I believe in a God who comes in the stillness of the night,
> who enters the manger of our lives,
> who walks beside us on the dusty roads of our journey,
> who sets banquets to satisfy our hunger,
> who triumphs over the trials we encounter,
> who rolls away the stones which imprison us,
> who rises in glory through the darkness which surrounds us,
> whose only language is LOVE.
>
> I believe in a God who graces our lives,
> who comforts our sorrows,
> who stirs our hearts to respond in deeds of love,
> who binds us to one another in peace,
> whose Spirit fills the whole world. Amen.[98]

The 'disloyalty' of conservative Ottawa Anglicans had already been demonstrated in a pronounced way the year before, when traditionalists who had joined the Anglican Catholic Church of Canada consecrated their cathedral church of the Annunciation in the city in October 1986.

Dr Hankey, however, before leaving for Rome expressed his faith in the preservation of orthodox worship and teaching, in spite of the despair of the present:

> Traditional Anglicanism is not going to die. The General Synod and General Convention . . . will not be able to kill it because they are losing their authority and monopoly on Anglicanism. Traditional Anglicans around the world still in communion with the Archbishop of Canterbury are reaching to link up with faithful Anglicans who have been pushed out of their national churches or are being persecuted within them.[99]

97 *ibid.*
98 'Anglicans Have New Creed', *The Messenger*, Epiphany 1993, 3.
99 'Editorial', Michaelmas 1987, 19-20.

In 1994, Bishop Anthony Burton of Saskatchewan outspokenly defended not only the Book of Common Prayer, but the Canadian Prayer Book Society itself, as

> the liveliest, fastest growing, and most stimulating church group I know.

Startlingly, it is the directness of the Prayer Book liturgy that he prizes, unhindered by the 'lobby-groups or the fads of twenty years ago':

> It presents an uncompromisingly biblical faith, balanced and easy to understand.

He notes, from his own experience of parish ministry, 'how much children prefer it to modern-language liturgies' – an observation that has been frequently made: they 'love its order and the magic of its poetry'. And Burton rejects outright the modernisers' regular charge of the peculiar incomprehensibility of Cranmer, arguing that all liturgy is difficult to a degree and such difficulty should not be regarded as a shortcoming:

> Should we try to resolve the ideas we employ in our worship to something that anyone can completely command on first encounter? Shouldn't worship challenge, elevate, inspire, and draw us into a fellowship beyond the here and now? The hope that people are more likely to respond to a faith which sounds secular and which demands little of them is certain to be confounded.

Not surprisingly, the Canadian Prayer Book Society gave this endorsement, unusual from an incumbent bishop, let alone a young one, a front-page spread in its June 1994 newsletter.

*The Machray Review*, the twice-yearly journal of the Canadian Prayer Book Society, is named after the first Primate of All Canada, Archbishop Robert Machray, 'a Churchman full of missionary zeal' derived from 'Gospel principles, Catholic principles, Prayer Book principles'.[100] The first number has articles addressing the various aspects of conservative liturgical concern, including a re-evaluation of the Book of Common Prayer by J.I. Packer (Professor of Theology at Regent College, Vancouver), rejecting the alleged obstacle of the difficulty of Cranmer's language:

> We do not complain of having to learn the language of computers, daisy wheels and bytes and floppies and so on; we simply learn it, in order to be able to use computers; why then should anyone baulk at learning the language one needs in order to worship God?

Critical of the *BAS*, he observes that 'the truth-content of worship gets watered down' in modern services. Instead of clarity being

[100] 'The Legacy of Archbishop Robert Machray', John Matheson, *The Machray Review*, no. 1, April 1992, 12.

achieved, 'liturgical expression becomes vague'.[101]

Addressing 'Gender and God', William Ralston focuses on the feminist desire to address the Father as 'Mother'. This is not an innovation, he argues, but an old practice found in the Old Testament, where the goddess was not a nurturing figure, but 'involved with blood and human sacrifice'. Might not Our Mother in Heaven turn out to be as oppressive as the Father is alleged to be?

> It is ridiculous for proponents of the goddess to inscribe licence for battle and murder to a 'masculine' deity. The old girl is even more cruel and more bloody.[102]

And Rhea Bright takes issue with inclusive language, arguing that women who were never aware of the fact that the liturgy was discriminating against them have been made so by the feminist thought-police. A female worshipper known to her, having been 'thoroughly and effectively indoctrinated against the Prayer Book', although unaware for thirty years of the 'exclusion which she now feels so keenly', finds that as soon as she hears the words 'Dearly beloved brethren', Morning Prayer 'is ruined for her'.[103]

Michael Carreker takes up the same issue in the fourth number of *The Machray Review*, arguing that the feminist programme of inclusive language is based on the same secular principle of feminism – to empower women, but

> we do not come to church in order to 'empower' our peculiar experience and ideology. If we have any true self-knowledge, we know 'there is no health in us'. We come to church to make sense of our lives, to order our *selves* through the authority of God's commandments.[104]

*The Machray Review* is a publication with an even balance of clerical and lay contributors, a range of churchmanship, an appearance of scholarship but, more often than not, an impassioned tone which places it somewhere between the two journals of the English Prayer Book Society in character.

As in Britain and North America, traditionalism in the Australian Church has produced active Prayer Book Societies (in several States), the new alignment of conservative Anglo-Catholics and Evangelicals (in a country where the division between them had been extreme, Sydney being the most conservative of Evangelical dioceses in the Anglican Communion, dioceses such as Brisbane and Adelaide being amongst the most 'advanced' of Anglo-Catholic centres) and, most

101 'For Truth, Unity and Hope', 19, 20.
102 30.
103 'The Dangers of Inclusive Language', 33.
104 'Balanced Language', February 1994, 54.

recently, the formation of the breakaway Anglican Catholic Church dedicated to the preservation of 'the faith and order of the Church of England'.

The introduction of *An Australian Prayer Book (AAPB)* in 1978, after a series of experimental rites in the preceding decade, has led to the virtual disappearance of the Book of Common Prayer from mainstream worship. Part of the story of the accelerated momentum of the movement for independence from English influences in Australian life in this period, *AAPB* was introduced as an 'alternative' to '166'2, but has since replaced it at the principal services in most cathedrals and in all but a handful of parish churches, throughout the country.

In spite of well-organised criticism from the Australian Prayer Book Societies, and other conservative bodies, such as Ecclesia and the Anglican Society, and the assurances of several bishops, through the years, that the Book of Common Prayer would and should be kept actively in use, the modern liturgy is now all but universal and is ubiquitous in the theological colleges and Church schools. As in Roman Catholicism, a generation of Australian Anglicans (including seminarians) has grown up and been trained without any significant exposure to the traditional worship and spirituality of their Church. Although plans to incorporate Cranmerian rites into the revision of *AAPB* had been greeted with interest and some sympathy, it could not be reasonably supposed that, if this had occurred, many of the clergy would, in practice, favour '1662' over the new orders to which they have become accustomed and to the theology of which they are committed, or that they would celebrate even the occasional Cranmerian service.

It is not too much to say that in Australia, as elsewhere, the most damaging factor in the demise of the Book of Common Prayer has been the failure of theological colleges to keep it as a regular part of their worship and as a fundamental text in the study of Anglican spirituality. In spite of the polemic about the involvement of the laity in 'worship committees' and so forth, the influence of the vicar or rector, who will express the worshipping priorities of his training, on the style of liturgy and the rites used is paramount. In one historic inner-city church, the newly appointed rector quickly became notorious, in the years of radical liturgical change, for enforcing his ideas and then, after they were securely in place, calling a series of elaborate forums to 'discuss' liturgical change, as if it were a matter for open-minded debate. He became agitated when any of his parishioners disagreed with his plans, refusing to marry couples who requested the traditional service, in spite of the fact that he would fervently proclaim his commitment to congregational participation, to the role of the laity in 'decision-making' and other shibboleths. Most recently, the several clergy of the parish, including the rector, styled themselves 'Associate Ministers', with 'a commitment to mutuality in ministry'. In this strategy, no-one in particular is a leader or ruler ('rector'), everyone is in charge – except those who are not (the laity) – yet when a controversy arises, as was recently the case over the parish's music, the rector suddenly emerged autonomously supreme in his rulings. All the propaganda notwithstanding, the authoritarianism of the episcopate and of parish clergy is at least as evident in this age as in any other – is more strident, in fact, in church now that their influence in the world is non-existent – and is the more sinister for being exercised in covert rather than explicit ways, for being denied even when its triumph is plain.

Unedifying evidence of the clerical shoring-up of power and position (in Australia, as elsewhere) is to be found in the rapidly burgeoning phenomenon of priests' pursuit of higher degrees, particularly doctorates, which bring with them a title supposedly indicative of higher learning, as in the American-style D. Min., conferred by institutions of dubious academic standing, which do not even require a primary degree as a prerequisite. Such disreputable professional self-elevation by the clergy sits oddly with their polemic of egalitarianism – in liturgical pronouncements, for example.

In an article, 'Laity in the Aisles', Dr Muriel Porter – a Doctor of Philosophy, not of Ministry – a lay representative on the Anglican Consultative Council, traces

> the major, if subtle, power shift that has occurred in the worldwide Anglican communion during the past two decades.

Not only the laity, in her view, but the inferior clergy too

> have been inexorably losing ground as power has concentrated in the hands of the bishops.

The 1998 Lambeth Conference, she opines,

> will inevitably be a triumphalist display of episcopacy . . . being restricted to bishops, it offers no representation to the clergy or laity, and so is a denial of the concept of synodical government that has become central to the ecclesiology of modern Anglicanism. . . . Bishops alone will effectively 'seek God's will' for the rest of the church.[105]

Whoever is in charge, whether priests or bishops, if they have no sympathy with, or experience of, the Book of Common Prayer in 'living worship' (to use Dr Runcie's phrase) – and it may be supposed that the majority of Anglican clergy now fall into one or other of these categories – then the preservation, or the even more difficult process of the reintroduction, of traditional worship will simply

105 *Eureka Street*, June/July 1994, 26-8.

not occur, no matter how determined the committed conservative members of a parish (usually, in any case, a minority of the laity) may be. The same is true of Roman Catholicism. If seminarians have no Latin and are not trained to celebrate the *Novus Ordo* in that language, there is little prospect of Latin masses returning in the future, the vigorous activities of the Association for Latin Liturgy and the traditionalist bodies notwithstanding.

The Australian Prayer Book Societies, unlike their overseas counterparts, have not established their own periodicals, but distribute the English *Faith and Heritage* and *Faith and Worship* to their members. These are, unquestionably, encouraging and informative publications for those devoted to traditional liturgy, but they are also quintessentially English. The popularity of these periodicals amongst Australian Cranmerians emphasises an element of anglophilia in the conservatives' Christianity which, while not necessarily reprehensible (the Irishness of Australian Roman Catholicism is a flavoursome ingredient of that faith), does suggest to their opponents, committed to making Anglicanism relevant to today's 'multicultural' Australia, that an aspect of traditionalist fervency for the retention or recovery of the Book of Common Prayer is a nostalgic desire to reclaim something of the lost Englishness of Australian social and religious life – undoubtedly, a futile quest.

In a nation where it is now possible to have an avowed atheist as the Queen's representative (in the person of Governor-General Bill Hayden), the once quasi-established character of the Anglican Church and its majority share of the church-going population are now only memories of the ageing. Today, 15 per cent of Australian Anglicans attend church regularly – about half the number who attended in the 1960s. Anglican church attendances in Melbourne, with a population of some three million, average only 27,000 on Sundays, mostly elderly women, compared with 216,000 at Roman Catholic masses.[106]

If it is to survive as a significant element in the Christian life of the country, Australian Anglicanism must find ways of combining its English genesis with native elements. This had been successfully achieved in the past in such organisations as the famous Bush Brotherhood, where the distinctively Australian romance of the outback was combined with Evangelical simplicity of life and witness and a Catholic style of worship and corporate organisation. Then, Bishop Howll Witt, the 'Bush Bishop' (although Welsh born), attractively combined traditional and home-grown qualities in a way with which Australians of his generation could identify.

But the romance of the outback is now exhausted, the huge coastal

[106] Stephen Freed, 'Praying for an Identity', *The Sydney Morning Herald*, 8 November 1993, 19.

cities are no longer overgrown country towns, looking by turns inland and 'homeward' to the British Isles, but internationalist in mood and perspective. The Anglo-Saxon monopoly of culture has passed into 'multiculturalism', and even Christianity (English, Irish, Scottish, Italian, Greek or whatever) must take its place in a 'multifaith' and increasingly predominantly secular milieu.

Aware of these phenomena, Christian commentators such as David Millikan developed the notion of 'ocker Christianity' in the 1970s, the 'ocker' being the average Australian 'bloke', speaking a language at once laconic and luridly colloquial, and embodying the gregarious and uncritical hedonism, deeply suspicious of any forms of transcendentalism or intellectualism, of the 'sunburnt country'.

The high point – or low point – of ocker Christianity was reached in 1987 when the Bible Society announced that it was to release an Australianised Bible for the bicentennial celebration of Australia's European foundation in 1988. This version would feature a gum tree on the front cover and an Aboriginal-style depiction of the crucifixion. The Scriptures would be translated into 'the common language of Australian people', with special attention to 'Australianising' key expressions.

If this programme were to be faithfully followed, as Peter White demonstrated in a satirical article, the universal message of the New Testament would be reduced, through parochial slang, to subcultural insignificance:

> Presumably the miracle of the loaves and fishes, for example, will end up something along the lines of an account of how Peter and the disciples invited a few mates of a Saturday arvo and, because it was hot, they brought all their kids and relatives with them for a swim in the pool. It looked like there wouldn't be enough food to go round until Christ threw another prawn on the barbie and, stone the crows, if there wasn't more than enough and a whole heap of potato salad left over as well.

Or St Paul's encounter with the voice of Jesus on the road to Damascus would read:

> Stun the mullets, cobber, but don't you think it's time you stopped coming the raw prawn with me?[107]

A *reductio ad absurdum* of the principle, Peter White's examples nonetheless expose the limitations of 'ocker Christianity', as of all attempts at 'inculturation', the procrustean process of constraining Christianity by the terms of temporal and societal priorities. To begin with, in an age acutely conscious of sexism, ockerism is unashamedly masculinist. Further, its vocabulary is essentially that of Anglo-

107 'Jesus: Prophet or Country Mug?' *The Sydney Morning Herald*, 6 October 1987, 13.

Saxon Australians. It is already dated and, as the Americanisation of Australian society continues apace, it will become increasingly outmoded. Most Australian young men of today, for example, speak not of 'blokes' but of 'guys', the 'cobber' of my father's generation is never heard now, and even the 'mate' of mine is being challenged by 'buddy'. Along with the mores of the country, the distinctive vocabulary and phraseology of Australia are on the wane. With the European and Asian sections of the population growing rapidly also, the 'ocker' is an endangered species. By the twenty-first century, his lingo could be at least as elusive to most Australians as that of the Authorised Version.

Consideration of the possibilities of an indigenous language of worship, however, indicates the erroneousness of the claims of the proponents of *An Australian Prayer Book*, on its appearance in 1978, that it was written in a language that would speak directly to 'today's Australia'. If only it were as lively and colourful as ocker-speak! In fact, the new liturgy is written, like all contemporary Anglican liturgies, in the anonymous international newspeak of liturgical commissioners, with one or two poeticisms from Professor David Frost which serve to emphasise the banality of its usual manner. So far from being vitally Australian, *AAPB* is written in the dead language of later twentieth-century officialese, as concocted for use on public ceremonial occasions, whether sacred or secular, at once inoffensive and unmemorable. After twenty years of weekly attendance at the modern language rites of the Australian Anglican Church, I could not begin to recite from memory the order for Holy Communion from *AAPB*. Yet I still know most of the Book of Common Prayer by heart (even the occasional services), although I had fewer years' exposure to it, and that in now distant youth.

The next production of the Liturgical Commission, *A Prayer Book for Australia*, is due for publication this year (1995) and will replace *AAPB*. There is little reason to suppose that its cadences will be any more memorable than those of the present volume, for while some members of the Commission, such as Dr Charles Sherlock, are aware of and sympathetic to the criticisms of the banality of the prose of modern liturgies, they are also conscious of demands for liturgical language to be simplified further and made more relevant to local culture.[108]

While the Australian Prayer Book Societies produce no journal, the Anglican Society has published a quarterly, *On Anglicanism*, edited by a layman, Michael Mansbridge-Wood, from its offices in the heart of the liberal archdiocese of Perth, Western Australia. The Anglican Society is opposed to 'present trends' in the Church, in

108 Interview with the author, 28 June 1994.

particular:

Moves to 'revise' the language of the Bible and the liturgy
Abandonment of the Church's historic faith
The 'ordination' of women
Standards of morality
Bishops and clergy who fail to teach the faith.[109]

*On Anglicanism* reports world-wide events in the Communion and has as many features on the Continuing Churches as on mainstream Anglicanism. It is journalistically forthright in style – the editorial of August 1987 has the exclamatory title 'Schism! Schism!' and speaks bluntly of getting things straight – while the 'Reverend Babs' cartoon, a satire of 'priestesses', is a regular feature (see Appendix). But the preoccupations of the magazine, as of the Anglican Society, are theological rather than liturgical. And the theology is amateuristic and sensationalist.

A different emphasis emerges from *Anglican Catholic News*, the periodical of the Anglican Church in Australia. By March 1990, this continuing body possessed a bishop in the Rt Revd Albert Haley, formerly an Anglican parish priest in Brisbane, a religious 'order' in the Augustinian tertiary, Brother Raymond (formerly a Franciscan friar), and some ten parishes sprinkled around the country.

While the *Anglican Catholic News* carries items of theological and historical interest, its largely photographic content demonstrates the importance placed by the Anglican Catholic Church (ACC) world-wide on traditional liturgy of the kind that used to be known as 'Walsingham standard'. It is appropriate that one of the parishes of the ACC, in the Queensland city of Rockhampton, is under the patronage of Our Lady of Walsingham.

Although its services are conducted in unprepossessing buildings, the liturgies are celebrated with an Anglo-Catholic solemnity and pomp in a style now unknown in Anglicanism and Roman Catholicism. Birettas and lace cottas predominate, the maniple has been restored as a eucharistic vestment, altars and shrines are elaborately adorned in baroque style, old-fashioned Stations of the Cross decorate the wooden walls, and the montage of photographs of the enthronement of Archbishop Mercer of Canada (in the November 1989 number) shows his triumphal, jewel-encrusted mitre, of the kind which even the Pope has abjured. Evensong has been restored in Cranmerian style, but so too has Benediction of the Blessed Sacrament and, of course, auricular confession. The term 'mass' is freely used. The polemic of the ACC stresses its return to the Book of Common Prayer. The *Anglican Catholic News*, however, indicates that if this is Prayer Book worship, it is according to *The English Missal*. In

[109] *On Anglicanism*, April 1987, 11.

other words, it shows the fragility of the alliance between conservative Anglo-Catholics and Evangelicals.

The fundamental similarity of all these periodical publications, and the problem which inhibits their mission, is that whatever the differences between them – of national origin and character, of churchmanship, of breadth or narrowness of conservative concern – each of them is preaching to the converted. Moreover, in the unlikely event of liberal, modernist or radical Anglicans consulting *Faith and Worship* or *Anglican Catholic News*, their chances of coming across an article, letter or photograph of the more strident traditionalist kind, serving only to confirm *their* prejudices, is as likely as their happening upon a scholarly, objective and restrained item.

Most of the polemic material in the journals can be summarised as a quest for arguments and reasons, of varying validity and profundity, for sustaining a liturgical and theological viewpoint that derives as much from spiritual and emotional sources as from detached inquiry and intellectual rigour. It is not the less worthy for this, but it is less conducive to the persuasion of opponents. This is not to say, on the other hand, that reformist propaganda is not also characterised by subjective discourse. One only has to read the works of Bishop Colin Buchanan to support this judgement. But it is because of the prevalence of these irrational elements on both sides that reasoned dialogue between them is difficult to achieve.

The conservative journals, whose proliferation is a clear index of the variety and vigour of the traditionalist movement throughout Anglicanism, serve the purpose, principally, of sustaining and encouraging their regular readership. Their frequent appearance, the quasi-institutional orderliness of their respective designs and arrangements and their support by various foundations with resonant titles give a sense of established Christian community (however sub-cultural) to many who have experienced painful ostracism by their Church.

## V

For Anglicans, the 1980s closed disturbingly, with the scandal following the suicide, in 1987, of Dr Gareth Bennett (author of the 1987-8 *Crockford's* Preface), the disunity of the 1988 Lambeth Conference (over the issue of the consecration of women bishops), the quincentenary celebrations, in 1989, of the birth of Cranmer (which emphasised the extent to which the Church had discarded his work), and – along with the secularisation of Western civilisation in which Anglicanism has an increasingly marginalised role – a deepening sense of *fin de siècle.*

These different preoccupations were expressed in various publications of these years: *To the Church of England* (1988), an edition of the writings of Gareth Bennett, including the controversial Preface, with a memoir by Dr Geoffrey Rowell; *The Crockford's File* (1989), a study of 'Gareth Bennett and the Death of the Anglican Mind' by Dr William Oddie; and in liturgy, *A Way of Life* (1989), a representative collection of essays from the Australian Prayer Book Society, defending Cranmerian worship, but in a constructive, forward-looking spirit; and *Towards Liturgy 2000* (1989), a symposium by members of the Alcuin Club, the long-established Cambridge-based liturgical group.

If a dominant theme is to be discerned in these disparate works, it is a conviction that the absoluteness of either the traditionalist or modernising positions is decidedly not in the best interests of the Church in the twenty-first century. In different ways, and even from contradictory starting points (and, in the case of Dr Bennett, in spite of episcopal misrepresentations, with fatal consequences), the authors point towards a condition of comprehensiveness in theology and liturgy, to a recovery of respect for the Anglican tradition of reasoned divinity, constrained by scriptural learning and a Catholic and Reformed tradition, which has been destabilised in the latter half of this century – initially by the party of theologians and liturgiologists, the 'liberal establishment', who might have been supposed to have keenly defended it, and then by the extremism of the inevitable conservative backlash.

The suicide of Gareth Bennett had positive aspects. It drew worldwide attention to the condition of the Church of England and it made all Anglicans – not only those actively involved in ecclesiastical controversy – aware of the deep divisions in their Communion. The decorous pretence that, in spite of the usual bickering, all was essentially well with the Church, could no longer be sustained by anybody.

The report of the suicide in the international news magazine *Newsweek*, 'Anglicans in Turmoil – A Death Comes to the Archbishop', pointed out 'how close to schism' Anglicanism had come:

> If Runcie and his fellow liberals continue their modernizing ways, some dissidents predict, eventually there will be an exodus of either Anglo-Catholics or Evangelicals – or both – from the Church of England. The liberals insist on adjusting to the times even as Anglo-Catholics want to retain pre-Reformation traditions and Evangelicals want a morally erect – and non-papist – church of the realm. The lesson for the Church of England: unlike the Trinity, it cannot be three things at once.[110]

Like many other articles, *Newsweek*'s focused on the criticism of

110 December 22/29 1987, 203.

Bennett's Preface by Archbishop Habgood of York, who denounced it as 'scurrilous, sour and vindictive', implying that such pillorying of Bennett led directly to his suicide.[111]

What is remarkable for those readers of the *Crockford's* Preface who have turned to it as a result of the publicity is to find how mild it is. As one reviewer noted:

> What I read took me by surprise. The preface is scholarly, well-written, even-tempered, factual and persuasive; everything is in good taste. . . . Bennett's preface is sober and responsible almost to the point of being dull. Its major fault in the eyes of the Church of England's Establishment, clearly, is its traditionalist and orthodox point of view.[112]

For the modernisers to have reacted defensively to a donnish analysis does suggest a certain neurosis on their part about their position and influence.

Liturgically, Bennett emphasises 'the uniting effect of the Book of Common Prayer, a liturgy of considerable literary power', in the English Church:

> Though it was possible to have different theological interpretations of the texts there was a common liturgical language which became part of the heritage of all Anglicans.[113]

In the scholarly way, he supports his point by reference to Professor Stephen Sykes' study *The Integrity of Anglicanism*, where Sykes found 'the essence of Anglican unity in a common tradition of worship based on the Book of Common Prayer':

> The liturgical tradition to which he points and on which he bases so much is fading as fast as the Cheshire Cat's smile (p.194).

This is as facetious as Bennett becomes. He continues in his more usual analytic vein:

> No change in Anglicanism during the last thirty years has been more remarkable than the virtual disuse of the prayer books based on the English Book of Common Prayer. . . . In England within a generation the Book of Common Prayer has been virtually eliminated by services which are in theory only permissible alternatives to it.

So far from being an intransigent reactionary, Bennett can claim that

> it may well be that there were good and valid reasons for all the churches to produce modern liturgies.

But he makes the historian's point about learning from the past – here, with ecclesiastical implications:

111 For a detailed account see William Oddie, *The Crockford's File*.

112 Thomas Reeves, *The Christian Challenge*, April 1988, 14.

113 'The Preface to Crockford's Clerical Directory', in G. Rowell (ed.) *To the Church of England*, 192.

> Nothing is more apparent than Anglicanism's break with its liturgical past, and any attempt to define Anglicanism by reference to its tradition of worship is now on very insecure ground (pp.197-8).

The new liturgies 'are not so much a factor for unity as a sign of increasing diversity'.

For Bennett, these developments are making a profound spiritual and theological impact:

> Anglican theological colleges . . . have now trained a whole generation of priests with a minimal knowledge of classical Anglican divinity or its methods. Clergy without a sense of there being some authority in the historic experience of the Church may well come to think that theology is the latest fashionable theory of theologians (p.201).

The consequences of such trends in ECUSA, he indicates, should be heeded elsewhere:

> Episcopal seminaries are centres of a liberalising theology which bears little or no resemblance to traditional Anglicanism; training in the spiritual life is widely discounted and few seminaries have any daily corporate prayer; the sexual mores of both staff and students appear to have broken with the standards usually associated with the Christian ministry (p.206).

While the implications of these comments are serious, this is scarcely the acrimonious outpouring of a priest embittered because (as was alleged) of his failure to gain promotion in the Church, and who had taken the cowardly opportunity to hide behind a custom of anonymity. Rather, as Dr Rowell's inclusion of other pieces written by Bennett over the years indicates, the Preface is an outcome of a lifetime's public speculation and scholarship on Church history and theology. In an essay on Thomas Ken, for example, Bennett had written:

> we sometimes imagine that our faith is enhanced by discarding the experience and tradition of the past.[114]

And in 'Tradition and Change in the Church', he reflected:

> It is always dangerous to interfere with a people's religious system. It is far easier to destroy religious communities than to build them up, and there are many examples of supposedly rational persons who did violence in ancient societies by not understanding what gave them their identity.[115]

What is notable about these reflections, and the *Crockford's* Preface (which is meant to be topical and controversial), is not the stridency of Bennett's claims, but – if anything – their gentility, even tentativeness. His is a warning voice, seldom castigating. He is not

[114] *ibid*, 74.
[115] *ibid.*, 135.

emotional about Cranmer, but historical and theological; he does not reject liturgical experimentation or *The Alternative Service Book*, but argues for the retention of the Book of Common Prayer as an influence for unity, a work of aesthetic distinction and a compendium of spirituality. The onus, once again, is on those who have worked strenuously for its abolition to explain why they regard its attributes as dispensable and undesirable. But they preferred to stigmatise Bennett rather than answer his criticisms in the courteous spirit in which they were made.

For William Oddie, in a way that Gareth Bennett would probably have found excessive, the Oxford don is a martyr for the traditional faith and practice of the Church of England. He was, Oddie writes, 'a brave, distinguished, and prayerful priest whose heart in the end was broken by the Church he served':[116]

> If the Church of England were other than it has become, *then* he would be alive today.[117]

If Bennett's death is not martyrdom, Oddie concludes, 'it is not far from it'.[118]

The irony of such an assessment, of course, is that on traditional teaching suicides, by their actions, place themselves beyond salvation, and Dr Oddie even includes an anecdote recalling Bennett's orthodox distaste during a theoretical discussion of suicide. That a self-murderer might be canonised for his mortal defence of traditionalist Christian theology and spirituality is a concept as paradoxical as the bizarre precepts of the modernisers against which Gareth Bennett, and more furiously, William Oddie, inveigh. Dr Rowell, in his address at the Oxford requiem, was more realistic:

> When pain and darkness drove him to a hell of despair, the God we trust who met him there was the God who in Christ crucified went down into the darkness. To that God we now commend him.[119]

Oddie's report of the Gallup poll conducted within a week of publication of the Preface shows that 'twice as many clergy supported the analysis . . . as rejected it'. This indicates, he argues, how out of step with their Church its liberal leaders have become, for Bishop John Taylor of St Albans had commented that 'few in the Church of England will have any sympathy with the views he has expressed'.[120] Indeed, Oddie's facts and his own book should have dissuaded him from his premature thesis that the 'Anglican mind' had died with Bennett.

116 *op.cit.*, 108.
117 *ibid.*, 3.
118 *ibid.*, 227.
119 'In Memoriam Gareth Vaughan Bennett', *ibid.*, 254.
120 *op.cit.*, 14.

The new willingness of some conservatives to contemplate a theological and worshipping future where reconciliation (or at least a tolerant tension) between contemporary doctrinal insights and the values of the modern liturgical movement and traditional orthodoxy and worship might be sustained is expressed in the collection of essays *A Way of Life*, the proceedings of a national conference on the Book of Common Prayer held in Melbourne in 1988.

The most important of these reflections are by the Revd Dr Evan Burge, Warden of Trinity College in the University of Melbourne who, some years before, was a prominent advocate of the new services which culminated in *An Australian Prayer Book* (1978), but who, in recent years, has drawn closer to the conservative viewpoint. Like Bishop Gordon Arthur, sometime Chairman of the Australian Liturgical Commission, who celebrated 'masses of reparation', in Cranmerian language, to atone for his labours in liturgical revision, Dr Burge has had second thoughts about the wisdom of an irreversible progression from the Book of Common Prayer to the new rites.

'For better or worse', he comments ambiguously (wittily quoting from the Prayer Book), 'An Australian Prayer Book has now established itself as the *de facto* norm of Anglican worship in Australia'.[121] But the burden of his essay is less enigmatic:

> A devotion to the continuity of our tradition is not a mere antiquarian hobby. It is an acknowledgment that God nourishes us with his grace not only as individuals but as members of his apostolic and catholic church.

'I am always deeply saddened', he continues, 'when pastors of Christian congregations, or even theological seminaries, in an excess of zeal only for things new deny their flock the older treasures'.[122] Dr Burge, at least, cannot be accused of neophilia. In the chapel of his College both traditional and modern eucharists are celebrated, his theological students being reminded thereby of the historical dimension of Anglicanism and participating in it.

Another essayist, Bishop James Grant, hopes (in vain, as it has turned out) that 'the principal services of the Book of Common Prayer . . . are bound up in the next edition of *An Australian Prayer Book*'. It is not the conservatives who are inflexible, the bishop contends, but the modernisers:

> Intolerance has not been an Anglican vice to date. Why has it now reared its ugly head?[123]

And the late Archbishop David Penman, a conspicuous liberal in

[121] 'Foreword', E.L. Burge (ed.) *A Way of Life*, 7.

[122] 'Nova et Vetera', in *A Way of Life*, 17.

[123] 'The Book of Common Prayer and the Recent Liturgies: The Rock and the Lapping Water?', in *op. cit.*, 27.

this conservative enclave, showed nonetheless that he was not intolerant of the traditionalist position in an essay pointedly entitled 'Love One Another: the Pastoral Implications of the Use and Non-use of the Book of Common Prayer', where he quotes approvingly from Bishop Arthur:

> My hope is that . . . many Australian Anglicans might begin to discover the treasures they have lost.[124]

At least, in *A Way of Life*, both conservatives and liberals show a willingness to seek common ground.

In *Towards Liturgy 2000: Preparing for the Revision of the Alternative Service Book* – a surprisingly poorly written volume from a collection of scholars with strings of degrees whose professional business is language – this compromise is presented as essential.

Produced by the Alcuin Club, it is almost entirely a clerical production, thus reflecting the monopoly of liturgiology held by clergy in the age when the emphasis on the laity's participation in worship has dominated liturgical theory. Furthermore, the writers largely ignore the vitality of the liturgical debate outside liberal circles. Bryan Spinks writes blithely of the 'success' of the *ASB* in the 1980s (a term which the present study of opposition to it contradicts) and, looking to the future, announces that liturgiologists 'are in a position to create even more satisfying liturgical forms'. Yet, even in the midst of this confidence, Spinks admits that

> It is certainly true that we have not yet created a twentieth century (or twenty-first century) English liturgical style which is evocative.

And then he presents, as original, illuminating perceptions, truths of liturgical composition which Cranmer recognised and acted upon nearly five centuries ago:

> Increasingly liturgiologists are dissatisfied – perhaps also bored – with this concise style of corporate prayer. . . . It could in fact be argued that the passion of prayer requires evocative images and embellished phrases, that complex sentences need not be obscure, and that the brevity of prayers does not necessarily lead to better comprehension.[125]

Then Martin Dudley, a parish priest, admitting that the two- or three-year cycle of the modern lectionary has been a failure, confesses that

> There is an undeniable power in the hearing of the same epistle and gospel on a given Sunday year after year, a power amplified by it being always heard in the same translation. The resonances created by language and texts frequently re-

[124] *op.cit.*, 63.
[125] 'What Kind of Book?', *Towards Liturgy 2000*, 8-10.

peated should not be underestimated.

In other words, there is a 'power' and 'resonance' in the Book of Common Prayer:

> What was used was well known, frequently known by heart and well loved. There is no evidence to suggest that this loss was compensated for by a movement towards general liturgical renewal or by a renewal in the biblical apostolate.[126]

Next Kenneth Stevenson admits, contrary to the propaganda, that the language of the modern rites, so far from being the language of 'today', is 'not actually spoken by anyone'.[127]

Of the funeral liturgy, Michael Perham writes that the prayers for the dead in the *ASB*

> have neither the theological nor literary power to carry the emotions of the mourners, and most clergy have to search elsewhere for adequate words.

He suggests that the revision of *ASB* might contain the Orthodox kontakion, 'Give rest, O Christ, to thy servant':

> By one means or another we must bring the people close to the coffin and help them say 'Farewell' with words that have resonance and ritual that has meaning.[128]

It is strange that an Anglican priest, searching for such a liturgy, has to resort to the numinous rites of the East, when the traditional Prayer Book of his own Church contains such material in abundance.

In 'The Ambience of Liturgy', his second essay in the collection, Martin Dudley praises 'the mysteriously exhilarating cadence of liturgical Latin or Tudor English' and admits that the *ASB* 'has not proved to be a remedy' for the transcendental yearning of the modern age.[129] And Michael Perham, in his second essay, 'The Language of Worship', while predicting that 'the main texts of any future service book will be in modern English', recognises that the concerns of traditionalist worshippers have to be respected. 'Their fears have been understood and their needs respected.' Such future texts will 'begin to reconcile and heal a Church where liturgy has been a source of discord'. He is correct to observe that 'we cannot define Anglicanism as the acceptance of a particular style of liturgical language',[130] but this is a truth to which modernisers as well as conservatives must assent. The former have been at least as likely to regard Cranmerians as beyond the pale, as conservatives have been prone to accuse them of disposing of Anglicanism in jettisoning the Book of Common Prayer.

126 'The Lectionary', *ibid.*, 38.

127 'The Eucharistic Prayer', 44.

128 'The Funeral Liturgy', 56, 58.

129 'The Ambience of Liturgy', *ibid.*, 60.

130 'The Language of Worship', *ibid.*, 67, 71.

The importance of a study such as *Towards Liturgy 2000* is that this forward-looking volume, produced by liturgiologists committed to renewal, recognises the deficiencies of services which are no longer 'new' but have had more than a decade's trial and, in doing so, acknowledges that at least some of these shortcomings might be eradicated through a resuscitation of Cranmerian liturgical principles. Now that the 'new' rites have been tested and found wanting in several ways, absolute claims about the worthiness of the revised texts can no longer be entertained.

## VI

Many today doubt whether Anglicanism, as an identifiable and viable part of the Catholic Church, has any future at all. Its decline from its stature in its golden age, in the seventeenth century, as described by George Herbert (in his *Musae Responsoriae*), seems complete:

> See how
> The lovely Church outspreads its wings and sheds
> Its radiance far as heaven. Far and wide
> The neighbour nations wonder, and, their minds adazzle,
> Want to learn a ritual in harmony with ours.
> Angelic hosts increase our company;
> And Christ Himself, watching from the skies,
> Taking in the houses of the world at a glance,
> Says that only England offers Him a finished worship.

A.N. Wilson has dated 'the last days before the final eclipse' of the Church in the 1940s, in the works and witness of C.S. Lewis, T.S. Eliot, William Temple and Dorothy Sayers.[131]

If Anglicanism does have a future it must recover and assert its fidelity to a measure of authority in doctrine and worship, respecting differences in interpretation and opinion, but possessed of the will to preserve, in combination, balance and tension, the principles of its heritage: scriptural and Catholic, liturgical and Reformed, spiritual and intellectual. In other words, it must confront its age-old, but now urgent, problem of the lack of a unified and central authority, as perceived by Gareth Bennett (with characteristic understatement):

> There is clearly an imbalance between the strength of the provinces and weakness at the centre. . . . As the Englishness of the Communion becomes less apparent, there are signs of a certain incoherence.[132]

[131] *C.S. Lewis: A Biography*, 182.

[132] 'The Bishop as Focus of Unity', in *To the Church of England*, 169.

Roman Catholicism has been more successful in surviving its *aggiornamento* because its Vatican authority is not dependent upon liturgical fashions or undermined by the heresies of errant theologians and bishops. For Anglicanism to survive, its sense of a *consensus fidelium* must be revitalised. Dr Runcie's enthusiasm for the role of the pope as the Bishop of a Universal Church, of which Anglicanism would be a constituent part, preserving its cultic distinctiveness, but looking to the pontiff as the focus of Christian unity, was, from a liberal prelate, a surprising solution to his Church's profound problems of doctrinal anarchy, with their liturgical consequences, but it may be the only possible solution. However, it is not a solution that the majority of Anglicans are ever likely to accept.

Dr Runcie's successor, Archbishop George Carey, has given little hope to defenders either of conservative orthodoxy in doctrine or traditional liturgical language in worship. In spite of some token gestures of appreciation of the Book of Common Prayer, it appears that the Evangelical Dr Carey has little time for the aesthetics of devotional prose. Angela Tilby, in her review of the Archbishop's collection of sermons and addresses *Sharing a Vision*, notes that while Dr Carey 'is a warm and engaging communicator',

> he is not a man who enjoys using words to worry an idea through. . . . Yet even in this age of visual, feely-touchy communication, it is a disadvantage to be deaf to the resonances of language.[133]

'The Archbishop's prose', she opines, 'is thin and colourless'. Such a writer is not likely to respond instinctively to Cranmer or the arguments for his retention, based – as they usually are – on ideas of the aesthetics of the numinous.

And for the doctrinally conservative, Dr Carey's reputation could scarcely be worse. While 'the present Pope, the spiritual head of the largest body of Christians in the world, is fulfilling his vocation as the primate of all Western Catholic Churches by his unflinching, unambiguous, and wholly faithful adherence to the ancient convictions of the Christian family',

> that old ball of fluff, the present Archbishop of Canterbury, huffed and puffed about a new obstacle to ecumenical discourse and union (as if he had not already jettisoned any realistic plank we possessed, and himself on it). He is a comic figure, wrapped in woolly delusion, presiding over the funeral rites of our beloved Mother Church of England. Who really cares what he thinks or says? What difference does he make to anything or anybody?[134]

133 'Faith Plainly Dressed', *The Tablet*, 6 November 1993, 1453.

134 The Revd William H. Ralston, 'Primacy and Patriarchy', *The Parish Paper* of St John's Church, Savannah, GA, 19 July 1994, 1.

# 4
# THE BOOK OF COMMON PRAYER AND ENGLISH LITERATURE

Reference to the influence of the Cranmerian Prayer Book and the Authorised Version in the evolution of literature in English has been a principal focus of the conservative critique of the disposal of those volumes. It is argued that if authors, from Shakespeare to our contemporaries, will turn readily to this diction, for its resonance and subtlety of expression, in a variety of literary genres, addressing different historical periods and cultural circumstances over the centuries, then the infinite adaptability and perennial meaningfulness of that prose-poetry (allegedly suddenly outmoded and irrelevant in the later twentieth century) has been – and continues to be – copiously demonstrated. Furthermore, the criticism by modern poets and prose-writers of the new versions of the liturgy in English (whether Roman or Anglican) has been heartening for conservatives. However, it seems of little or no importance to liturgiologists, for whom literary and aesthetic concerns are less urgent than theological and pastoral priorities.

## I

From the seventeenth century until the mid-twentieth century, English Christian worship and so, to a large degree, English life were imbued with the language of the Anglican liturgy. As the upbringing of virtually every famous writer included first-hand knowledge of the Authorised Version of the Bible and the Book of Common Prayer, English literature abundantly records and reflects this influence, as reference to any dictionary of quotations will show. Today, as that language disappears from use in church and school, so its echoes in literature are silenced and the literature, too, substantially dies. In company with much of the music written for the traditional liturgy, it is another casualty of liturgical renewal.

In the works of writers who were the children of parsons – Joseph Addison, William Cowper, Coleridge, Jane Austen, the Brontës,

Charles Kingsley and Matthew Arnold, to give but a tiny handful of examples – the words of worship and Scripture are inevitably present. The Australian historian Manning Clark – himself the son of an Anglican priest – observed:

> if you are the son of a clergyman, you're brought up in an environment in which you are introduced to great literature – the Old Testament, the New Testament, the Book of Common Prayer. You're surrounded from earliest times by serious thoughts.[1]

Such writers from clerical families could be expected to echo the words of the liturgy and Bible to which they were exposed day by day. More remarkable is the witness of the host of authors born into professedly, though not 'professionally', Christian homes. The most noteworthy are those who, in adulthood, rejecting the tenets of Scripture and Prayer Book and even the mores of a Christian society, were yet unable or unwilling to discard that language, such was its power. Agnostics and atheists – the *fin de siècle* trinity of Samuel Butler the younger, the poet Swinburne and Lytton Strachey, for example – express artistic tribute to Cranmer and the Authorised Version even as they bitterly repudiate their teaching. They, like the believers, recognised the potent vocabulary and beguiling rhythms of a diction to which they had been introduced as children, which – whatever they might subsequently have done or read or thought – remained a part of them. The most influential of these, Bertrand Russell, recalled the incidental phrase 'sundry places' (from the Introduction to Morning and Evening Prayer) some seventy years after his compulsory churchgoing days were over, mischievously exploiting its unintended double meaning:

> I had remembered . . . a stony bay which I had imagined to be one of the 'sun-dry places' mentioned in the Prayer Book.[2]

Such evidence refutes an argument often put forward for the disposal of the Book of Common Prayer and the Authorised Version – that children and young people find them unintelligible and, therefore, boring (an argument based itself on the questionable premises that matters of doctrine and spirituality should or can be easily comprehended and ought to be immediately entertaining). On the contrary, the tantalisingly mysterious and peculiar ingredient seasoning what is substantially a plain vocabulary captivates and excites the curious and receptive mind of infancy. 'I was brought up on the Bible', D.H. Lawrence reflected,

> and seem to have it in my bones. From early childhood I have been familiar with Apocalyptic language and Apocalyptic

1 'Growing up with Reverend Father', *Good Weekend* magazine, *The Sydney Morning Herald*, 13 February 1988, 25.

2 Russell, *Autobiography*, 561.

> image: not because I spent my time reading Revelation, but because I was sent to Sunday School and to Chapel, to Band of Hope and to Christian Endeavour, and was always having the Bible read at me or to me.

His rebellious nature rejected the institutionalism of this discipline, but no artistic sensibility could resist its diction:

> I did not even listen attentively. But language has a power of echoing and re-echoing in my unconscious mind.[3]

The moral and prophetic spirit of Lawrence's novels, as a result, is strikingly scriptural in cadence and allusion – the principal symbol in *The Rainbow*, for example, recalls the Old Testament metaphor of God's covenant with His people.

The mystery writer Dorothy Sayers had a special devotion to the Prayer Book and remembered falling in love with a phrase from the creed – 'Catholic and Apostolic Church' – long before she was challenged by its persistence in her mind to search for its meaning. 'The ecstasy of great words and great phrases never deserted her', her biographer notes. 'She was convinced that all children could be trusted to revel, as she had, in grand, incomprehensible words . . . and moreover that anyone who did not understand this knew nothing whatever about children.' Children's minds, Sayers wrote, are 'open and sensitive to the spell of poetic speech':

> It is the language that stirs and excites. . . . I will swear that no child has ever heard unmoved 'when this corruptible shall have put on incorruption and this mortal shall have put on immortality'.[4]

That today no child has the opportunity to be so moved is described by the novelist and playwright Allan Sillitoe as 'an atrocity against our heritage'. For he remembers an excellent teacher in his childhood, a 'young woman at Canal Street School in the middle of Nottingham', who

> started us at five on the story of Abraham and Isaac. In those days they just read the beautiful King's English from the King James' version.[5]

What John McManners has called the 'dim lust for intelligibility of reforming clergy of our own generation'[6] and Evan Burge describes as the 'fetish of comprehensibility' in modern liturgiology have prevented children from relishing 'big, beautiful-sounding words'.[7]

Antithetically, we have the example of John Donne – brought up in recusant hostility and ignorance of the liturgy of the Church of

3 In *Prose Studies*, September 1983, 196.
4 James Brabazon, *Dorothy Sayers: A Biography*, 18, 193.
5 'He Used to Read to Us', *Times Educational Supplement*, 31 July 1992, 17.
6 In Michael Perham (ed.) *Model and Inspiration: The Prayer Book Tradition Today*.
7 Interview with the author, 8 July 1994.

England, but who, in converted adulthood, came to love its language of worship to the point where it intimately shapes his art. His celebrated poetry and prose – treated in undergraduate courses in secular English departments but never opened by Anglican theological students – show that 'the English Bible is the most potent of all influences which have helped to mould his style'.[8] Eccentric in a different way was Donne's near contemporary John Milton, who deviated from a cradle Anglicanism to a succession of increasingly peculiar variations of Protestantism. Yet for all his wilful repudiation of the Established Church, the poet could never divorce himself from its language of faith. In the last of his anti-episcopal pamphlets, Milton writes:

> I conceived myself to be now not as mine own person, but as a member incorporate into that truth whereof I was persuaded

– 'echoing majestically', as A.N. Wilson has noted, 'that liturgy he professed to loathe and abominate'.[9] The spell of the prose artistry of the Jacobean Church, cast in his youth, was destined to remain with the Cromwellian always – as his lines prophesied:

> But let my due feet never fail
> To walk the studious cloisters pale,
> There let the pealing organ blow
> To the full-voiced choir below,
> In service high and anthems clear,
> As may with sweetness, through my ear,
> Dissolve me into ecstasies,
> And bring all heav'n before my eyes.
> (*Il Penseroso*, ll.159-66).

Earlier in the Renaissance we have the example of Shakespeare – in his sonnets, for instance. In 'Sin of self-love possesseth all mine eye', the fourth line, 'It is so grounded inward in my heart', reflects the Prayer Book phrase 'grafted inwardly in our hearts', which – as his editor has noted – 'he heard in church all his days'. Then the opening lines of this well-known sonnet,

> Let me not to the marriage of true minds
> Admit impediments

echoes the marriage-service in the Prayer Book; while in 'That you were once unkind befriends me now',

> it is interesting to observe the religious language of the poem – 'transgression', 'trespass', 'ransom': all of them words that Shakespeare was familiar with from early days in church[10]

– words which have been specifically proscribed, liturgically, as in-

8 Evelyn Simpson, 'The Literary Value of Donne's Sermons', in Helen Gardner (ed.) *John Donne*, 140.

9 *The Life of John Milton*, 107.

10 A.L. Rowse, *Shakespeare's Sonnets*, 3rd edn.

comprehensible today while no-one simultaneously suggests that Shakespeare should (or could) be rewritten in order to empower and enhance the profundity of his thought. And his works are as popular as ever.

In the different cultural milieu of the eighteenth century, the passionate convictions of the previous age were contrasted with a studied commitment to reason. The trembling apprehension of the awful nearness of God and His judgement was replaced by a distancing conception of the Almighty as the impersonal *primum mobile* and of Christianity as but a worthy moral guide in a supremely social age. Alexander Pope satirises a Dean of Gloucester who thought it impolite to refer to Hell.[11] Yet those sixteenth- and seventeenth century documents, the Prayer Book and the King James Bible, composed in the heat of Reformation, when the 'Last Things' of death, judgement, Heaven and Hell were realities for all, being catholic in their character and appeal, captivated the altered sensibilities of the new epoch as surely as those of the previous age, while we are supposed to believe that they are suddenly out-of-date in the twentieth century. That most Augustan spirit, Edward Gibbon, in an observation exhaling the temperate sensibility of his times, reflected:

> In the prayers of the Church our personal concerns are judiciously reduced to the threefold distinctions of *mind, body* and *estate*[12]

– effortlessly resorting to the phrase from the prayer for all conditions of men. And in Handel's masterpiece, *Messiah*, Prayer Book and Bible are intertwined: 'the text', as Geoffrey Cuming has observed, 'is drawn from the use of Scripture in the Prayer Book'.[13] Much of the third part of the oratorio, indeed, is a setting of the words of the Burial Service. Handels inspiration was also that of William Byrd.

But it is to the greatest literary figure of that epoch, Samuel Johnson, that we turn for the most powerful evidence of the influence of traditional Anglican worship on the artistic sensibility. James Boswell, his biographer, records that Johnson was nurtured by Cranmer from infancy:

> Mrs Johnson one morning put the common prayer-book in his hands, pointed to the collect for the day, and said 'Sam, you must get this by heart'. She went upstairs, leaving him to study it: But by the time she had reached the second floor, she heard him following her. 'What's the matter?' said she. 'I can say it', he replied; and repeated it distinctly, though he could not have read it over more than twice.[14]

[11] 'Epistle to Burlington', II, 149-50.

[12] *Memoirs of My Life*, 107.

[13] Booklet accompanying the Mackerras recording.

[14] *The Life of Samuel Johnson* (Penguin: Harmondsworth, 1986), 38.

Evidence of a precocious child, it is also a testament to the memorability of the Cranmerian collect. In adulthood, Johnson's piety continued to be sustained by the Prayer Book services:

> He carried me with him [Boswell notes] to the church of St Clement Danes, where he had his seat; and his behaviour was, as I had imagined to myself, solemnly devout. I shall never forget the tremulous earnestness with which he pronounced the awful petition in the Litany: 'In the hour of death, and at [*sic*] the day of judgement, good LORD deliver us'.[15]

Not surprisingly, Johnson declared: 'I know of no good prayers but those in the Book of Common Prayer',[16] and his own copious composition of prayers, notable for their rotundity and incantatory pulse, echoes the Cranmerian idiom.

Witnessing the apotheosis of Reason, the eighteenth century – as if in spite of itself – also spawned burgeoning movements of passionate commitment to politics and religion. The prevailing rationality seems to have especially incited revolutionaries and evangelists. The results, in the early years of the nineteenth century, were the Romantic movement, the Evangelical revival, Tractarianism and the rise of democracy. In eighteenth-century English religion, John and Charles Wesley are the harbingers of the new age. Although dissociated from the spirit that animated Gibbon and Handel, they found Cranmerian liturgy and the Jacobean Bible similarly inspirational. John Wesley determined 'to express Scripture sense in Scripture phrase'. For him, the King James version was the inspired Word of God, capable of striking to the hearts of the simple as well as the erudite. So, in his preaching, he used its diction:

> The Bible is my standard of *language* as well as sentiment [he emphasised]. I endeavour not only to think but to speak *as the oracles of God*.[17]

In literature, Jane Austen best reflects the transference from sense to sensibility *circa* 1800. In *Mansfield Park*, a novel about ordination, she contrasts the worldly Dr Grant, representative of the high and dry eighteenth-century school, and her hero Edmund, with his heartfelt vocation. Even the flippant Henry Crawford, in this most theological of her books, has an arresting reflection on the condition of the Church of England. 'Our liturgy', he observes,

> has beauties, which not even a careless, slovenly style of reading can destroy.[18]

We sense that this is as much Austen's observation as his.

15 *ibid.*, 163.

16 *ibid.*, 318.

17 In Isabel Rivers, 'John Wesley', *Prose Studies*, December 1981, 264.

18 Austen, *Mansfield Park*, 337.

Because of the revival of religion and the religious preoccupation of most of the famous Romantic and Victorian poets and prose writers, the advances in education and literacy and the expansion of the Anglican Communion through the world, the nineteenth century was the golden age of the influence of the Bible and the Prayer Book in human history. From the extremity of profound faith to that of neo-paganism, the presence of the sacred texts is felt. So John Keble, in his 'Advertisement' to the collection of poems based on the Prayer Book calendar and services, *The Christian Year*, announces:

> Next to a sound rule of faith, there is nothing of so much consequence as a sober standard of feeling in matters of practical religion: and it is the peculiar happiness of the Church of England to possess in her authorised formularies, an example and secure provision of both.[19]

Oliver Taplin reminds us that the Victorian translators of Homer turned to the Authorised Version for a suitable English idiom:

> a familiar, noble, weighty language, archaic, yet read and, even more to the point, heard constantly.[20]

The Cranmerian liturgy and the Jacobean Bible were, for the nineteenth century, quintessential expressions of that Englishness epitomised by Wordsworth:

> We must be free or die, who speak the tongue
> That Shakespeare spake; the faith and morals hold
> Which Milton held.
>
> ('National Independence and Liberty', I, xvi)

## II

Although the twentieth century congratulates itself on its liberation from that language and those principles, an impressive array of literary practitioners in our time has protested about the disposal of the Prayer Book and the King James Bible. But the complaints of the poets and novelists have gone unheeded by Church officials and liturgiologists in a neo-Puritan revulsion against the aesthetic or, more simply, an ignorant philistinism.

'Oh pray for the Church of England!' exclaimed the Anglican novelist Barbara Pym, after attending (as she puts it) 'a rather dire little service at St Albans Holborn. Series 4 I should think.'[21] When the poet W.H. Auden was invited to sit on a committee to revise the Psalter in the early 1970s, he frustrated every attempt at revision, on the principle that liturgical language that was 'out-of-date' was a blessing rather than a curse. It was a token of the timelessness of its

19 Keble, *The Christian Year*, 1.
20 *Times Literary Supplement*, 24 October 1980, 1197.
21 Diary entry for 31 October 1972, in *A Very Private Eye*, 272.

teaching. And he drew on Cranmerian cadence in his own poetry, as in *The Orators*:

> in the moment of vision; in the hour of applause; in the place of defeat; and in the hour of desertion, O Holmes, Deliver us.

The wit and point of the reference is lost on those who do not know their Prayer Book. And T.S. Eliot, the most influential of modern poets and critics, and a devout Anglo-Catholic, observed that

> if the Church re-writes its Bible and its liturgies to conform with every successive stage of deterioration of the language, the prospect is gloomy.

In his criticism and in his own incantatory poetry, Eliot emphasised the 'music' of the traditional translation of Scripture and of Cranmer – 'the music of the phrase, of the paragraph, of the period' – and argued that this musicality gave life to the reading of gospel and epistle in the liturgy in 'the music of the spoken word'.[22] Enlisted, like Auden, to sit on a liturgical committee, the modernising poet's only contributions, ironically, were to speak up for the retention of hallowed phrases. After these experiences (and a similarly negative result with Philip Larkin), liturgiologists have determined to avoid poets. But that inconvenient race cannot be silenced. Stevie Smith made her objections known, in her distinctive style, in several poems:

> Why are the clergy of the Church of England
> Always altering the words of the prayers in the Prayer Book?
> Cranmer's touch was surer than theirs, do they not respect him?
> For instance last night in church I heard
> (I italicise the interpolation)
> 'The Lord bless you and keep you *and all who are dear unto you*'
> As the blessing is a congregational blessing and meant to be
> This is questionable on theological grounds
> But is it not offensive to the ear and also ludicrous?
> That 'unto' is a particularly ripe piece of idiocy
> Oh how offensive it is. I suppose we shall have next
> 'Lighten our darkness we beseech thee O Lord *and the darkness of all who are dear unto us*'
> ('Why are the Clergy. . . ?')

Then, more positively:

> Admire the old man, admire him, admire him,
> Mocked by the priests of Mary Tudor, given to the flames,
> Flinching and overcoming the flinching, Cranmer.

22 'New Translation of the Bible', *Theology*, September 1949, 337; and see Dennis Nineham (ed.) *The New English Bible Reviewed*, 101.

. . . . Admire the Bishop,
The old man, the scholar, admire him.
Not simply, for flinching and overcoming simply,
But for his genius, admire him,
His delicate feelings of genius, admire him,
That wrote the Prayer Book
(Admire him!)
And made the flames burn crueller. Admire Cranmer!
('Admire Cranmer!')

The Irishman Samuel Beckett, the most experimental of dramatists, was yet indebted to this most traditional speech:

> The basic influences on Beckett's style will always have been those that he absorbed in youth: the Authorised Version of the Bible, the Book of Common Prayer, and the Early Fathers. From the 'Christ have mercy upon us' of *Waiting for Godot* to the lilies of the field of *Enough*, in the exquisite verbal simplicity of Beckett's prose, these persist.[23]

Most recently, the popular mystery writer P.D. James gives ample evidence of the influence of these same volumes on her mind and art and shows that for all the efforts of the Church to dispose of them, these texts stubbornly survive in the cultural consciousness of English speakers and, so far from being dated, fit admirably into the contexts of her contemporary stories. James has given the title *Devices and Desires* to her latest book, the phrase coming from the confession at Morning and Evening Prayer: 'we have followed too much the devices and desires of our own hearts'. In *The Skull Beneath the Skin* (recalling the line of Eliot about Webster), her heroine, Cordelia, thinks of a 'biblical text . . . brutally explicit in its meaning . . . "Whoso shall offend one of these little ones" ',[24] and the title of the third part of the book also has a biblical resonance: 'Blood Flies Upwards'. In *A Taste for Death*, James calls Evensong 'the most aesthetically satisfying portion of the Anglican liturgy', while one of her characters quotes from the Burial Service: 'in the midst of life we are in death'.[25] James has been active, indeed, in the English Prayer Book Society, writing a pamphlet for them with the title 'Bad Language in Church' and contributing to Michael Perham's collection of 1993, *Model and Inspiration: The Prayer Book Tradition Today*, where she argues that the Church has a duty to preserve the Prayer Book:

> We have to ask ourselves whether we really want a philistine Church whose services will be repugnant to those who seek to worship God in the beauty of holiness, a Church in which

[23] Harold Hobson, 'Chances of Salvation', *TLS*, 17 December 1982, 1382.
[24] James, *The Skull Beneath the Skin*, 122.
[25] James, *A Taste for Death*, 434, 230.

> dignity, excellence of word and music, quietude and good order are all sacrificed to the demands of fashionable social, theological, sexist and liturgical theory including, God help us, inclusive language.

Like Baroness James, Ian Curteis, the dramatist and television playwright (of *The Onedin Line, Upstairs Downstairs* and so on), is a member of the English Prayer Book Society, as is his wife, the novelist Joanna Trollope. In 'The Media and the Book of Common Prayer', an address to the Society's conference in 1993, Curteis refers to the

> grandeur of mind in Cranmer, a majesty of thought which is reflected and fulfilled in his English – which, quite literally, cannot be fulfilled in the thinner English we have today.

Curteis' view, in other words, is Hooker's:

> Signs must resemble the things they signify. If religion bear the greatest sway in our hearts, our outward religious duties shew it as far as the Church hath outward ability. Duties of religion performed by whole societies of men, ought to have in them according to our power a sensible excellency, correspondent to the majesty of him whom we worship.[26]

Curteis notes in particular the appeal of Cranmer to the young people in his own parish:

> the young . . . attend the monthly 1662 celebration of Holy Communion in our little village of 182 souls in greater numbers than they attend any other form of the eucharist.

For an explanation, he cites the observation of Stella Gibbons (of *Cold Comfort Farm*) that the English are 'plain, ordinary people with poetry secretly burning in their souls'.[27]

A.N. Wilson's novel of 1993, *The Vicar of Sorrows*, is the story of the decline and fall of the Church of England – a decomposition that is articulated by the author largely through liturgical and spiritual metaphors and in the characterisation of its central figure, the unbelieving clergyman Francis Kreer, for whom only the words of the old liturgy can provide any solace in his misery:

> Often a phrase in the liturgies choked him . . . because it was so beautiful. 'To pass our time in rest and quietness . . . who hast taught us to make prayers and supplications and to give thanks for all men . . . O God who alone can order the unruly wills and affections of sinful men . . . whose service is perfect freedom'. All these phrases were so familiar to him that he had barely noticed them for years; now he would find himself stumbling as he recited them, so moved that he could no longer speak.

In contrast to the tragic Kreer are the success-stories of modern

26 Hooker, *The Laws of Ecclesiastical Polity*, 5.6.2.
27 *Faith and Heritage*, Spring 1994, 7.

English Christianity:

> an evangelical church which wanted to re-order its sanctuary, remove the High Altar (reredos by Bodley and Garner) and install audio-visual equipment and a movable cinema-screen. . . .

and the Reverend Terry Widger, whose 'voice was not in the least euphonious; there was a harsh timbre to it, and he could easily have made himself heard, in that comparatively small church, without a microphone'. Widger's retreat to the puerile in liturgy is satirised by Wilson:

> The children . . . were told to climb into the pulpit and hold up some balloons on strings. On one of the balloons there was a large letter S, on another the letter I, and on another N. . . . Now when I ask the children to bust those balloons. . . . [28]

The title of the novel, referring to Kreer, recalls the anticipation of Christ, in the Authorised Version, as 'a man of sorrows and acquainted with grief', immortalised by Handel in *Messiah*.

As Wilson's recent novel and the entire tradition of literature in English show, Cranmer and King James not only survive in, but continue to enrich that literature. Had they been allowed to survive in the liturgy in English, conservatives contend, they would have continued to enrich it also, as they have done for four centuries.

[28] Wilson, *The Vicar of Sorrows*, 84-85, 193, 253.

# 5
# FEMINISM AND RENEWAL

## I

The source of the most radical and recent revisions to liturgical language and hymnody has been the contemporary rise of feminism, which has made a momentous impact on the theological preoccupations of a Western Christianity sensitive to the spirit of the times and has called forth, in consequence, febrile conservative rebuttals of its more extreme claims and an extensive critique of its manifestations in worship, even from women themselves: the Movement for the Ordination of Women (MOW), for example, spawned Women Against the Ordination of Women (WAOW).

In their attention to the discourse of Scripture and of liturgy and hymnody, feminists have argued that it reveals and sustains the patriarchal character of traditional Christianity, which they repudiate as a perversion of the gospel. The masculinist bias of biblical language and of liturgical prayer has not only marginalised women for centuries, they contend, and subordinated their role in all aspects of Christian life (most notably in the ordained ministry), but has even forced them to deny their God-given womanhood and womanliness. Harriet Blodgett succinctly enunciates this linguistic sexual theory:

> Because men control meaning by controlling language, women must either internalise man-made language and become alienated from the female experience it fails to encode, or else keep silence.[1]

On this view, patriarchal vocabulary and symbolism have been deliberately used by men to impose their world-view on women. In the male interpretation and manipulation of the human condition, women are misconceived to be either 'daughters of Eve' (in Milton's phrase) – liable, if not restrained, to lead men into sin – or impossibly immaculate virgins:

> Women use a language encoded by the dominant male-group to suit its own perceptions, not those of the subordinated (and

1 'A Woman Writer's Diary', *Prose Studies*, May 1989, 63.

> hence muted) group of females. Females may not speak spontaneously, but must instead monitor their expression and transform their meanings to conform to male requirements, to be heard and understood.[2]

The compromising of women by language and imagery is a denial of their very creation. Feminists, unlike modern liturgiologists, have a keen appreciation of the persistent power of the traditional discourse of Scripture and worship, even in the modern world.

Yet feminists also stress the equality of men and women in the eyes of God – 'we should be . . . neither he nor she', Stevie Smith has written, 'but human',[3] a favourite text for this position coming from Galatians:

> There is neither Jew nor Greek, there is neither bond nor free, there is neither male nor female: for ye are all one in Christ Jesus (3:28).

Conversely, critics of this view, citing Genesis: 'male and female created he them' (5:2), while acknowledging equality, argue that it does not entail identity. They would contend for a diversity of God-given functions between the sexes, including, most contentiously, those of leadership and support. However, the ideas that authority must be based on a sense of duty and benevolence towards those it governs (so the pope is called 'the servant of the servants of God'), and that service might be perfect freedom, are paradoxes undreamt of in feminist philosophy. Authority, to the extent that it is the province of men, is always and everywhere oppressive, while to serve another is burdensome servility. Yet 'the Son of man' himself (in the sexist language of traditional Scripture) 'came not to be ministered unto, but to minister, and to give his life a ransom for many' (Matthew 20:28). While, if Mary was magnified, it was as the 'handmaid of the Lord' (Luke 1:38), not as an empowered woman freed from a relationship with patriarchy. Feminists have little time for the most prominent female in the New Testament.

Amongst the issues focused on by Christian feminism, abortion has had the most conspicuously secular profile. The prohibitions of the prelates are seen to be striking examples of male disregard for, or oppression of, women, substantiated by conservative theology. 'Keep your rosaries off our ovaries', chant the feminists.

The only solution to this time-honoured and ecclesiastically sanctioned subjugation of the female, feminists argue, is a radical refashioning of word and image. 'If women are ever to speak a genuinely female text', it is necessary for them (in the words of Julia Kristeva)

2 *ibid.*

3 'The Better Half?' in J. Barbera and W. McBrien (eds) *Me Again*, 178.

> to break the code, to shatter language, to find a specific discourse closer to the body and the emotions, to the unnameable repressed by the social contract.

They must 'deconstruct the phallogocentric discourse' that has been the tool of their repression, in the Church and in the world.[4] They must dispose of the 'phallusy' of history.

Their success in secular discourse has been notable, having been supported by anti-discrimination legislation and affirmative action (where the female is deliberately preferred to the male, to correct the imbalance of the centuries). Violence has been done to the language in the process (as Kristeva prophesied) – a 'chairman' is now a 'chairperson' or (absurdly) a 'chair', a 'man-hole' is a 'person-hole', 'actresses' no longer exist, it has to be explained that Stevie Smith is a 'female author' as 'authoress' is proscribed, the 'history seminar' must now be complemented (or replaced) by the 'herstory ovular', women no longer menstruate but 'femstruate' and so on. Tortuous grammatical constructions evolve in sentences from the necessity to add 'she' to 'he' (which can no longer serve, as before, for both sexes). Even the phrase 'men and women', to replace the sexist 'mankind', is frowned on as privileging the male by naming men first, and 'ladies and gentlemen', which might appear to solve this problem, is prohibited as the term 'lady' is perceived to spring from a masculinist fantasy about women being better than they are. Anyone resisting this Newspeak is liable to prosecution for sexual harassment. There is the sense that Big Sister is watching you.

The Church, as ever, is charged with being dilatory in embracing this secular movement. In particular – according to feminist theologians – the most oppressive of masculinist doctrines, those of God the Father, the deification of patriarchy and of the maleness of Christ and his apostles, must be reformed or even disposed of. Sue Donath and Janet Gaden have prepared a liturgy in which God is invoked in maternal terms and in the curious modern style of liturgical writing when the petitioner appears to be informing God of His/Her role: 'you told your people that they would be carried at the breast and on your knees' (with the sense, here, that the Almighty has fallen short of His/Her promises). Mary Daly, who sees 'Christolatry as idolatry', has described the Incarnation as 'inherently sexist and oppressive' (Jesus being undeniably, inconveniently and regrettably a man, whatever might be said of the sexuality of the Being he repeatedly referred to as his 'Father', even 'Daddy') and Elizabeth Schussler Fiorenza dismisses the 'all-male Last Supper' as 'a betrayal of true Christian discipleship and ministry', arguing that the New Testament documents must be 'assessed theologically in terms of a

4 In Blodgett, *op. cit.*, 63.

feminist scale of values'.[5] (Paintings of the Supper with Christ flanked by females have been approved – by such as the Revd Harry Herbert, general secretary of the Board for Social Responsibility of the New South Wales Uniting Church – as a kind of apostolic affirmative action.) How the New Testament would survive such an assessment does not appear and, indeed, Dr Barbara Thiering has conjectured that the Scriptures – being irretrievably androcentric – will have to be abandoned to facilitate the feminist Christian cause.

Meanwhile they are being rewritten, as is hymnody. The 'wise men' became 'wise persons' in the Christmas sermon of at least one (male) priest (which began with the acclamation, 'In the Name of God, Life-giver, Salvation-bringer, Wholeness-maker', to avoid the masculinist names of the Trinity), at a service where 'It Came upon a Midnight Clear' was rewritten: 'Peace on the earth, goodwill to all' (the poet's 'men' being deleted), where 'While Shepherds Watched their Flocks' was 'degendered' in two lines: 'to you and humankind', 'henceforth from heaven to all'.[6] Apart from the fact that such strategies are an arrogant violation of the integrity of the texts thus censored, and of the works of Christian poets writing, by their lights, under divine inspiration, it has been observed that replacing male-specificity with nothing-specificity does not make women visible.[7] It destroys the poetry and irritates at least as many people as it satisfies.

The most significant gains made by the feminist movement in Christianity have occurred in the Episcopal Church of the United States, with the ordination of practising lesbians by the Bishop of New York, the installation of the avowedly lesbian priest, Carter Heyward, as Dean of Faculty at the Episcopal Divinity School and the consecration of Barbara Harris (a divorcee with no tertiary qualifications and a champion of feminism and 'gay rights') as the first woman bishop – suffragan, in Massachusetts – in February, 1989. This took place at a stormy ceremony during which a representative of the American Prayer Book Society denounced the act as 'a sacrilegious imposition' and a priest implored the congregation not to proceed with a service that was 'contrary to the unbroken tradition of 2,000 years of apostolic order'.[8]

In November 1993, some fifty Episcopalian women attended an ecumenical conference in Minneapolis, a defining point of which

[5] All quoted in the Newsletter of the Association for Apostolic Ministry, Australian Branch, December 1989.

[6] The author thanks the Revd John Beer for passing him the pew-sheet for Christmas Day services at St James' Church, Sydney, 1993.

[7] The Revd Charles Sherlock, interview with the author, 28 June 1994.

[8] 'First Woman Bishop breaks Hallowed Ground', *The Sydney Morning Herald*, 13 February 1989, 10.

was the presentation and use of the name Sophia, or 'Divine Wisdom' as personified in the Book of Proverbs, as a feminist name for God. Organisers developed elaborate worship rituals using feminist imagery.

Other events at the conference included:

• An unscheduled gathering of roughly 100 lesbians on the dais, followed by a standing ovation from the audience.

• A panel on Jesus, in which seminary professor Delores Williams was quoted as saying, 'I don't think we need folks hanging on crosses and blood dripping and weird stuff. . . . We just need to listen to the God within'.

• A closing worship service featuring a ritual of milk and honey rather than traditional bread and wine, which included the words:

> Our Sweet Sophia, we are women in your image. With the nectar between our thighs, we invite a lover, we birth a child; with our warm body fluids we remind the world of its pleasures and sensations.[9]

Such emphasis on the femininity of God also appears in a book of prayers submitted for approval in the United States by the nine-million strong United Methodist Church. Of the 281 prayers in the book, only ten address God as 'Father', while others refer to Him as 'Mother God', 'Bakerwoman God', 'God, our Grove'.[10]

In the Episcopal Church, the General Convention in 1985 had ordered the development of 'inclusive language' rites. In a paper prepared for the Convention's Standing Liturgical Commission, it was argued that

> our anthropology informs our theology.

Jesus used 'Father' in addressing God to stress the intimacy of their relationship. The masculinity of the term and, so, any concept of the relationship peculiar to Father and Son, apart from the matter of intimacy itself, was irrelevant. When the first version of the rites was published in 1987, as *Liturgical Texts for Evaluation*, 'Rite II Adapted' eliminated 'Father', 'Son', and 'Lord', and the associated personal pronouns. The *Benedictus*, for example, became

> Blessed is the One who comes in the name of our God.

The *Leaders' Manual* to accompany the new eucharistic rites expressed the Committee's desire that

> another generation will reform and renew the perceptions of God sufficiently to actually call God 'Mother'.

The biblical names of God were merely cultural products to be

9 'Mainline Conservatives Protest Feminist Theology Conference', *Episcopal Life*, February 1994, 27.

10 *Faith and Heritage*, Autumn 1992, 29.

changed as desired.[11]

The idea of female attributes of God is, however, far from new. The difference is that, before, His femininity was included in His fatherhood, whereas today feminists would exclude that fatherhood from even the possibility of femaleness, establishing a separate female deity – an exclusivity accomplished in the name of inclusivity. In 'Praise, My Soul, the King of Heaven', for example – a hymn that will either have to be rewritten or banned as its very opening line is masculinist and monarchical – the third stanza reads:

> Father-like he tends and spares us;
> Well our feeble frame he knows;
> In his hands he gently bears us,
> Rescues us from all our foes.
>
> Praise him! Praise him!
> Praise him! Praise him!
> Widely as his mercy flows.

In a truly inclusive language, the fatherly functions of God include and, more importantly, are defined by quintessentially maternal qualities of tending and bearing, and of abundant mercy. The same is true of the twenty-third psalm.

In July 1993, the Anglican diocese of Melbourne issued 'Guidelines on Inclusive Language' which began cautiously and uncontroversially with the statements that

> 'Inclusive language' is difficult to define precisely. . . . Inclusive language is about people.

The document acknowledged that, in the past, 'male terminology included the female', so the hymn 'Rise Up, O Men of God'

> was written to challenge both women and men to respond to the call of God.

Today, however – the document continues – such challenges fail to communicate with women who feel excluded by the 'male terminology'.

The anonymous author of the 'Guidelines' does not speculate how this changed perception of language on the part of women came about and whether it might be due, indeed, to documents such as this which inform the reader, without argument or demonstration, that this shift in (and impoverishment of) interpretation and understanding has occurred and, therefore, that it must be rectified.

If women are indoctrinated to believe that language is excluding them from experience and are put on the alert when they encounter such words as 'man' and 'mankind' in texts – as used for the whole human race by writers such as Shakespeare and Milton, the biblical translators and the hymn-writers, through the centuries – then they

11 David Mills, 'PECUSA's "Inclusive Language" Liturgies', *Faith and Worship*, Autumn 1991, 14-20.

will come to feel not only excluded from the meanings of those texts, but embittered about the agents of this exclusion: men. Feminist theorists teach that, through the ages, men have been involved in a conspiracy in language (as in every other sphere of life) to render women silent and invisible, to oppress them and deny them access to power.

In a review of Katie Roiphe's exposé of dictatorial feminist ideology on American campuses, *The Morning After: Sex, Fear and Feminism*, Catherine Runcie argues that such propaganda is crucial to the survival of the feminist movement (and the career structures that it has established). It needs 'new recruit victims to sustain itself'. In the feminist orthodoxy that 'turns women into fearful little girls', Runcie and Roiphe identify an army of 'guerilla feminists', militant watchbitches who encourage the younger generation of women to believe that 'all men were guilty until proven guilty' – linguistically, historically, sociologically, matrimonially, sexually. Doing the thinking on behalf of womankind (Runcie alleges), in a proliferation of publications – language guidelines, sexual harassment pamphlets and so on – they hope to stir up fear and resentment in the context of an absolute submission to an ideology. 'Where on earth is a woman safe from rape?' is the rhetorical question posed on a poster seen displayed on doors and noticeboards in the University of Sydney. A woman like Roiphe, enjoying 'men, romance and sex' and feeling 'able to cope with it all', finds herself ostracised by the 'suffering sisterhood'. Runcie asks:

> Who benefits from all this? Not men. Not women who want and trust a man as friend, partner, husband. Not children. The benefits go to bureaucrats, administrators . . . up and coming feminist professionals.[12]

Certainly, in the Church, where the feminist professionals are the women priests, those women (not to mention men) who have failed to submit to their propaganda have found the self-proclaimed inclusivists to be unpleasantly exclusivist. In 'The Censorship of Dissent', Mark Thompson writes of a number of women

> who have been harassed, abused, badgered and isolated because they do not 'toe the line' on women's ministry.[13]

Yet the Melburnian 'Guidelines' announce that it was in the former masculinist dispensation where rigidity prevailed, and the new inclusive order will bring 'mutual gentleness, patience and forbearance'.

Various strategies are proposed, linguistically, to bring this brave new world into existence: 'invisible mending', the revision of pronouns, and – more radically – 'complete re-writing'. The so-called

12 'The New Orthodoxy that turns Women into Fearful Little Girls', *The Press*, 23 July 1994, 10.
13 *The Briefing*, issue 132, 6.

invisible mending is nothing of the sort:

> omitting 'men', or replacing it with 'one' or 'person', can often resolve the matter.

Yet this very visible mending of texts may not be sufficiently corrective:

> it may still leave [women] 'invisible', and so not necessarily seen or felt to be included.

In other words, for women to be visible the general human references are inadequate. 'For us men and for our salvation', in the Nicene Creed, could be 'mended' to 'for us and our salvation'. But that is probably insufficient. Obviously, the only solution, if women are to be made visible, is to revise the creed thus: 'for us women and men and for our salvation'. Yet that prioritising of women may begin to render men invisible.

Acknowledging this possible outcome, the 'Guidelines' warn that the revision should not eliminate certain images to which men are (allegedly) naturally drawn:

> such as appropriately used military metaphors, with which men have traditionally identified.

The writer, in one stroke, reveals a patronisingly stereotypical conception of the male sensibility and a condescendingly dismissive evaluation of the female intellect – confining men to masculinist metaphor and judging women incapable of entering into a world of imagery beyond their usual experience, in spite of the fact that it had been earlier asserted that, in their unenlightened past, women were able to apply the language and imagery of 'Rise Up, O Men of God' to their own spirituality. A document allegedly single-mindedly inclusivist in intention is doubly exclusivist in practice.

## II

Feminist demands for the revision of Scripture and liturgy led to the resignation from the Australian Liturgical Commission in 1986 of one of the leading liturgiologists of the Anglican Communion, Professor David Frost. In his letter of resignation, Frost, commenting that 'it is time for me to call a halt, after 17 years in liturgical revision', quoted, as an example of the influence he was repudiating, a feminist rewriting of the Blessing – 'In the name of the Father, the Son and the Holy Spirit' – as 'In the name of the Parent, the Child and Holy Spirit'.

The significance of Professor Frost's criticism of such radical revision – which, he contends, will leave the Church with 'liturgy like a dodo'[14] – is that until his resignation he was a committed and con-

14 'Reforms Will Ruin Liturgy, says Academic', *The Sydney Morning Herald*, 11 June 1986, 7.

structive advocate of liturgical reform, his translations of the psalms and his compositions for other parts of the liturgy being used throughout the Anglican Church.

In a paper 'Truth, Language and Liturgy' – the Oxford Movement Anniversary Lecture for 1987 – Frost had argued that the extremism of the claims by feminists in the Church actually exceeds what has been achieved by their sisters in the world, that their changes to the language of Christian prayer would be more radical than those of secular feminists in ordinary discourse, making the liturgy a conspicuous vehicle of 'the lingo of a faction' and certainly not an expression of the 'majority-usage' of the present day. This opinion has been echoed by Professor David Martin, who derives feminist linguistico-liturgical correctness from 'quite limited ideological micro-climates in the middle class'.[15] For Frost

> the demand for 'inclusive' language is not merely a dispute about a handful of words, but part of a larger demand that originates from outside Christianity and strikes at central doctrines of the Christian faith. . . . You cannot serve God and radical feminism.[16]

In his view, the origins of the Christian feminist movement are to be found in the revolutionary turmoil of the 1960s, when the ideologues, failing 'to forge a revolutionary axis with the workers', decided that 'western capitalism could only be de-stabilised by an assault on the family'. In Marxist terms of a necessary class war, 'men (husbands and fathers) were the oppressors, women exploited, and all married women prostitutes': the feminist movement developed a theory of some universal conspiracy by the men, extending over thousands of years and in every country of the globe, to oppress and subjugate women.

Frost does not deny the masculinist bias of language, whether in English, Greek or Hebrew, and understands that this will arouse 'pastoral instincts' when the feminists 'like the Aborigines or the poor', make their emotive complaints:

> Why should their demands not be met, since it means only tinkering with a few phrases and upsetting a handful of wordsmiths? To Christians weary of the battle to convert hearts and minds, verbal change seems to offer one painless victory: a chance by manipulating language to engineer an improvement in human attitudes, making it that much more difficult to think wrong things. And for once the Church would be with, not against, secular society; for the women's movement, with

15 '"In Tune with Heaven" Examined', *Faith and Worship*, Summer 1993, 9.

16 See *Australian Journal of Liturgy*, vol. 1, no. 2, October 1987 for the full text of the paper.

> its proper demand that women should be able to fulfil their talents, is part of a larger social and economic change.

But it is precisely this sentiment that Frost warns against. 'We should not put our feet on a slippery slope where, once we have begun to move, there is no rational stopping-point':

> Objections to the language of liturgy lead inevitably to attacks on the language of the Scriptures from which that liturgy derives; from there to assaults on the basic metaphors and symbols by which the faith is taught; and finally to demands that doctrine itself be changed.

Frost's analysis of Jesus' vocabulary shows that 'the overwhelming and apparently unconscious 'sexism' of Christ's thought and expression makes him a prime candidate for feminist re-education (leaving aside his failure to promote according to the principles of Equal Opportunity)'. The argument that Christ simply subscribed to socio-cultural fashions of his time is rejected, 'for on other matters (such as Sabbath observance or ritual purity) he clearly defied their expectations'.

By submitting to the feminist correction of male bias in Scripture, the 'Great Sexist-Language Slide', and thus abandoning the principle that translation must be honest to the original texts, 'it becomes impossible to draw a line between what may, and may not, be changed'.

Frost concludes with uncompromisingly conservative statements of Christian orthodoxy, which he regards as non-negotiable:

> Traditional Christianity holds that God intervened in history to reveal his nature in Jesus Christ. It teaches that there is both equality *and* subordination within the Trinity itself, whereby Christ, though equal and co-eternal with the Father, is obedient to the Father's will, as we are required to be subordinate and obedient to Christ. The relationship within the Trinity is an archetypal pattern that serves as the model for human relationships, and destroys all worldly notions of hierarchy, status, domination and submission. The woman is to be subordinate to the man as the Church is subordinate to Christ; yet Christ, coming to us as one who serves, redeeming us to be his brothers and sisters before God, gives up his life and dies for us, as the husband must give up himself for his wife, and the Christ-like bishop and pastor must give up his life for his people. It is only the heathen who lord it over one another.

Christianity takes its name from Christ, who 'is recorded as making no criticism of and advocating no adjustment to the time-honoured Jewish roles of women as wives, mothers, help-mates, nurturers, sustainers and comforters'. For Frost, 'Christian feminism' is a contradiction in terms.

## III

The best-known conservative riposte to feminist polemic is William Oddie's *What Will Happen to God? Feminism and the Reconstruction of Christian Belief*, on the cover of which is a photograph of 'Christa', the sculpture of the 'female Christ' by Edwina Sandys. This had been unveiled and displayed during the Maundy Thursday vigil in the Episcopal Cathedral of New York in 1984 but had to be removed after the ensuing outcry. A decade later, in Manchester Cathedral in October 1993, 'a *Christa*' was carried in procession 'in the presence of the bishop' – an indication of the growing acceptance of the feminist perspective in Christian theology and worship. The hymn, 'I Vow to thee my Country' was rewritten for the occasion to become 'I Vow to thee my Sisters' (rendering men invisible) and ended 'And God, she'll stand among us and join our victory song'. The triumphalist militaristic metaphor, usually regarded by feminists as indicative of the masculinist patriarchal phallocentric perversion of the gospel, was allowed, in this context, as the victory that was proposed in the regenderisation of the hymn was that of Christian feminism.[17]

'Christa'

[17] 'The Church in Danger', *Faith and Heritage*, Spring 1994, 26, and '"Feminist Triumphalism" Detected', *The Church Times*, 26 November 1993.

Dr Oddie's comprehensive treatment of the feminist issue in *What Will Happen to God?* bears the following diplomatic dedication:

This book is dedicated
with love to
THE FEMALE SEX
particularly to
my mother, my wife and my daughter,
and to
THE GLORY OF GOD THE FATHER.[18]

Dr Oddie, who left Anglicanism for Rome, might not be a feminist, but he is careful (like David Frost, who closes his paper in quotation from his wife) to show that he is not a misogynist.

As Frost does, Oddie argues that the maleness of Christ and the masculine bias of his discourse present insuperable problems for feminists who would remain Christian. So far from modifying the patriarchy of the old dispensation (as some feminists, anxious to appropriate Jesus to their cause, have claimed), the Lord accentuates it:

> in the Old Testament, God is described as 'Father' only eleven times (and not once actually addressed in this way): Jesus, in startling contrast, uses the term at least 170 times.[19]

Of the feminist revision of the Nicene Creed:

> We believe in one God, Holy Immortal Almighty,
> Maker of heaven and earth,
> Of all that is, seen and unseen,
> We believe in Jesus Christ, Image of the invisible God,
> An eternal showing of the Almighty,
> God from God, Light from Light, True God from true God,
> caused to become human. . . .

Oddie comments:

> Nothing could be further away from the atmosphere of profound spiritual reflection surrounding the composition of the Nicene Creed than the cold calculation of this revision. 'Criteria' have been applied, stock devices from feminist handbooks deployed: God the Father simply disappears with a stroke of the blue pencil. The resulting document reminds one of nothing so much as a new edition of the Soviet Encyclopaedia, from which all mention of some luminary who has suddenly become a non-person is unaccountably discovered to be eliminated. The objection to this particular expurgation is clear enough: Christian prayer and worship should follow the model of Christ himself, who never used any other form of

18 Oddie, *What will Happen to God?*, v.
19 *ibid.*, 104.

> address than 'Father', and his explicit instructions in his gift of the Lord's Prayer.[20]

Again, like Frost, Oddie claims that the increasing influence of feminists in the Church (culminating, in 1990, in the election of the first woman diocesan bishop, Penny Jamieson, in Dunedin, New Zealand), can only have a deleterious effect on Christianity:

> the more powerful the Christian feminist movement becomes, the more abundant will be the Church's bitter harvest of division, anger, suspicion and all uncharitableness.[21]

## IV

There has been no shortage of female Christian critics of Christian feminism in its linguistic manifestations. A recent analysis of the feminist revision of liturgical and scriptural language comes from Dr Caroline Moore, Fellow in English at Peterhouse, Cambridge. In a monograph entitled *Divisive Language*, published by the 'Church in Danger' group (an alliance of Evangelical, liberal and Anglo-Catholic parliamentarians and journalists), she confronts the arguments of the English Liturgical Commission for 'inclusive language'.

First, Moore meets the proposal to accommodate feminist demands with the contention that the Commission's 'attitudes and assumptions'

> have been shaped by certain extremely deterministic schools of feminist linguistic theory, which are by no means accepted by all linguists, or, indeed, by all feminists (pp.2-3).

And she shows how the Commission's feminism and its inclusivist goals are already outdated, for advanced feminists (such as Deborah Cameron, in *Feminism and Linguistic Theory*) are arguing that 'non-sexist language is an illusion' and designed to support a masculinist pretence of neutrality (pp.3-4). Feminists are recognising – as the modernisers in the Church are failing to do – that changing language will not necessarily alter attitudes and beliefs. It is more likely that the process works in reverse, and that the imposition of new forms of language on a resistant society could reinforce rather than eradicate the very prejudices it would destroy. The burgeoning satirical literature critical of 'political correctness' is evidence of this backlash – *Politically Correct Bedtime Stories*, revisions of 'Little Red Riding Hood' and so on by James Finn Garner, for example, in which feminist Newspeak is wittily lampooned, was on the American 'best-seller' list in 1994.

In any case, if the Church is traditionally and profoundly sexist

[20] *ibid.*, 107-8.
[21] *ibid.*, 155.

(as feminists allege), changing 'man' to 'human' will not prevent 'human' being used as if it referred to men. It would only be tokenism. Next, Moore asks 'at whom these proposals are aimed':

> no very clear evidence has been adduced to show that ordinary women in practice find the generic use of 'man' offensive.

And churchwomen, in particular, have demonstrated that they experience neither ostracism nor oppression:

> It is hard to maintain that women feel themselves to be effectively excluded from a church in which, statistically, they are in the majority. . . . They, like their sisters throughout the ages, have been able to feel themselves part of the Mystical Body of Christ (p.6).

Like Frost, Moore argues that, before cultural priorities, Christians owe their allegiance to Christ and his Word. Jesus, she insists, did not bring his message into conformity with a 'culturally acceptable form, to make it apparently easier of access, more "inclusive" ':

> What he demanded, instead, was something far more radically challenging: the ability to move beyond the merely cultural altogether. And this, paradoxically, often involved the superficial appearance of exclusivity. Christ often seems, deliberately, to make his message hard.

For Moore, discrepancies between late twentieth century modes of thought and those of the first century, are forces for good rather than deficiencies:

> What appears to be a difficulty will actually make it less likely that we will become self-trapped by a deadly literal-mindedness (p.15).

Scriptural forms of language 'simultaneously stretch and humble the mind, making one aware of the greatness and littleness of man':

> They enhance our awareness of how easy it is to be trapped in merely human terms; but simultaneously enhance awareness of the miraculously creative and God-given nature of the power that enables us to transcend and transform those terms, with an act of understanding that alters what it sees (pp.15-16).

Caroline Moore's thesis is based on the biblical teaching that 'the letter killeth, but the spirit giveth life' (2 Cor. 3:6). The preoccupation of the Liturgical Commission, on the other hand, with inclusivist language reform to accommodate Christian feminism is evidence of a preoccupation with, rather than a liberation by, *the word*, which, so far from being inclusive, Moore argues, will foster a 'feminist ghetto-mentality' (p.13) that will be divisive and destructive.

## V

The renewal of the discourse of faith by Christian feminism raises numerous problems for the Church, as exposed in conservative polemic. Proposed, like secular feminism, in the name of empowerment and animated by a desire for vengeance on men, this latest attempted reformation of Christianity has proceeded in defiance (or ignorance) of at least three fundamental principles of religion – generally, that it is a critique of the aspirations of those in 'the world' (for whom the attainment of power and the seeking of revenge are cherished goals: 'Getting Even' was the recent aptly double-edged title of a television programme on women's struggles to achieve equal representation on legislative bodies), and particularly that the acquisition of power and the pursuit of vengeance are contradictory of the teaching of the gospel. Yet Sister Carolyn Osiek, a Professor of New Testament Studies and a feminist who travels the world in the name of the Christian women's movement, has urged women to articulate their powerlessness by taking vengeance – to

> demonstrate their importance yet lack of power in the Catholic Church by choosing one Sunday to put nothing in the collection box and to do no voluntary work.

A Sacred Heart nun who has regularly considered leaving her order and the Church, Osiek has decided 'to stay and concentrate on transforming it'. Church leaders, she opines, restrict the ministry of women who do most of the parish work but are denied 'positions of power in parishes and dioceses'.[22]

Within Roman Catholicism, Christian feminism and the renewal it proposes are in the paradoxical situation of attempting to advance its cause in a Communion that teaches that

> it is the bishops of the Catholic Church, together with the Pope, who have the task of teaching with authority those things which Christ has revealed as the sure way of truth[23]

and whose opposition to feminist polemic is clear. Yet Roman Catholic feminists defy the magisterium which enunciates the doctrine of the faith which they claim to profess.

In response to a letter from the pope in 1993 to bishops, rejecting the possibility of women ever becoming Roman Catholic priests and indicated that further debate on the matter was unwelcome, Sister Jo Armour, a Dominican nun who is the Chaplain of the University of South Australia, has announced that, contrary to the pope's teaching, the ministry of women is 'one of the biggest unresolved issues for the Catholic Church today'.

22 'Women's Church Work "Ignored"', *The Sydney Morning Herald*, 30 July 1994, 11.

23 Pastoral Letter from the Archbishops and Bishops of England and Wales, read at all masses in England and Wales on 2 May 1993.

For Chaplain Armour, the ordination of women as priests is 'a matter of justice'. She regards the pope's pronouncement as merely one of the 'differences of opinion in the church' and judges his letter to the bishops 'inappropriate'.[24] Catholicism, on this reading, is indistinguishable from Congregationalism.

Amongst the 'differences of opinion' in the Roman Catholic Church to which Chaplain Armour does not refer are those of a new generation of young women who (not unlike their secular counterparts) are increasingly distancing themselves from the stridency of middle-aged feminists. Responding to the pope's teaching at the Catholic Youth Conference, 'Summit 94', in Sydney, several young women not only assented to his edict but rejected the feminist critique of it as 'thinly focused' and divisive.[25]

The matter of the relevance of feminism to the younger generation is being ignored by Churches which are busily (if belatedly) assimilating the movement's precepts. Yet there is increasing evidence (in the phenomenon of the so-called 'retro-feminism', for example) of a reaction against its more extreme manifestations. Even the high priestess of Women's Liberation, Germaine Greer, has confessed to second thoughts, has joined the choir of the most conservative of Anglo-Catholic parishes in Cambridge, and has even had some good words to say about the traditional family unit. In tardily absorbing feminist theology and liturgy, in a spirit of justice and charity towards a vocal minority of victims and malcontents, those Churches which are embracing inclusive liturgy and other items of the feminist agenda may find after disposing of their allegedly sexist texts of Scripture and worship and (in Anglicanism) of the apostolic tradition of male priesthood that they have committed themselves to a phenomenon that the world has already rejected – or, at best, only selectively sustained.

In its much-prized, if recent pursuit of relevance to the spirit of the times, the Church could discover, early in the twenty-first century, that its irrelevance has been aggravated by the very feminism it imagined would ameliorate it. There is nothing so *passé* as the revolution before last.

If the evidence of undergraduates, female and male, on university campuses in the 1990s is any guide, it is environmentalism, rather than feminism, that inspires their hearts and minds today. Young women, in particular, naturally accept the tremendous benefits in their own lives which have been achieved for them by the women's movement of their mothers' generation. But – such is the way of the young – they are simultaneously rebelling against its orthodoxies.

24 'Nun's Call for Debate Defies Papal Edict', *The Australian*, 27 June 1994, 3.
25 'Women Back Pope's Ordination Veto', *The Australian*, 30 May 1994, 3.

Erica Jong's explanation is that the radicalism of feminists such as Glenda Jackson – who attempt to persuade younger women that they need to develop beyond any immature interests they might have in men, sex, romance, home-making and family life, in order to develop their potential as independent adult career women – is fatally flawed. For human nature being what it is, the majority of young women find these to be attractive quantities, and certainly more alluring than the role-models presented by the older feminists such as Dr Greer, who describes herself as 'fat, 55, dishevelled'.[26]

## VI

The most serious aberration of feminism, however – whether within the Church or without – is its critical construction of masculinity, that is, its negative appraisal of half of the God-created human race. The victimism of feminism, presupposing the male oppressor, and its vengefulness – the inevitable outcome of women's view of that oppression – stirs up distorted images and parodies of masculinity, bitterness and even enmity in confrontation with the masculine in all its forms, including language. Now that men are becoming victims – of a sustained campaign of vilification – they too are fighting the oppressor. In 'The Masculine Mystique', the novelist Tim Winton recalls that in the 'ideological grid' of his university years,

> I struggled privately with the feminist orthodoxy which argued that men's natures made them violent. They were all thugs and rapists, even if they hadn't 'offended' yet.[27]

In this environment, not only 'men' but 'family' were words 'uttered as expletives'. To challenge the feminist propaganda about masculinity was daunting,

> because the stream of grievance and loathing was too strong, its proponents too hurt and twitchy, their 'discussion methods' brutal and vindictive.

To disagree was to 'challenge a victim's veracity' and in the age of the victim in which we live, a 'culture of forbidden questions' has arisen in the context of the 'ideology of sensitivity' whereby the unquestioning acceptance of alleged 'hurt' has 'trumped the search for truth'.[28]

Winton's experience of men, however, in his extended family in particular, is that 'they were good or just plain harmless'. The focus of power and strength, in fact, was the women:

> the matriarchs made all the running. . . . They were stronger-willed and altogether more fierce as personalities. . . . They

26 'Stay in Touch', *The Sydney Morning Herald*, 17 October 1994, 24.

27 *Good Weekend Magazine*, 27 August 1994, 61-5.

28 See Charles Sykes, 'The Ideology of Sensitivity', *Imprimis*, July 1992, [1]-6.

> were more vengeful than their men and they were always the final authority. My grandmothers ran their families by sheer force of character, by brilliant organisation and hard work, or by mean-spirited sabotage and humiliation. Their husbands, by comparison, were mild and ineffectual.

The men Winton knew in his working-class childhood and adolescence were 'not the titans the gender myths would have them be'. He does not deny that men have flaws, but argues that the feminist insistence that these are peculiar to the sex is erroneous:

> Men's flaws are human flaws. Women have them too.

Again, it is in an anti-feminist context that we encounter an inclusivist teaching true to the gospel. At present, the most strident of the

> Shrieking voices
> Scolding, mocking, or merely chattering

assailing the Word are those from the feminist lobby. It remains to be seen in the Churches which have accommodated their liturgies to that discourse, whether the proclaimed inclusivity, by which they justify that accommodation, leads rather to the exclusion of men (and women who do not toe the feminist line), and thus accelerates the decline of those already numerically declining communions, into the invisibility of sectarianism and secularism, with an inculturated language of worship indistinguishable in vocabulary and ideology from that of the world and its evolving priorities, and in direct contradiction of Christian revelation as recorded in the New Testament.

# 6
# CHURCH MUSIC AND RENEWAL

## I

The effect on church music of the contemporary reforms in worship has, if anything, been even more bitterly criticised than the revision of liturgical language. It is all but impossible to find a distinguished ecclesiastical musician, organist, choirmaster or chorister, in the Anglican or Roman Catholic Churches, to defend *aggiornamento* unreservedly, in the context of musical art, and to argue that the liturgy has been improved, devotionally and aesthetically, in its musical component, by the so-called renewal. Writing in 1990, in *Why Catholics Can't Sing: The Culture of Catholicism and the Triumph of Bad Taste*, Thomas Day (a Roman Catholic Church musician) points out that

> today, a large number of Roman Catholics in the United States who go to church regularly – perhaps the majority – rarely or barely sing any of the music. . . . A great many people in Catholic churches do not even open their mouths to sing – ever.

Day argues that there is a 'sullen rebellion' taking place amongst the laity: that the 'once noble ideal' of 'participation', enforced by liturgical disciplinarians – trend-setters who demand that everybody subscribe to their views about the correct, up-to-date approach to God – is being resisted and has become a 'symbol of coercion' to be repudiated.[1]

As in the case of language, fictions with regard to music have been propagated by modernising liturgiologists about the former worshipping arrangements, in order to discredit them and validate 'renewal'. Just as it is erroneously alleged that Latin and Tudor English were incomprehensible to congregations for four centuries, it is asserted that the church music of the past was operatically polyphonic and so monopolised by choirs as to exclude the people from singing the Lord's song or joining in the worship chorally offered. Such an argument, also, is based on the literal-minded definition of 'partici-

[1] Day, *Why Catholics Can't Sing,* 1, 3, 167.

pation' in corporate prayer as occurring only when a worshipper is audibly saying or physically doing something – which in any case in music, the modernisers in Roman Catholicism at least have spectacularly failed to achieve. Musically, contemporary Roman Catholic parish worship is, as Day puts it, a weekly 'display of failure'.[2]

Certainly polyphony and other ornate musical forms demanding choral expertise were normal in most cathedrals and those parish churches with strong musical traditions. But in the later nineteenth century, in Roman Catholicism, the primitive accompaniment to the Latin mass, the Gregorian chant, had been recovered after some centuries' neglect and provided a mode for liturgical singing as unadorned as could be imagined. Similarly in Anglicanism, with the post-Tractarian revival of the eucharist as the principal Sunday service, the sixteenth-century setting of the Prayer Book by Merbecke provided a singing line, at the communion, like Gregorian chant, shaped to the cadence of the speaking voice, properly placed in the middle range convenient for all singers and adapted to the aural and accentual qualities of the text. This was music in which people could participate.

These settings possessed the timelessness of plainchant – dating from at least as early as the sixth century – and, thereby, a universality and stability of idiom in contrast to subsequent musical fashions. Yet, as Thomas Merton perceived from his familiarity with Gregorian chant in the monastic choir, it is the paradox of plainsong that its apparent simplicity will, after repeated use, yield devotional subtleties:

> Gregorian chant that should, by rights, be monotonous because it has absolutely none of the tricks of modern music, is full of variety and infinitely rich because it is subtle and spiritual and deep. . . . Those Easter 'alleluias', without leaving the narrow range presented by the eight Gregorian modes, have discovered colour and warmth and meaning and gladness that no other music possesses.[3]

The same testimony comes from Lois Lang-Sims about the use of plainchant in Canterbury Cathedral:

> Such music is passionless, and anonymous; and yet no human passion could be so intense, and no expression of human individuality so tender and intimate.[4]

Both emphasise the numinousness of this music, how it is evocative of the transcendental, yet profoundly human in character.

Modernisers, who have largely succeeded in disposing of

[2] *ibid.*, 3.
[3] In Furlong, *Merton*, 128.
[4] *Canterbury Cathedral*, 62.

Gregorian chant, of polyphony, Merbecke and most of what used to be known and celebrated as the 'Anglican cathedral tradition' (having eliminated Mattins and Evensong, for which much of this music was written), as well as vandalising hymnody in the name of the eradication of sexism, militarism ('Halt, Christian Soldiers', as one wit has put it), authoritarian paternalism, Zionism and so on, regard such perceptions as irrelevant. As Judith Rice notes, in 'Places Where They Sing', those who have abolished centuries of inspired artistry have done so on the conviction that choruses, 'folk and charismatic tunes', are 'the only medium for evangelism',[5] particularly amongst youth, in spite of the fact that the best-selling classical-music CD as *Canto Gregoriano* had, as the majority of its purchasers (70 per cent), people aged between sixteen and twenty-five. A recording of Gregorian chant, by EMI, by the monks of the Spanish Benedictine Abbey of Santo Domingo de Silos, *Canto Gregoriano*, sold more than a million copies world-wide in the space of a few months in 1994. Knowing the 'youth market' better than the liturgiologists – the CD is more popular than Madonna – its distributors have placed it in the 'pop and rock' section of music stores. In any case, as with modern liturgical language, the 'pop' music churches provide is not the same as that enjoyed by youngsters in the secular world, but a lame parody of it.

Graham Williams, accounting for this surprising phenomenon, reveals how the chant – 'highly spiritual music that engages man's natural spirituality' – is fulfilling a profound need of young people (and its other, older purchasers) today, and how the Church, in disposing of it and resisting attempts to restore it, has misjudged the aspirations of humanity to the numinous:

> In a world of conflict, death and mayhem . . . the power of this most ancient of Christian music [will] calm the spirit, still the anxious mind and . . . induce deep tranquillity and meditative states.

A consequence (if not intention) of the Vatican Council, he continues, in 'the "renewal" of . . . 32 years ago', was that 'parishes around the world' were encouraged to 'abandon this and other great sacred music':

> Desperate to attract and keep young people, they embraced pop, folk and even gospel music – instantly accessible and emotion-charged music, much of which is dismissed as banal and trivial.

Abandoned by the churches because of 'suspicion or ignorance' by the clergy, who prefer 'McDonald's music', the chant and other traditional forms have become 'part of the secular, popular culture'

5 *The Tablet*, 18 May 1991, 610.

which the Church had imagined that it was embracing.[6]

Similarly, in Anglicanism, it has been observed that at Winchester Cathedral today, 'a growing number of young people attend the Sung Eucharist . . . wanting to hear great religious music in its proper liturgical setting'[7] and the *Rector Chori* of Southwell Minster reports that the service which the boy choristers there enjoy singing most is the 1662 Communion Service:

> the fascinating thing is that when the boys have to be involved in a Rite A [modern] service they don't like it at all. . . . They're very ordinary boys. They would see themselves as very trendy boys. But when it comes down to it, they like the traditional words

and, therefore, the traditional music which accompanies them.[8]

In Anglicanism, the disposal of the heritage of genius in the works of its Tudor composers has eradicated music which, as C.H. Phillips argued, is strikingly simple to perform and easily receptive to understanding and appreciation by all. It is not the exclusive property of accomplished musicians:

> Tye's *O come ye servants (Laudate nomen)* is little more than a hymn-tune with a 'point' set in the middle, and the contemporary *Lord, for thy tender mercy's sake* of Hilton . . . is similar. . . . Tallis offers two little gems, *If ye love me* . . . and *O Lord, give thy Holy Spirit*, and Byrd a deeply felt *Ave verum corpus*, while Weelkes provides in *Let thy merciful ears* a tender miniature of no great difficulty.

That this body of work came into existence was due to the fact that these composers were 'moved into utterance' by great texts:

> In music written for the church service the notes must catch fire from the words, themselves aflame with the deep meaning behind them. The composer must be moved by the words into music.[9]

In the sixteenth century, as Phillips argues, there were both the words from Cranmer and gifted composers to appreciate them and set them.

The contemporary division and debate between what Erik Routley has called 'the trend-seekers and the traditionalists'[10] in church music is brought into clear focus in an ecumenical collection of essays, *In Spirit and in Truth*, by eleven English writers, most of whom are full-time church musicians. The editor, Robin Sheldon, who is on the side of 'renewal', denigrates what remains of old musical customs in worship as 'a hangover from the culture of the privileged classes', with 'triumphalistic affirmations of the Lordship of

6 'Charge of the Chant', *The Sydney Morning Herald*, 16 April 1994, 12A.
7 Judith Rice, *op.cit.*, 610.
8 *Faith and Heritage*, Spring 1992, 29.
9 *The Singing Church*, 98, 183.
10 *Church Music and the Christian Faith*, 134.

Christ which is so often different to real life as lived from Monday to Saturday'.[11] 'Real life' (undefined) and 'relevance', the buzz-word of the liturgical movement, are refrains in several of the essays in the collection:

> we need great sensitivity to the way in which music of cultural relevance can convey by its own nature the power of the gospel being proclaimed.[12]

That the power of the gospel might abide in its irrelevance to cultural priorities – 'be not conformed to this world' (Romans. 12:2) – is undreamt of in this philosophy.

'Culturally appropriate' music in church, it follows, must be attuned to 'pop', as Graham Gray insists in 'Justice, Rock and the Renewal of Worship', a title embracing the trinity of sociology, populism and *aggiornamento*:

> rock and pop music must be taken seriously. . . . Rock music with its great variety of styles and forms is the music of most ordinary people and it is essential that music in worship be accessible and appropriate to ordinary people.[13]

With condescension to the very 'ordinary people' (whoever they might be) he is supposed to be sensitive towards, Gray sets clear limits on the aspirations and capacities of worshippers – if you are an 'ordinary person' you could not possibly be inspired by Tallis, Palestrina, Bach or Stanford, nor should you be expected to be – and denies any desire they might have to be lifted out of 'ordinariness' to the vision of extraordinariness which, some would argue, it is the fundamental purpose of worship to convey. And what of those Christian people who are not 'ordinary'? If Gray's suppositions are true, why should these people be subjected to the lowest common musical denominator? But his intentions are political and sociological rather than theological and spiritual. Through music, he would

> break down the elitist barriers between different musical styles and social groups.[14]

Ambiguously affirming 'renewal' while revealing a conservative temper, Stephen Dean (of the *Music and Liturgy* magazine) argues, in his essay on 'Roman Catholic Music: The Recent Past and the Future', that satisfactory forms of musical accompaniment for the new vernacular mass have not been produced for the simple reason that leading composers have failed to be inspired by 'the poor quality of the texts'.[15] Folk mass settings have been popular, he acknowledges, 'in spite of the crudity of their

11 Sheldon (ed.) *In Spirit and in Truth*, 1.
12 *ibid.*, 2.
13 *ibid.*, 23.
14 *ibid.*, 26.
15 *ibid.*, 38.

words and music'.[16] But it should not be supposed, he warns, that such wide usage is due to congregational preference for this banal material. Rather, he suggests that the faithful are induced to use it through appeals to their 'sense of duty'. He has yet to observe 'real enjoyment or motivation to do so',[17] and he closes:

> [Christian music] should point to the beyond, rather than maroon us in the here and now.[18]

Going to the heart of one of the main reasons for the acrimony produced by the liturgical movement at large, the Director of the Royal School of Church Music, Lionel Dakers (in 'The Establishment and the Need for Change'), exposes the clerical manipulation of the liturgical changes which are nonetheless introduced in the name of improving the laity's worship, and the ignorance of most of the clergy in these matters.

The liturgical movement, in this sense, is an extraordinarily conservative phenomenon, for it is the expression – perhaps the last, in our culture – of the will of an authoritarian power group (the ordained ministry) being imposed upon a passive constituency (the laity). But, as Dakers argues, many lay people today are better educated musically than their priest or minister, 'through records and tapes, radio, television and the concert hall', and are less likely than previous generations,

> to accept a lessening of musical standards or quality when they are worshipping.[19]

If this is forced upon them, by the clergy, they will simply stay away:

> [as] the clergy are for the most part musically uneducated, is it any wonder that through ignorance or disinterest they repeatedly come up with the wrong answers? . . . When clergy equate their authority with autocracy, is it surprising that disastrous consequences result?[20]

The principal errors Dakers identifies come from the convictions that what is appropriate in church music today is 'the casual, the unstructured, the quasi do-it-yourself approach', from the obsession with 'virtually non-stop participation' and a 'seemingly relentless urge to discard moments of silence'. The catastrophic result is that 'there is little encouragement for serious musicians nowadays to contemplate working for the Church',[21] whether as performers or composers.

The most extreme espousal of the iconoclastic approach in this

16 *ibid.*, 39.
17 *ibid.*, 45.
18 *ibid.*, 47.
19 *ibid.*, 77.
20 *ibid.*, 86.
21 *ibid.*, 77, 81, 84.

collection comes from Philip Lawson-Johnston, in 'Power in Praise – Worship, "Cloud", and the Bible'. He emphasises the movement in contemporary worship 'towards everyone being fully involved and giving out rather than sitting back and receiving', perpetuating the modernisers' myth about the spiritual indolence of previous generations of Christians, and – surprisingly, from a musician – failing to recognise that some, in any congregation, are incapable of 'giving out' musically. Modern choruses

> provide a good and simple means for us to express the feelings of our hearts to the God we love.[22]

This, and much more in this mode, reveals a simplistic conception of faith that excludes that host of Christians – perhaps the majority today – who find that to pray, worship and live the Christian life is not a matter of straightforward platitudes, patient of a 'good and simple' means of expression, but a complex issue, vitiated by doubts, backslidings and even despair, but supported by moments of insight, understanding and vision, of ecstasy and exaltation: 'sometimes a light surprises / The Christian, while he sings', as William Cowper wrote. To reduce everybody's faith to the level of jejune sentiments, infantile lyrics and rhythms may achieve participation, on the same debased stratum, by everybody. But participation in worship to the point where all intellectual and spiritual discernment, and its variety of expression through the Christian centuries, are denied is a mockery of religion in its liturgical dimension.

Unexpectedly, even Lawson-Johnston, much later in his essay, begins to perceive the limitations of his polemic:

> It seems that when you try to please the maximum number of people by including something with which each one feels comfortable, then you run the risk of pleasing no one, because no one feels that you have included enough of their own particular preference.[23]

The most persuasive voice for the alternative, classical tradition of liturgical music, in this collection, is Christopher Dearnley's, coming from his experience as organist of St Paul's Cathedral. Of 'pop' music in church, he remarks:

> by its very nature [it] has to be constantly updated, but classical music has an enduring quality that can speak anew long after it was originally composed. It has the power and subtlety to express faith and the longings of the spirit that can rarely be contained, through its *naiveté* and over-simplification, in ephemeral music.[24]

22 *ibid.*, 162.
23 *ibid.*, 170.
24 'English Cathedral Music – A Glorious Habit', *ibid.*, 128.

Like Erik Routley, who denounces a former Bishop of Leicester's call for 'popular' music in church as a 'repulsive piece of ignorant philistinism evincing an attitude of deliberate misunderstanding which is painful in the ill-informed but catastrophic in the influential',[25] Dearnley berates the Church for so rudely discarding its heritage:

> No civilised society, however primitive, neglects its arts or, in the long run, ignores the insights and inspirations of its men of genius in the field of the arts.[26]

Yet the society of Christians, having done that, has impoverished its spiritual life. The Western, Christian, musical tradition provided an 'ambience for purposeful listening', space to 'loiter with God':

> a framework for those who commit themselves to prayer, a 'zone of stability' for searchers for areas of calmness, in busy lives, or just an opportunity to eavesdrop on a godly conversation.[27]

Routley similarly sees the purpose of church music 'not to attach [the worshipper] to the sensations of this world', but to facilitate transcendence:

> its purpose is to assist the believer in his journey towards God.[28]

Those who want music that, in style and expression, is 'easy and familiar', are driven by 'a lust for quick results'. This is music that requires no effort or imagination and, thus, seeks 'to bring men to Christ by a route which bypasses the way of the Cross. Music come by in that frame of mind will not profit the people of God'.[29]

## II

The strongest protests, however, have been against the revision of hymnody, which has been most radical, for it is perceived as the musical domain in which the laity most actively participates. As with liturgical language, lay people are told by the clergy what is in their best interests as worshippers, and if they complain they are rudely rebuked.

So, the Bishop of Chester, the Rt Revd Michael Baughen, having received a flood of criticisms of the 'dreadful doggerel' in *Hymns for Today's Church* (the result of ten years' labour and for which he was Consultant Editor) responded, not with the eirenic analysis one might have expected of an episcopal reviser of poetry, but simply with abuse

25 *op.cit.*, 78.
26 *op.cit.*, 128.
27 *ibid.*, 122.
28 *op.cit.*, 85-6.
29 *ibid.*, 96, 67.

irrelevant to the precise critique:

> 'Who wert and art and evermore shalt be' – that is really ridiculous. How on earth can you sing that in Toxteth [an inner-city area of Liverpool]?[30]

Not everyone lives in Toxteth and no argument is given for taking it as the measure of literary standards in the Church, nor is the layman's correct description of the version of the twenty-third psalm, in this collection, as 'doggerel' answered:

> The Lord my shepherd rules my life
> and gives me all I need.

To sustain this crass rhythm, language must be tortured:

> Though in a valley dark as death
> no evil makes me fear –

producing a syntax, taxing even in Toxteth, more complicated than Coverdale. There is laborious emphasis:

> ◡ / ◡ / ◡ / ◡ /
> While all my enemies look on

and perversion of meaning:

> Your goodness and your gracious love
> pursue me all my days. . . .

For in contemporary meaning 'pursuit' has the connotation of hostility – as in 'hot pursuit' – alien to the psalmist's concept of pastoral solicitude.

In the liberalising Protestant Churches, the very home of hymnody, revision has known no bounds. Supposed sexism having been eradicated, the modernisers then turned their censorious attention to alleged militarism. 'Onward, Christian Soldiers', 'Fight the Good Fight', 'A Mighty Fortress is Our God' and so on have had to go, for 'we are starting to realise our language is militaristic'.[31] This revelation, however, does not appear to have been accompanied by the appropriate corrective that this is the language of poetry. For the Revd Dick Wotton, hymnody with imagery from soldiering and battle, and even scriptural references to 'putting on the armour of God' and, incredibly, 'fighting against the devil',

> teaches children from the start that fighting and warring is OK. We just don't have to sound like warmongers when we talk.[32]

Incapable of understanding that St Paul, the psalmist, and the hymn writers were using military symbolism not to urge Christian people to worldly battle, but to spiritual warfare, Wotton has apparently never heard of a metaphor. Yet he has the temerity to revise poetic language.

30 'Tory Outcry over "Trendy" 23rd Psalm', *The Australian*, 10 November 1982, 6.

31 The Revd Dick Wotton, 'Halt, Christian Soldiers, Says Uniting Church', *The Sun-Herald*, 13 June 1982, 28.

32 *ibid.*

It is the sexism of traditional hymnody, however, that has most preoccupied the modernisers. Shamelessly revealing her iconoclastic temper, Judith Maizel, of the working party for the new Methodist hymn book, remarked that she took 'great glee in ruining ['Rise Up, O Men of God'] for a number of people who have not noticed that [masculinist] imagery before'.[33]

The problem with this zeal, driven by feminism, is that it requires the revision of most of the hymns in such collections as *Ancient and Modern Revised*. And such revision, in many cases, amounts to elimination, for the offensive imagery is present not only in passing phrases, which can be reformed according to feminist ideology, but informs the entire metaphorical and narrational structure and process of numerous works. And if these hymns, composed by such purveyors of sexism as Charles Wesley, are censored and destroyed, then to whom shall we go today for worthy replacements?

That well-known paean of adoration, 'At the name of Jesus / Every knee shall bow', concludes, in its seventh stanza, after an elaboration of metaphor, thus:

> Brothers, this Lord Jesus
> Shall return again,
> With his Father's glory,
> With his angel train;
> For all wreaths of empire
> Meet upon his brow,
> And our hearts confess him
> King of glory now.

Sexist, patriarchal, monarchist, imperialist, implicitly militaristic – there is nothing to redeem this stanza (or the hymn as a whole, for this is the culmination of its imagery) from its ideological unsoundness. And to make matters worse, it was written by a woman!

In a review of *Hymns for Today's Church* in the *Times Literary Supplement*, Michael Trend remarks that the principles upon which the revision of Anglican hymnody has proceeded 'spell misery', and he argues that the volume is likely to be strongly resisted in parishes, for worshippers, having endured the turbulence of the 'recent years of liturgical experiment and change', draw solace from the traditional hymns that have continued to be used in services otherwise in modern language.[34]

The audacity of revisers in disposing of the works of some of the greatest poets and composers in the tradition, to replace them, moreover, with their own ephemeral and second-rate productions, drew

33 'He becomes Thee as Hymn Book Sheds Sexist Tones', *The Sydney Morning Herald*, 1 April 1981, 7.

34 'Ancient, Modern and More Modern Still', 26 November 1982, 1996.

the ire of Richard Ingrams in his review of *Hymns for Today's Church*, entitled 'Look what they Done to your Songs, Lord'. This work of revision, if it must be undertaken

> should be done, like all works of restoration, by people with some respect for their predecessors; in the case of hymns, by people with some feeling for music and poetry. Otherwise, as with the new Church of England liturgy, the result is disastrous.

From *Hymns for Today's Church*, Newman's 'Lead, kindly Light' has been omitted, so too has George Herbert's 'Teach me, my God and King', and Christina Rossetti's 'In the Bleak Mid-winter', with music by Gustav Holst. Blake's famous words for 'Jerusalem' are rejected – 'their meaning is presumably thought to be obscure' – and 'the compilers have not hesitated to change the words even of writers like Milton'.

Ingrams is referring here, no doubt, to 'Let us with a gladsome mind', which becomes 'Let us gladly with one mind', with the outrageous notation – 'after John Milton'.

No fewer than twenty-six original compositions by the Revd Michael Saward, then vicar of Ealing, are included in this compilation which judges the poetry of Herbert, Newman and Christina Rossetti inferior and unworthy, in spite of the fact that those writers have touched the souls of countless worshippers. Ingrams quotes one of Saward's verses:

> Fire of God, titanic Spirit,
> Burn within our hearts today,
> Cleanse our sin – may we exhibit
> Holiness in every way. . . .

commenting:

> Quite apart from his audacity in rhyming 'spirit' with 'exhibit', it may strike some people as rather extraordinary that a man who has devoted so much time to pruning what he thinks are obsolete words and phrases from other people's hymns should use the word 'titanic' which if it means anything to 'today's churchgoers' is the name of an expensive and ill-fated hulk lying at the bottom of the sea.[35]

Clearly, Ingrams foresees the same fate for *Hymns for Today's Church*.

Ingrams' point about the selective updating of allegedly incomprehensible language is copiously substantiated in this collection. Saward, who could not allow Milton's flavoursome and joyous 'gladsome' to stand, yet permits – in the very next hymn – 'pavilioned in splendour' to survive. If the ignorant laity (as they are envisaged by

35 Originally in the *Spectator*, reprinted in *The Sydney Morning Herald*, 5 February 1983, 33.

liturgiologist-priests) cannot cope with 'gladsome' (as they have somehow managed to do for three centuries), with its simple Old English derivation, how are they to understand and envisage the rococo 'pavilioned'?

But the most thorough analysis of the contemporary revision of hymnody is the critical essay of 1990 by Professor Margaret A. Doody, 'Changing What We Sing',[36] which reviews the past decade's rewriting and censorship of 'the standard Christian hymns of the Protestant tradition'.

As an Episcopalian professor of literature, she argues that hymns are poems –

> hymns are songs reaching to the divine, and also moments of the divine touching the human, and they are the product of individual human persons, men and women, who can be individually named as makers. Toplady himself was a real individual; 'Rock of Ages' had its origin in an experience of his own, as he tells us, when he was sheltering from a storm (p.316).

To subject these individual utterances, as various Church committees have done, to 'wholesale and merciless revision', is to deny the integrity of the experiences they record and the inspired creative act and expression in which their writers recorded it. Presenting us with such 'tinkered and adulterated goods', the revisers are revealed in self-parody. For they are 'denying God and denying his presence, potential or actual, among real live human beings':

> Their denial of authorship, imagination and individual creation spells a certain assent to the proposition that there is no Author of Creation (p.336).

By what authority do they make these changes? Doody notes that the 'revisers' overt attention is always benevolent' (pp.316-17). So, in the new hymn book of the First Congregational Church in Amherst, Massachusetts, where military metaphor is banished in the name of pacifism, the negro spiritual 'We Are Climbing Jacob's Ladder',

> has had the last line of the first verse altered from 'Soldiers of the Cross' to 'Bearers of the Cross' (a different statement) (p.317).

In America, all monarchical metaphors associated with the deity in hymnody must be purged, in the interests of republicanism, so Robert Grant's 'O Worship the King' has been rewritten thus:

> We worship thee, God,
> All glorious above.

But with this censorship in metaphor goes the power of the original

36 In Christopher Ricks and Leonard Michaels (eds) *The State of the Language.*

poetry. Doody recalls the qualities of Grant's poetics, derived largely from Cowper, of which arresting symbolism is the most prominent.

However, the revisers, having placed monarchical metaphor on their Index of proscribed language, literally and figuratively emasculate the hymn. They also dislike its imperative voice, Doody argues, because, in the best modern way, they 'have an aversion to all exhortation':

> Nobody should order anyone to do anything. . . . All imperatives (including those of the 'let us' variety) seem to have been changed into calm statements of fact. 'We worship' – so there's no need for anyone to *tell* anyone else what to do (pp.318-19).

What has happened in such revision is that translation has occurred 'from English into another English', often ungrammatical and senseless, as in the rewriting of Charles Wesley's well-known hymn:

> O for a thousand tongues to sing
> My great Redeemer's praise,
> The glories of my God and King,
> The triumphs of his grace!

The censorious blue pencil of 'inclusive language' is applied, and this is the result:

> O for a thousand tongues to sing
> My great Redeemer's praise,
> The glories of my God to bring,
> Who wins our hearts by grace!

Professor Doody responds:

> Now there is no vulgar triumph about God – no implied victories of grace, nor anything that might seem nasty-nasty military. And nothing as horrible (indeed unspeakable) as a King appears. Getting rid of 'King' while keeping the first line must have cost these new-fledged rhymesters considerable trouble and some headaches. Or perhaps it did not – they cannot surely have troubled themselves too long about it, because they came up (and were content) with the totally inane and meaningless line 'The glories of my God to bring'. This is an incomplete clause which as it stands is a nonsense. How do I 'bring' the glories of God? Where do I bring them? – bring to notice, to book, to light, to the 'bring and buy' sale? When sung, the expression comes off as 'to bring who', which sounds not only ungrammatical but puzzling. The revisers evidently cannot see that the old – that is, Charles Wesley's – construction had 'praise', 'glories' and 'triumphs' as a sequence of three noun objects of the verb 'to sing'. If these rhymesters are not to be trusted with sentence construction, why must we trust them with our hymns? Their new fake line is a grammatical and

> linguistic disaster, and makes the hymn a parody of itself (p.320).

Such censorship and revision is nothing less, Doody contends, than a 'rewriting of history', attempting to delude congregations into believing 'that we always thought as we do now', on the arrogant premise that we have nothing to learn from the insights of previous generations. This is another twentieth-century tyranny, as the past must be revised in subservience to ideology:

> Everything that has come down to us is to be subjected to drastic alteration, refurbished and tricked out to look unlike itself, like antique furniture smartly enamelled (p.322).

The revisers of hymns, in current literary-critical terminology,

> are engaged in a new postdeconstructionist activity . . . 'unlimited rewriting' – erasing the original text and making it unquotable. They willingly and wilfully execute their own wills upon texts, without acknowledging any limitation (p.327).

The most preposterous example she cites of this process occurs in the replacement of the word 'King' in Wesley's Easter hymn, 'Christ the Lord is Risen Today', which contained the line

> Lives again our glorious King.

The revisers have changed this to

> Jesus lives, eternal spring

thus 'getting rid of all might, majesty, dominion, and glory, and turning the Lord into a season rather than a person'.

Woe betide the laity who might protest!

> We are to be fobbed off with bad and even ungrammatical language, but if we make a fuss then we are acting in a bad, naughty, uncharitable manner. As congregations, we are less than dust (p.337).

Liturgiologists, Doody concludes, are ideological dictators, who 'despite lofty ideals about the community they are writing for', are

> mental overlords who compel obedience without calling for discussion or entertaining protest (p.338).

Liturgical revision

> is an undeclared onslaught which is presented (ah, how like imperialism) as a modern set of benefits conferred. These revisers have left us poorer than they found us, and, while they think they are making us progressive, they are suiting us for dictatorship. And it is one of the evils of dictatorship that one is forced to go along with ugly and ungracious words (pp.338-9).

It should be noted by those who imagine that criticisms such as these could come only from a reactionary that Margaret Doody is

> a liberal from way back, a card-carrying feminist, and, if not a convinced republican, at least an ardent democrat with socialist tendencies (p.322).

The conservative critique is not confined to political and social conservatives.

Christians are being indoctrinated to believe that their worship has been improved by the eradication from their hymnals (as in the latest edition of *Hymns Ancient and Modern*) of ideologically unsound poetry like Wesley's 'Gentle Jesus, Meek and Mild', Heber's 'The Son of God goes forth to War' and 'From Greenland's Icy Mountains', Keble's 'Lord, in thy Name thy Servants Plead', Philip Pusey's 'Lord of our Life, and God of our Salvation' and so on, and the addition – in that collection – of nine hymns by Fred Kaan, a United Reformed Church moderator, of which this is a typical sample:

> We thank you, O God, for your goodness,
> For the joy and abundance of crops,
> For food that is stored in our larders,
> For all we can buy in the shops.
> But also of need and starvation
> We sing with concern and despair. . . .[37]

It is the conservatives, indeed, who are concerned and despairing.

[37] In John Whale, 'Ancient Hymns Kinkered', *The Sunday Times*, 5 June 1983, 3.

# 7
# THE LANGUAGE OF LITURGY

Consider the Epistle to the Hebrews – where is there in the classics any composition more carefully, more artistically written? Consider the book of Job – is it not a sacred drama, as artistic, as perfect, as any Greek tragedy of Sophocles or Euripides? Consider the Psalter – are there no ornaments, no rhythm, no studied cadences, no responsive numbers, in that divinely beautiful book?

John Henry Newman, *The Idea of a University* (1852).

There is a kind of clearness of statement which suits material objects but which simply does not apply to spiritual things; and it is plain that such clearness is avoided as a danger both in the Bible and in the Fathers. . . . Human language can but dimly adumbrate . . . divine mysteries. . . . It is a shallow rationalism and intellectual indolence . . . which crave for clearness of statement beyond the measure allowed for us who 'see through a glass, darkly' – the craving must be gratified only with great reserves.

Charles Gore, *The Body of Christ* (1902).

We cannot order chunks of liturgy in the kind of way we get various items from the laundry. I say this because I believe that this essential understanding of what is a literary art as well as a theological art has been somewhat lost sight of in the way we have set about it in our proceedings.

Michael Ramsey (1973).

Our explanatory and moralizing liturgy needs figures whose very mystery is our hope, metaphors that surprise us and lead us on (where?), poetry which 'means nothing' but makes us think and imagine (what?), music which does not give us information but which moves us (how?) and the gesture which commits us (to what and to whom?).

Joseph Gelineau, *The Liturgy Today and Tomorrow* (1978).

The paradox at the heart of the debate that I have described over the revision of liturgical language is the same as that at the centre of the Christian religion, as revealed in the mystery of the Incarnation. Liturgical language should be both evocative of the eternal and intelligible within the discourse of the times and cultures in which it is used. The result is the 'tension' powerfully described by T.S. Eliot, who recognised the burden borne by language, particularly in poetry, when the medium of human discourse strives to transcend its inherent mutability and evoke the eternal:

Words strain,
Crack and sometimes break, under the burden,
Under the tension, slip, slide, perish,
Decay with imprecision, will not stay in place,
Will not stay still.

Debased or demotic idioms – 'shrieking voices / Scolding, mocking, or merely chattering' – also threaten the elevation of language to the transcendental.

In such cacophony, the voice of God may not even be heard. It could be submerged in the verbiage of worldliness and mortality and the other fancies and illusions which might encompass and overpower it:

The Word in the desert
Is most attacked by voices of temptation,
The crying shadow of the funeral dance,
The loud lament of the disconsolate chimera.[1]

The problem for liturgiologists in all times, as indeed for biblical translators, has been to sustain the numinousness of the Word while renewing its ability to speak to successive generations, to make the language of God incarnate in the ages of humankind.

These two matters of the eternal signification of liturgical language and its requirement of comprehensibility are recognised by all who are concerned with the words of worship, but conservatives stress the numinous and 'reserve' in the communication of sacred truth, while reformers characteristically concentrate on the issue of intelligibility, arguing that (as the Preface to the Book of Common Prayer puts it) the Church's prayers must be 'easy and plain for the understanding both of the Readers and Hearers'. More radically, they contend that this will be achieved only if liturgy is written both in the language of today and in the various idioms of cultural groups. In other words, it must be always being rewritten, for language and culture are constantly evolving, as the generations pass.

Insufficient attention has been paid to detailed definition and demonstration of the characteristics of numinousness and compre-

1 'Burnt Norton', V, *Four Quartets*.

hensibility, as revealed in liturgical language. Too often, mystery and clarity are invoked as self-evidently and exclusively commendable, by opposing sides in the debate, without argument and analysis.

## I

The conspicuous example of numinous liturgy, in the West, has been the Latin rite. Here was a language of worship, removed from daily speech, which was valued because of its detachment. It was the liturgical embodiment of the *Disciplina Arcani* of the primitive Church – the practice of an element of restraint in the communication of ultimate mystery, which was revered, for example, by the Tractarians.[2] Yet, at the same time, it possessed aesthetic qualities, an aural appeal and an incantatory pulse, propitious for emotive impact and memorability. That much of the mass was said *in secreto* added to the sacredness of this discourse. Millions could recite and sing the *Pater noster*, to plainchant, who had never studied Latin. In combination with the ceremonies of the liturgy, as arcane as the language in which it was written, the architectural design of churches, and the eastward position of the celebrant at the distant, elevated high altar, these qualities created an atmosphere of mystery and other-worldliness redolent of the eternal. A momentous testament to the aural and numinous qualities of the Latin liturgy is the repertoire of musical settings of the rite, including those by the great composers.

Its language is resonant – *Gloria in excelsis Deo* (with those open vowels) – and intimately tender: *dona nobis pacem* (with the succession of quietening consonants). It is insistent – *Credo in unum Deum* (with the pointed rhyme) – and all but sensuously transcendental in a word such as *requiem*, with its verbal closure: its several repetitions in the mass for the dead emblematise and emphasise the pervasive experience of the end of life. There is no quality of poetry that the Latin liturgy does not possess. Above all, it was the strangeness of this text – for even when it was familiar in worship, it was not heard elsewhere – that was the secret of its elevating quality, its other-worldliness. Here was a higher language, the mysterious discourse of Heaven.

The price which the Church had to pay for such a peerless possession, however, was that its people were often unclear or simply ignorant about the precise meanings of words and phrases in their liturgy. To non-Catholics without Latin, it could be simply 'hocus-pocus' (the satirical contraction of the formula for consecration in the canon of the mass: *Hoc est enim corpus meum . . .* etc.). Both within

[2] See G.B. Tennyson, *Victorian Devotional Poetry: the Tractarian Mode*, 144-5.

the Church and outside it, the liturgy was scarcely evangelistic, for all its beauties and timelessness. Yet the incomprehensibility of the Latin rite has been exaggerated. Particularly from the early twentieth century to Vatican II, the provision of translations in the vernacular in bilingual missals resolved any difficulties while preserving the qualities of the Latin text, recited at the altar. But if it was permissible for the laity to *read* the prayers in their own language, should they not be *recited* audibly by the priest in the vernacular too?

The linguistic argument against vernacularisation was that the sacred qualities that Latin brought with it, by virtue of its poetry, would then be lost to worship. Indisputably, this has occurred. Similarly discounted are the arguments from stability and universality – that Latin, as the Renaissance scholar Alexander Gill put it, represents 'that inviolable spirit of Christ which governs the universal company of Christian teachers', spreading the gospel through 'a language common to no people and therefore not liable to changes', or as his contemporary, Richard Mulcaster, argued – a language 'absolute, and free from motion', 'shrined up in books, and not ordinary in use, but made immortal by the register of memory'.[3]

But the view that the intelligibility of liturgy was even more important than its numinousness, universality and stability has prevailed, to the point where this preference is taken for granted. And the same has been true (if less rigorously imposed) in the Anglican Communion – where, again, a treasury of distinguished music had been based on the prose-poetry of its Cranmerian Prayer Book and Jacobean Bible.

## II

The problem with the reform of worshipping language in the name of comprehensibility or intelligibility is to define, in theological, liturgical and, indeed, linguistic terms, what is meant by 'comprehensible' and 'intelligible'. Today, it is taken as axiomatic that liturgical language should be immediately understandable and that comprehensibility will be be achieved automatically if the contemporary vernacular tongues are used.

Far from being self-evident truths, however, these assumptions are highly contentious. Ian Ramsey described religious language as, at best, 'significant stuttering about the Inexpressible',[4] while Evelyn Underhill, that impassioned transcendentalist, argued that 'all worship ever looks away from the transitory and created to the Abid-

3 Both in Judith Anderson, 'Patterns Proposed Beforehand: Donne's Second Prebend Sermon', *Prose Studies*, September 1988, 41.

4 *Words about God: The Philosophy of Religion*, 219.

ing and Increate, . . . where it is emptied of this unearthly element . . . worship loses its most distinctive characteristic'.[5]

The truth of religion, the knowledge of the love of God, is a matter of grace and faith. While instruction in Christianity, whether for neophytes or seasoned believers, is an essential function of liturgy – performed principally in the recitation of the creeds, in the liturgy of the Word and in preaching – the ultimate purpose of worship is to lift the soul to God. This is not to argue that worship should be predominantly emotional in character (although, in some traditions, this is so),[6] but to restrict liturgy to the function of didacticism is to misrepresent it and to impoverish it. Worship, like religion itself, should engage the whole person, heart and mind, and then transport him beyond himself – as C.S. Lewis argued: 'in worship . . . I transcend myself; and am never more myself than when I do'.[7] This is 'participation' in liturgical prayer and ceremony of a divine kind, beyond its literalist reckoning by modernising liturgiologists.

For this reason, the obsession with making every phrase of the liturgy as clear and contemporary as possible, without a concomitant concern with the poetic qualities of language propitious for evoking a sense of eternal mystery and with the power to stir the emotions, is an imbalance which reflects a theoretical view of the way people should worship that is in itself questionable and limited, and which, in any case, is removed from the expectations and experience of most worshippers. For, as Stephen Prickett has argued, 'a language of discomformation and ambiguity is not merely a concomitant of religious experience, but is actually characteristic of, and historically central to, man's experience of God'.[8] Yet, ironically, as Cardinal Newman observed, the arcane language of liturgy becomes 'a portion of the vernacular tongue, the household words, of which perhaps we little guess the origin, and the very idioms of our familiar conversation' – by virtue of its innate power of language. For him, the 'Protestant Bible and Prayer Book . . . remain as perfect and original a work as Euclid's elements or a symphony of Beethoven', yet – at the same time – they have 'seized upon the public mind'.[9]

The doctrines that liturgy expresses and enacts – such as the resurrection of Christ – are irretrievably mysterious, 'so ambiguous', Prickett observes, 'as to resist any modern attempt to reduce [them] to a direct simple statement'.[10] This does not mean that they must,

5 *Worship*, 8.

6 See Douglas Kennedy, *In God's Country: Travels in the Bible Belt, USA* for a vivid account of anti-intellectual fundamentalist evangelical worship.

7 *An Experiment in Criticism*, 141.

8 *Words and 'The Word'*, 224.

9 *The Idea of a University*, 313.

10 *Words and 'The Word'*, *op.cit.*, 7.

therefore, be embodied in incomprehensible language, although to argue for the mimesis of word and idea is not disreputable, but it is certain that to achieve this embodiment, inspiration of the kind Hilaire Belloc recognised in Cranmer is required:

> he was master of the Word, he possessed the secret of magic. He had been granted power in that which is perhaps the highest medium we know of expression among men, English at its highest.[11]

These subtleties are suppressed in the argument that by simplifying and modernising the vocabulary in which such verities are couched worshippers will be best equipped to come to a spiritual understanding of their truth. A simplified and readily accessible contemporary expression could traduce the profundity and complexity of doctrine, devaluing its inherent mystery and compromising its universality. True liturgical language, Evelyn Underhill observes,

> enchants and informs, addressing its rhythmic and symbolic speech to regions of the mind which are inaccessible to argument, and evoking moments of awe and love which no exhortation can obtain. It has meaning at many levels, and welds together all those who use it; overriding their personal moods, and subduing them to its grave loveliness.[12]

It is understandable, in an age of scepticism and rationalism, not to mention unprecedented rapidity and brevity in the communication of information, and where the unchurched vastly outnumber the churched, that Christian apologists should be anxious to present the faith forcefully, succinctly and plainly. In 1991, in the Diocese of Sydney, 'plain English' liturgies were being tested to see if they might be meaningful in evangelistic outreach, especially amongst those with little formal education:

> we were concerned because our Prayer Books [that is, both BCP and AAPB] require a high degree of literacy for comprehension.[13]

On the publication of *Experimental Services* in 1993 a diocesan spokesman on liturgy, Dr David Peterson, referred to

> those who seek more radical changes of language and style. Especially in churches where every effort is being made to attract inquirers or new converts, it is felt that our liturgical forms do not always speak with sufficient clarity and relevance.

Even services in modern English

> are often thought to be too complicated and written in

11 *Cranmer*, 257.

12 *Worship, op.cit.*, 113.

13 App. 2: 'The local church and literacy', committee re Church Growth.

> unfamiliar language.[14]

But where does this slippery slope end, in the attempt to compose liturgical language that is clear, relevant and immediately comprehensible to everybody? Peterson contends that only those with 'a literacy level of 13 years of education or more' are able to understand the language of modern rites. But what does 'understanding' mean, in this context?

Joanna Southcott, an uneducated domestic of the late eighteenth century – to take but one example – understood the Book of Common Prayer well enough to be able to remark that there were no words 'more proper' than those found there.[15] Words communicate meaning on levels other than simplistic conceptions of comprehension, clarity and relevance. They accomplish much, for example, when they put the worshipper in a spiritual state of mind and sensibility – and that might be achieved as much by their cadence and aural appeal as by their precise meaning.

By which precepts are we to judge what is 'comprehensible' in liturgy and who it is who is capable of 'comprehension' in faith? Liturgiologists are always talking of comprehensibility and intelligibility, but these fundamental questions about the interpretation and application of the terms seem never to have occurred to them.

Moreover, precisely because we live in a civilisation dominated by humanistic philosophies (which the Church is bound to contradict) it could be argued that it is the numinous rather than the informative aspects of liturgy which require emphasis today. People are yearning for transcendental succour. The young American who observed that his parish church would be the last place he would visit to satisfy his craving for the contemplation of the supernatural sounded a warning to biblical and liturgical experts who imagine, with the 'breezy confidence' ridiculed by Stephen Prickett, that by providing a Scripture and liturgy that are comprehensible (as judged, again, by the narrowest linguistic criteria) they have discharged their commission.

As Michael Gilchrist has observed of the Roman Catholic defence of the revision of liturgical language in the interests of the young:

> The drift of young Catholics from mass attendance has occurred, ironically, despite the preoccupation of modern liturgists with their alleged needs. Dr Marcellin Flynn's finding that 84% of Year 12 [eighteen-year-old] students in 1982 thought the mass 'boring' confirmed a smaller 1979 survey . . . which revealed that 92% of teenagers were bored with the mass.

14 'New Trial Services Published', *Southern Cross*, November 1993, 31.

15 In David Martin, 'The Woman Clothed with the Sun', *Times Literary Supplement*, 26 November 1982, 1288.

The disenchantment of young people, it is argued, is due to the disenchantment of the liturgy. It had arisen, Fr Luis Mondonaldo of *Concilium* has written,

> not for lack of the Church's adaptation to the secular world, but rather because [the young] find the Church empty of her true, profound and specific substance.[16]

In his *De Doctrina*, St Augustine (as summarised by Rowan Williams) warned against the 'constant danger of premature closure, the supposition that the end of desire has been reached and the ambiguities of history and language put behind us':

> Obscurity in the words of revelation is one of the things that anchors us in our temporal condition: the search for instant clarity and transparency is like the Platonist's search for 'unattended moments' of ecstasy. . . . A language which indefinitely postpones fulfilment or enjoyment is appropriate to the Christian discipline of spiritual homelessness, to the character of the believing life as pilgrimage.

Augustine's warning against the 'folly of supposing we have rapidly and definitively grasped what is being said in a single successful event of communication'[17] contradicts the principal linguistic premise on which the modern liturgical movement is founded.

## III

A comparison of the Prayer of Consecration in the communion service in the Book of Common Prayer and the approved English translation of the Roman canon of the mass will bring into focus the disparity between liturgical writing designed ultimately to inspire and that intended primarily for instruction. In the Cranmerian prayer, both vocabulary and cadence are poetic, although in prose. The fallacy, still perpetrated by liturgical modernisers, that Cranmer wrote in the everyday language of the sixteenth century (to support their argument that they should write in the everyday language of the twentieth, which, in any case, they do not) is disposed of in the opening address of this prayer – 'Almighty God, our heavenly Father', with its expansive exaltation of diction, in those two epithets, which are then counterbalanced by the intimacy of a third – 'who of thy *tender* mercy. . .'. Far from being idiomatic speech, this is language approaching the extremities of evocativeness. As Anne Hall has observed, 'conservative linguistic forms and toneless chanting both contributed to a liturgical idiom at the end of the sixteenth and begin-

16 In Gilchrist, *Rome or the Bush*, 57.

17 'Language, Reality and Desire in Augustine's *De Doctrina*', *Literature and Theology*, July 1989, 142-3.

ning of the seventeenth centuries, the simplicity and solemnity of which stood in marked contrast to the brisk and giddy-paced language of modern debate'.[18]

The cadence is incantatory: 'who made there . . . and did institute . . . Hear us . . . and grant', with a dominant effect of accumulating intensity: 'a full, perfect, and sufficient sacrifice, oblation, and satisfaction. . .'. These phrases are essentially theological, with their insistence on the sufficiency of the Cross; but the doctrinal component is again complemented in the next clause by an atmospheric adjectivalism to strike to the hearts of the auditory; 'and did institute, and in his *holy* gospel command us to continue, a *perpetual* memory of that his *precious* death. . .'.

To conclude this preamble to the institution narrative, there is the petition:

> Hear us, O merciful Father, we most humbly
> beseech thee; and grant that we receiving
> these thy creatures of bread and wine,
> according to thy Son our Saviour Jesus
> Christ's holy institution, in remembrance of
> his death and passion, may be partakers of
> his most blessed Body and Blood. . . .

Again, adjectives such as 'merciful', 'holy' and 'blessed', the ejaculation 'O', and the sequence of rhythmically balanced couplets: 'bread and wine', 'death and passion', 'Body and Blood' are embellishments signifying the abundance of the divine economy. In more than 120 words, in this allegedly incomprehensible language, there are no more than two or three substantives ('oblation', 'satisfaction'), which, because of their technical theological implications, could be described as abstruse. They are key words, certainly, but their meaning is revealed by association: 'a full, perfect, and sufficient sacrifice, oblation, and satisfaction, for the sins of the whole world' – and, again, the magnitude of the matter is conveyed through an epithet which is as clear as day: 'the *whole* world'.

It is the genius of this language that it is both meaningful and arcane. It is impossible to conceive that the monosyllabic vocabulary of the phrase 'the sins of the whole world' was ever linguistically incomprehensible to anyone, even if its theological import is inexhaustible. Such aspects of the vocabulary as its conscious archaisms ('thee', for instance – dated, even in 1662) elevate its lucidity, touching it with appropriate strangeness. Such language embodies, as Stephen Medcalf observes, Cranmer's

> humanist, melodious balance of latinate and English words

[18] 'Richard Hooker and the Ceremonial Rhetoric of "Silly Sooth"', *Prose Studies*, September 1988, 29.

> ('create and make in us new and contrite hearts'), his temperate modifying of all richness ('whose service is perfect freedom' for the Latin *cui servire regnare est*, 'whom to serve is to be a king'), terse, purged metaphor ('lighten our darkness') . . .[19]

and so on, in the mode of poetry.

This is liturgical language 'understanded of the people', as the article of religion requires, but not *spoken* by the people, yet capable of being remembered and loved by them. It was consciously arcane, producing a numinous style to embody the mysteries of faith. In the modern cliché, the medium is the message. And such a mode of communication may be more powerful for Christian conversion and nurturing in the faith than a diction which strives for clarity. C.S. Lewis's latest biographer tells us that it was not by argument and textual analysis that the philosopher and literary critic was led to belief, but 'by his experience of the numinous, and by the exercise of his imagination'.[20] Cranmer's language has a power, lacking in modern liturgical writing, to stimulate the sensibility as well as to inform the mind.

In the English translation of the Roman canon of the mass, on the other hand, the most striking difference in the character of this vernacular idiom from Cranmerian diction is the immediacy of the address to God, as captured in the modernised use of the grammatical second person:

> We come to you, Father,
> with praise and thanksgiving,
> through Jesus Christ your Son. . . .

Reserving the special 'thee / thou' mode in addresses to the Almighty in prayer marked the unique character of that conversation by emphasising both its sacred nature – as prescribed in the Lord's Prayer: 'hallowed be thy name' – and by implying the elevation of the Godhead. Such sacral and hierarchical attributes of kingly power are, however, distasteful to the temper of twentieth-century secular life, and liturgiologists, convinced of the necessity of accommodating those mores in worship, have determined to minimise the kingdom and the power of the Father, but in the process they may have inhibited His glory. The preceding *Sanctus* might sing of these qualities, although in a rhythm that constrains holiness by banality:

> Holy, holy, holy Lord,
> God of power and might. . . .

but the statement (immediately following) that 'we come to you,

19 'On Reading Books from a Half-Alien Culture', in *The Context of English Literature: the later Middle Age*, 49.

20 A.N. Wilson, *C.S. Lewis: A Biography*, 166.

Father' is linguistically impoverished in the context, lacking the sonority of Cranmer and the adornment of the Tridentine Latin where the polysyllabic adjective enacts the effusion of praise: 'Te igitur, clementissime Pater'.

The defence of 'we come to you, Father' as opposed to 'Te igitur, clementissime Pater . . . supplices rogamus ac petimus' or 'Hear us, O most merciful Father, we most humbly beseech thee', is that it is plain and direct, immediately comprehensible and expressive of the direct access that the faithful have to God. Certainly, it is a simpler idiom, but in what sense is its meaning clearer? It is no more (or less) literally true than the similarly verbal request that the prayers be heard or accepted. And the approachability of God, for all the assurance Christians have of it, is a mystery; its mode (in the eucharist) is sacramental. That that approach, therefore, should be couched in a language where directness is vested in ceremoniousness seems closer to what is required than a statement that is merely forthright.

The suppression of such epithets as 'merciful' also has a theological as well as a linguistic purpose. This attitude of supplication sprang from the doctrine of a fallen humanity making petition at the judgement seat of God – a teaching that has become increasingly unpalatable to modernising theologians. Catholic apologists are now at pains to dissociate themselves from it. 'We've been taught that we are part of fallen humanity', comments the Revd Peter Maher, a Marist priest, 'when in fact [*sic*] we have been created good'.[21] This new emphasis, sitting uncomfortably with scriptural teaching ('in sin did my mother conceive me', etc.) could render superfluous even the doctrine of redemption – for if we are not fallen, we scarcely need to be redeemed from 'the sins of the world' – and redundant all liturgical images of and references to a sinful humanity beseeching the mercy of the Father.

The succeeding divisions of the canon – the intercessions for the Church ('We offer them [the elements of the eucharist] for your holy catholic Church, watch over it, Lord, and guide it . . .'), the communion of the saints ('In union with the whole Church we honour Mary . . .') and the Lord's supper itself ('The day before he suffered . . .') – contain nothing that is revolting, but neither do they contain anything that is notably inspired. This is not natural (or demotic) language, for it is in the stilted style of contemporary liturgical formalese. It is unnatural language – as still-born as Latin is alleged to be dead – but it is not *supernatural* language, lacking (unlike Latin) any poetic heightening. In contrast, in the prayer of oblation, in the Book of Common Prayer, belonging to the community of the Church is described in terms of being 'very members incorporate in the

[21] In 'The Sin Pill', *The Independent Monthly*, March 1991, 15.

mystical body of thy Son, which is the blessed company of all faithful people'. This is arcane and numinous language – largely by virtue of the epithets used at this point, which add resonance to the theological concept of the body of Christ – but it is not incomprehensible language. The few archaic or obscure words ('very' for 'true', and the over-technical 'incorporate', with its reminiscence of its Latin etymology) are explained, as so often in Cranmer, by the clarity of associated phrases – here, in the substantially Anglo-Saxon reference to 'the blessed company of all faithful people'. This is liturgical language that is both clear and transcendental, which 'shines [C.S. Lewis contended] with a white light hardly surpassed outside the pages of the New Testament itself'.[22]

## IV

The language of liturgy, teaching and inspiring, needs also to be expressive of the poetry of the emotions as they are excited by the momentous events in a Christian's pilgrimage. The 'rites of passage' in life – birth, marriage and death – should be consecrated, in worship, by a language and ceremonial that is not only theologically appropriate to the events commemorated in the occasional services, but evocative of the sentiments they embody: of joy linked to commitment and grief ameliorated by confidence in the resurrection.

The characterless didacticism of contemporary liturgical English, while arguably embodying advances beyond sixteenth-century perceptions in the theological interpretation of these rites, is yet wanting in the matter even more urgent to all but professional theologians – the evocation of the essential meaning of these events in the soul's understanding.

It is remarkable how a consideration of these services in the Book of Common Prayer disposes of the myths about traditional liturgy – that it is incomprehensible, verbose and circumlocutory. These services, if anything, are franker than their modern counterparts in never shirking the unromantic realities of life and drawing a clear distinction between this-worldliness and other-worldliness. Yet they simultaneously elaborate a poetic diction which animates and heightens their teaching to the point where even the most daunting truths partake of beauty:

> Almighty and everlasting God, who of thy great mercy didst save Noah and his family in the ark from perishing by water, and also didst safely lead the children of Israel thy people through the Red Sea, figuring thereby thy Holy Baptism; and by the Baptism of thy well-beloved Son Jesus Christ, in the

22 *Oxford History of English Literature in the Sixteenth Century*, 221.

> Jordan, didst sanctify water to the mystical washing away of sin: We beseech thee, for thine infinite mercies, that thou wilt mercifully look upon this child; wash him and sanctify him with the Holy Ghost; that he, being delivered from thy wrath, may be received into the ark of Christ's Church; and being steadfast in faith, joyful through hope, and rooted in charity, may so pass the waves of this troublesome world, that finally he may come to the land of everlasting life, there to reign with thee world without end.

The impetus of this prayer, at the beginning of the service of baptism in '1662', is provided by the apt aquatic metaphor with its scriptural sources in both Testaments linked by typology, and elemental sacramental significance, introduced in the opening address and resolved at the end as the passage through water concludes in arrival in 'the land of everlasting life'. It is a metaphorical vignette of the Christian pilgrimage on which the child is about to embark – a 'language stretched beyond the literal in order to talk of God'[23] – where the emphasis is not (as is often alleged) on the negativity of Original Sin and a punitive Father, but on the blessings of this life, if it is lived in a christian way: such emphasis being insisted upon in a striking triplicity of phrasing ('being steadfast in faith, joyful through hope, and rooted in charity'), numerologically evocative of the Trinity.

In contrast, the opening remarks of the order for baptism of children in *The Alternative Service Book* are starkly and baldly declarative: 'Children who are too young to profess the Christian faith . . .', 'N, when you are baptised, you become a member of a new family . . .', 'God is the creator of all things . . .'. There is nothing here, linguistically, to engage the imagination, to lift the heart – 'the hungry sheep look up, and are not fed', in spite of being filled with a baptismal theology which, in the best modern way, impeccably avoids the doctrine of Original Sin, that 'terrible aboriginal calamity' in which Newman insisted that the whole 'human race is implicated'.

At the culmination of the ceremony, the 'signing' of the child, the difference between the resonant, symbolic voice of the Cranmerian order and the spare declaration of the modern rite is clear:

> We receive this child into the congregation of Christ's flock, and do sign him with the sign of the Cross, in token that hereafter he shall not be ashamed to confess the faith of Christ crucified. . . . ['1662'].
>
> I sign you with the cross, the sign of Christ [*ASB*].

Of course, the second is all that is theologically needful. Much in the former is doctrinally superfluous. But so, too, are the attendants about King Lear whom his heartless daughter would cull:

23 T.R. Wright, *Theology and Literature*, 129.

Regan: What need one?
Lear: O! reason not the need; our basest beggars
Are in the poorest things superfluous
(King Lear, II, iv, 266-8).

The elaboration of liturgical language, like the retinue of kings, adds significance to essence and, so, becomes part of meaning, as doctrine is brought to life in the words of worship. For religious language, as T.R. Wright has written, is not simply an 'attempt to name metaphysical entities' but 'a symbolic expression of realities beyond human comprehension'. And when such writing is beautiful – as metaphorical writing, by its nature, tends to be – it is memorable too, and so the event and its significance might live beyond the occasion in the auditory imagination. In so living, even if only in the subconscious memory, its teaching waits to wake the spirit and conscience.

Of the occasional services, holy matrimony is conspicuous as the rite familiar to the unchurched. In personal attendance at weddings of family and friends, and in exposure to portions of the service through television and film, this liturgy is known to countless millions otherwise ignorant of Christian worship, let alone the Anglican rite. The wedding of Prince Charles and Lady Diana Spencer, in St Paul's Cathedral in 1981, with an audience of some 600 million, was seen by more people than any other single event, before or since, in the history of the human race. The order of service was from the Book of Common Prayer. An extraordinary opportunity for the Church of England to display to the world the reputed advantages of its new liturgy was thus forfeited because the Church recognised that the older order possesses a dignity appropriate to such a dramatic and solemn occasion – though it has proved to be equally apt in humble circumstances – and that the familiar words, known and hallowed through the centuries, would satisfy the expectations and appeal to the sensibilities of the public. Also, the royal couple requested that rite.

In elsewhere repudiating historical familiarity and disappointing personal nostalgia, contemporary liturgiologists pride themselves on their objectivity and modernity. But in doing so, they miss, in Auden's words, 'the essential human element', which is nourished by custom and memory – corporate and individual. The phrases of the marriage rite in '1662' are a liturgical speech that brings together romance and theology, in a unique combination, as the ministers of the sacrament, the bride and bridegroom themselves, pledge their love in a Christian poetry which – it is not too much to say – has become part of the racial memory of the English-speaking world:

I N. take thee N. to my wedded wife, to have and to hold from

> this day forward, for better for worse, for richer for poorer, in sickness and in health, to love and to cherish, till death us do part, according to God's holy ordinance; and thereto I plight thee my troth. . . .
>
> With this ring I thee wed, with my body I thee worship, and with all my worldly goods I thee endow.

Allegedly irrelevant and incomprehensible, this liturgical language, in each phrase, has passed effortlessly into vernacular speech in every century since its composition.

The authors of *The Alternative Service Book* recognised something of the qualities of 'The Solemnization of Holy Matrimony' by preserving echoes of it in their 'Marriage Service' of 1980, but rationalising the syntax, ruining the rhythm and debasing the vocabulary, they disposed of the poetry:

> I give you this ring as a sign of our marriage.
> With my body I honour you,
> all that I am I give to you,
> and all that I have I share with you.

Unobjectionable (though, if spoken quickly, it slides into gibberish), but instantly forgettable, this writing is dispossessed of the power of the former rite to recall couples, hearing the words down the years at others' weddings, to the occasion and solemnity of their own vows – not simply because the language is new, but because it is uninspired, therefore uninspiring, and unmemorable.

That these are essential qualities of liturgical language, capable of communicating meaning even to the subliterate, is arrestingly conveyed by Dolly Winthrop in George Eliot's *Silas Marner*:

> I can never rightly know the meaning o' what I hear at church, only a bit here and there, but I know it's good words – I do. . . .
>
> For what you talk o' your folks in your old country niver saying prayers by heart nor saying 'em out of a book, they must be wonderful cliver; for if I didn't know 'Our Father', and little bits of good words as I can carry out o' church wi' me, I might down o' my knees every night, but nothing could I say (Chapter 16).

Consideration, finally, of aspects of traditional and modern funeral services in the Anglican Communion prompts, first, the observation that liturgical language should speak for itself. One of the curious features of contemporary liturgy is that, in spite of the supposedly clear vocabulary of modern worship, its authors and celebrants often regard it as incumbent upon themselves to provide explanatory introductions and commentaries to what is about to be said or done. Such material is reminiscent of the opening paragraph of a weak student's essay, which sets out what the subsequent exercise will accomplish, instead of allowing the process to speak for itself, which – in most cases – it fails to do. In worship, it indicates a loss of faith in the power of liturgical language and ceremony to reveal and enact what it describes.

When leaders of worship add their own explanations to those already provided in modern service books – 'in this prayer, we will be asking for such-and-such', 'now I am going to do so-and-so' – the prevalent didacticism declines into a running commentary. An unedifying explanation of these interventions, condescending to congregations, by worship leaders is the new authoritarianism of priests and ministers which contemporary liturgies, with their flexibility and evasion of universality, invite and foster. In the conduct of public worship, and in much of its substance, objectivity has been replaced by subjectivity in the influence of the personalities of the pastor and the most prominent members of the parish. Such personalised liturgy may exclude and alienate the itinerant or uncommitted and irregular worshipper in its focus on the worshipping peculiarities of its leader and the group attuned to his or her liturgical preferences.

It would be reassuring to imagine that these commentaries spring from a wise recognition of the failure of many of the rites to catch and retain attention on their own merits, and to reveal the spiritual truths they should express. However, the real source, again, is the dominant obsession with clarity in matters (as we have argued) that are not only impatient of clarity but are, in essence, unclear; and a concomitant suspicion about the powers of language, especially metaphor and symbol, to convey such meaning as mystery will reveal.

To enter into mystery requires the nurturing of spirituality, which cannot be appropriated instantaneously, and which has its basis in personal prayer. But if the prayers of the Church are poor things, no-one will be moved to pray them.

In *An Australian Prayer Book*, the 'Funeral Service' is prefaced with a series of flat statements of mind-numbing obviousness:

We come together – to mourn a relative. . . .

This is followed by a 'prayer' which (with the possible exception of the exchange 'V. The Lord be with you. R. And also with you', where the vocabulary of an afterthought has been substituted for an identity in complementarity, 'And with thy spirit') contains that stylistic feature of modern liturgical composition in English which is most ludicrous to the intelligence and offensive to the ear:

> God our Father
> you alone are holy. . . .

– as the petitioner absurdly supplies information to the Omniscient about (of all phenomena) Himself. It is the *petitioners* who need to be reminded of the attributes of the Godhead, as in the usual form of the subordinate clause in the collects of the Book of Common Prayer:

> O God, from whom all holy desires, all good counsels, and all just works do proceed. . . .

But so pervasive is the manner of pointlessly informing the Father of what He is or has done – as in the funeral service in *The Alternative Service Book* –

> Heavenly Father,
> in your son Jesus Christ
> you have given us a true faith and a sure hope. . .

– that its absurdity is now entrenched. On those occasions, in the Book of Common Prayer, where the Lord is addressed in terms of His qualities – as in the *Te Deum*, 'Thou art the King of Glory: O Christ' – the ceremoniousness of the archaic second person pronoun poetically detaches the utterance from the directness of address, with its inherent futility, by oblique approach; such detachment being brusquely eliminated in the modern version of this verse, as found in the *ASB* funeral rite: 'You Christ are the King of glory'. One has only to repeat the opening words, 'You Christ', a couple of times for their aural ugliness to be discerned: there is nothing, linguistically speaking, of 'glory' here. The modern version of the *Te Deum*, Enoch Powell writes, could only have been constructed by the 'linguistically uneducated':

> Only draftsmen . . . in that condition could have dared . . . to replace the correct English equivalent 'we praise thee, O God' with the horrific mistranslation 'You are God, and we praise you'.[24]

Such linguistic vandalism is the despair of church musicians and composers. In any case, the *Te Deum* will have to be rewritten – 'King' being authoritarian and masculinist – as the Church proceeds with its accommodation of egalitarianism and feminism.

That insensitivity to language and its nuances is the blight of modern liturgical revision is plainly evident in the modern versions (from *AAPB* and *ASB*) of one of the best known passages from the order for the Burial of the Dead in '1662':

> Man that is born of a woman hath but a short time to live, and is full of misery. He cometh up, and is cut down, like a flower; he fleeth as it were a shadow, and never continueth in one stay.
>
> In the midst of life we are in death: of whom may we seek for succour, but of thee, O Lord, who for our sins art justly displeased?

[24] 'Grammar and Syntax', in *The State of the Language, op.cit.*, 484.

Yet, O Lord God most holy, O Lord most mighty, O holy and most merciful Saviour, deliver us not into the bitter pains of eternal death.

Thou knowest, Lord, the secrets of our hearts; shut not thy merciful ears to our prayer; but spare us, Lord most holy, O God most mighty, O holy and merciful Saviour, thou most worthy Judge eternal, suffer us not, at our last hour, for any pains of death, to fall from thee.

In *AAPB*, the first change that is wrought in this utterance (apart from the inconsequential deletion of the first indefinite article) is the replacement of 'a short time' with 'a few days'. That this is nonsensical, in the immediate linguistic context, is palpable. The very opening word, 'Man', brings with it the idea of a mature human being, who has lived several years. The original, more vague time-span – 'a short time to live' – is, in fact, logically precise. In seeking a poeticism too early, the Australian liturgiologists stumble and then fall, in their tampering with the Prayer Book's 'full of misery', at the end of the sentence, by giving us 'full of trouble'. The unusual and extreme phrase is replaced by flaccidity, for modernising theologians and liturgiologists are uncomfortable with the reality of the tragedy of life. They belong to what T.S. Eliot called, in his critique of them, 'the rosy tradition of Rousseau'.[25] Convinced that the emphasis on sin, suffering and death was a principal cause of the decline in church attendance in our age, they imagined that by minimising these dark elements – which remind worshippers, at every turn, in the old liturgies, that they are sinful and mortal – they would reclaim the disaffected and lure the unchurched. The extent to which this strategy was justified is apparent in the accelerating decline in church membership which has accompanied it. They have disturbed the subtle balance in the spirituality of Christianity, which has the forgiveness of sins at its heart, succinctly captured by such as Mother Julian – 'Sin is Behovely [inevitable], but all shall be well' – and everywhere in Cranmer, which recognised the disturbing truths of the human condition, but could resolve those disharmonies in cadences of hope and joy. Where misery is not acknowledged, mere trouble being substituted for it, where sinfulness is discounted or eliminated, then salvation is rendered superfluous and the heroism of the spiritual life, struggling with sin, the world and the devil, demeaned.

And the modernisers have destroyed the cumulative incantation of the old prayer:

O Lord most holy, O Lord most mighty, O holy and most merciful Saviour . . .

– neither *ASB* nor *AAPB* allowing this repetition of the phrases. Yet

[25] In *The New Criterion*, May 1927; in F.B. Pinion, *A T.S. Eliot Companion*, 37.

it is through rhythmic emphasis that prayers come to life, are learnt by heart and abide in the memory through what George Steiner has celebrated as the Prayer Book's 'exact stylised articulateness and music of thought'.[26] If, even only for a short time, they echo there, at least something of their meaning has the chance of becoming clear, in a way more lasting than any rubrical directions or painstaking explanations and commentaries, no matter how theologically impeccable. For while not every worshipper is receptive to doctrinal and liturgical sense, all – being human beings – are creatures of sensibility.

## V

In *The Development of the Anglican Liturgy 1662-1980*, an exhaustive account by R.C.D. Jasper, the long-serving chairman of the English Liturgical Commission, of changes in Anglican worship from the Book of Common Prayer to *The Alternative Service Book*, the reader waits until the thirteenth chapter for these crucial issues of language to be raised. Then, in the chapter entitled 'Questions of Language', linguistic problems are indeed enumerated – briefly, in a half-dozen pages – but left unresolved as the author returns, within that chapter, to his usual chronological account of the ongoing process of revision.

The position of this chapter in such an authoritative work by a liturgiologist influential in both the Anglican and Roman Churches, and its lamentable quality as a consideration of a matter central to liturgical composition, are indicative of the lack of interest and expertise in the literary dimension of liturgy of those responsible for the revision of worshipping language.

Jasper's frustration, moreover, with linguistic issues appears in the chapter's opening paragraph. Language was a 'problem' for the Liturgical Commission and it had 'difficulty in finding a satisfactory way of tackling it':

> This was not altogether surprising, for there had been no systematic study of liturgical language in this country: for too long writers had been content to imitate Cranmer.[27]

The vocabulary here is instructive: those who had drawn on the Cranmerian style (as in '1928'), it is alleged, were complacently derivative, lacking creativity. Jasper reduces the English liturgico-literary tradition, initiated by Cranmer, to the imitation of an individual's style and cannot allow that these liturgiologists, recognising the fertility of that tradition and its proven suitability to devotion, in several

26 *In Bluebeard's Castle*, 84.
27 *The Development of the Anglican Liturgy 1662-1980*, 286.

ages and by 'all sorts and conditions of men', were not only 'content', but felt obliged and were keen to perpetuate its linguistic manner and structure. For to concede this would be to give canonical status to that Prayer Book which it was the *raison d'être* of the Liturgical Commission to destroy, in spite of the customary casuistry rehearsed by Jasper that the alternative services were designed to be used beside '1662', and that if the use of the Book of Common Prayer declined this would be the result of a conscious decision by 'the people' (p.241). In fact, rarely has the parochially and pastorally divisive arrangement of a mixture of modern and traditional rites been sustained, and, as Jasper's *apologia* proves, influence upon the character, substance and development of liturgy comes not from the laity, but from liturgical commissioners, followed by the bishops and clergy, who are in turn supported by that minority of quasi-clerical lay people of the kind who are apt to be synod-goers.

Having isolated language as a difficulty, Jasper then turns to particular instances of the problem – such as that raised by one of the liturgical commissioners, Stella Brook, the philologist responsible for the classic study of *The Language of the Book of Common Prayer*. She pointed out that

> the difficulty [with liturgical composition in a contemporary idiom] lay in the divorce of spoken and written styles in twentieth-century English, to the detriment of both. Written style had deteriorated into a stylised and unnatural idiom, employing a vocabulary that had ceased to be a genuine part of living speech; while spoken style had also deteriorated, becoming slipshod, riddled with vague catch-words and limited in vocabulary. Such joint deterioration impeded the development of a good liturgical style; the former because liturgy needed to reach the hearts and minds of the worshipper, the latter because liturgy needed to express profundities in a decorous and comely language (p.286).

All that Dr Brook could postulate, before ill-health brought her premature resignation from the Commission, was that 'if there could be a vigorous cross-fertilization between written and spoken English, then a living liturgical style could well emerge again, as it had done four hundred years previously' (p.287).

Obviously, Brook was one 'content' to take Cranmer as her standard for liturgical English. Noting her incisive comment, and her warning –

> the idea of a wholly 'contemporary' liturgy . . . seems presumptuous. . . . The offering to God will be the poorer if the liturgy of a particular time has to express itself wholly in the current idiom of that particular time. . . . A wholly 'contemporary' lit-

> urgy . . . will have nothing to offer the future, when our own immediate idiom will have lost its currency: on the other hand it denies all virtue to our liturgical inheritance from the past (p.287)

– Jasper dismisses these learned reservations with the detached observation that 'despite her cautious approach, speaker after speaker pleaded for a "modern liturgy"'. Regularly, in this work, Jasper reverts to statistics to 'prove' his case and here minimises the import of Stella Brook's judgement in a lame epithet.

The next difficulty which he raises – only to sidestep it – is that of 'trying to produce a single set of texts for the entire English-speaking world', a problem succinctly stated for him in a contemporary Roman Catholic document, *English for the Mass*, where a 'solution', revealing a linguistic perception so facile as to astound, is provided for this particular puzzle:

> An idiom which is modern and contemporary to the liturgiologist in Chicago is very different from the idiom natural to a taxi-driver in London, a lawyer in Durban, a storekeeper in Karachi, or a bank clerk in Sydney. It follows that the final translation cannot be in any particular 'idiom': it must aim at good, straight, simple English which brings understanding to the learned and delight to the literate. Such writing demands the highest kind of literary art (p.289).

That so many and varied idioms in written and spoken English exist does not imply (let alone, necessarily) that a language devoid of idiom – whatever that lifeless thing might be – should be appropriated or invented for liturgy. What is needed for worship in English – and this is self-evident – is that idiom we know as liturgical English. To assume that an idiom-less, and therefore flavour-less, vocabulary and syntax, which is 'good, straight, simple' (adjectives of undefined meaning revealing the poverty of linguistic discernment of those responsible for liturgical revision in Western Christendom today), will at once bring 'understanding to the unlearned and delight to the literate' *and* be the embodiment of 'the highest kind of literary art' is risible.

Unchecked, Jasper pursues his tale of multiplying liturgies and endless committee meetings, quoting with approval 'this important point' made by Professor Nineham about biblical translations for use in worship:

> they did not go to church primarily for an aesthetic fillip; but to worship God and to hear the Word mediated to them through the Bible; and therefore, surely the first question was whether that was as good an instrument as they could find for purveying the meaning of God's Word and allowing that

> Word to have its maximum impact. That was the question which should be uppermost in their minds and not questions about whether the New English Bible was as beautiful or as dignified as it could be (p.295).

Jasper, moving on to considerations of hymnody, lets pass Nineham's dismissal of art in the cause of meaning by which he attempts to discredit the Authorised Version of the Bible and, thereby, a central truth of Christian experience, in several ages and amongst the learned and untutored alike – that the most profound meanings in Scripture and spirituality have been mediated through artistic expression: literary, musical and visual. The testimony of Penelope Fitzgerald about her uncle, Dillwyn Knox, of the family of famous brothers, recalls innumerable other such observations:

> Dilly, like all his brothers, could not forget or unlearn the words of the Authorised Version of the Bible, which had been interwoven since childhood with his daily life. He could never cease to be profoundly moved by 'Son of Man, can these dry bones live?'[28]

Such 'maximum impact' was achieved by the power of linguistic expression.

The final difficulty with language which Jasper encounters – and surmounts by overriding it – presented itself in the person of David Frost, who brought to the Liturgical Commission the specialist concerns of a literary critic who recognises (unlike Professor Nineham) that considerations of beauty have a high priority in Christian life and worship:

> liturgy should have some of the qualities of poetry, yielding further meanings at each repetition, exercising the hearts and minds of congregations. . . . Considerations of verbal beauty, subtlety and precision would then demand a wider vocabulary and a more sophisticated syntax [than previous texts by the Commission] (p.296).

As though referring to an entertaining diversion, Jasper notes that 'such criticisms proved healthy; discussion was lively' and then – ignoring Professor Frost's principles – goes into a detailed account of the haggling over the Lord's Prayer and the Psalter, with which the chapter closes.

As Jasper concludes his study with sections on Series 3 and *The Alternative Service Book*, without reverting to his unanswered 'questions of language' (though, with unintentional irony, devoting pages to details of printing and layout as one might admire the frame of a portrait: the *ASB* was 'a piece of specialist printing and design of a high order', worthy to be displayed next to the 'British Leyland

[28] *The Knox Brothers*, 72.

Mini' at the Design Council Centre in 1980 (p.359)), it is made obvious that he regards such questions as trivial, bothersome and wearisomely obstructive. 'Of course, there were the expected outcries [on the publication of Series 3] both in the daily press and in correspondence over the language question' (p.315), he notes – these coming, no doubt, substantially from the laity, and therefore worthy only to be sneered at by professional theologians and liturgiologists. Lay people, such as a member of the Prayer Book Society who had the effrontery to criticise the *ASB*, on its publication, are dismissed as cross-grained kill-joys, sounding a 'bitter note' while everybody else experienced a feeling of 'genuine excitement' (p.360).

Jasper's principal concern, as a liturgical commissioner, was to achieve orders of service which would be up-to-date theologically and precise and concise in their expression of doctrine. These are indisputably worthy aims, but to conceive of liturgical texts merely as statements of theology, doctrinal forms of words, reveals a misunderstanding of worship and worshippers that is humanly and spiritually impoverished.

Not once, in his 400 pages, does Jasper give any consideration to the nurturing of holiness of life in congregations by worship – such as in the encouragement of a private discipline of prayer, inspired and renewed by the texts of public devotion. He finds it dim of Archbishop Michael Ramsey to have asked, when the Doctrine Commission came up with a clever form of words about the departed, 'whether the sort of prayer that the report suggests is really a prayer that anyone wants to say' (p.319). Canon Jasper had expected better of the Archbishop who, after all, had commended the 'masterly theological analysis' of prayers for the dead by the Commission. What more than theological facility could possibly be required of a prayer? But Ramsey had the *goût pour la vie spirituelle*, and so he knew the difference even between the most unobjectionable doctrinal formula and a liturgical petition to stir the heart and mind.

For Jasper, liturgy has fulfilled its purpose if, for example, the form of words of the oblation in the eucharist and the position of the epiclesis can, by all kinds of linguistic contortion, satisfy at once Zwinglians and Tractarians. But he does not address any notion of the power of worship, in language and ceremony, to stir the people to make of themselves, 'their souls and bodies', a living sacrifice to the Lord, or mystically to mediate for them the 'holy comfort' of the Spirit.

He commends Leslie Houlden's argument that liturgiologists need to

> widen their horizons and enlist support from other disciplines, biblical studies, doctrine, anthropology, psychology, sociology (p.317).

Nowhere does he suggest that such enrichment might come from its source in the practice of prayer. Those who advocate the devotional qualities of traditional liturgy are scorned by Jasper, in the words of Philip Cecil (which he approvingly quotes) as 'witty bishops, comical clergymen and some of their less amusing supporters' (p.318) – the most biting indictment being reserved once again, it will be noted, for the laity.

Jasper expects us to take on trust his assurance that, if the *ASB* is used 'with love and imagination', if 'we work hard at it . . . it can still attain great heights' (p.366), but never does he demonstrate through linguistic exegesis how its language might assist the elevation of the spirit – an experience that cannot be quantified by statistics.

As disturbing, finally, as Jasper's dismissive attitude to language, the very vehicle of worship, in this depressing chronicle of what Bishop John Taylor described as a 'monstrosity of a process . . . not the way to write liturgy' (p.353), is his account of the gigantic expenditure of individuals' and the Church's resources of time, energy and money on liturgical 'renewal', by which even he is occasionally appalled. When one considers that the result – if one may use Jasper's favoured recourse to statistics – so far from producing growth in the Anglican Communion (the tangible sign of renewal), has accompanied its accelerating decline to its current death-throes, this tale of alleged 'development' in liturgy and mission can only be assessed as a scandalously wasteful squandering of Christian resources.

But still the Church, in Dryden's phrase, being 'subject to this curse' of tampering with itself, continues to 'physick [its] disease into a worse'. Archbishop Carey has declared that this 'development' must continue:

> Be willing to give away precious and cherished liturgies to share new life and grow.[29]

[29] Quoted in R.E. Spalton, 'Bread or Stones', *Faith and Heritage*, Spring 1991, 20.

# CONCLUSION

> Since Christianity is an historical religion that fulfils its task by engaging with rather than withdrawing from human culture, it is in constant danger of so adapting itself to the context in which it is set as to dilute and neutralise its own nature and message. It becomes an echo, not a prophetic word, a benediction on the spirit of the age rather than a challenge to it.
>
> The Rt Revd Richard Holloway
> Primus of the Episcopal Church of Scotland.

> The question which faces every Christian body today and which underlies all practical issues is this: is the Christian religion something revealed by God in Christ, which therefore demands our grateful obedience, or is it something to be made up by ourselves to our own specification, according to our own immediate desires? When we assent, as I am convinced we must, to the first alternative, we must also insist that the second is not only false but bogus, and that our true fulfilment and happiness is not to be found by following our own whims but by giving ourselves to God in Christ.
>
> The Revd Eric Mascall
> *Saraband* (1992).

The conservative reaction to the revision of liturgical language in the West since the vernacularisation which followed Vatican II, and the widespread replacement of the Authorised (King James) Version of the Bible and the Cranmerian Prayer Book in Anglicanism over the same period, is the expression of a variety of responses to 'renewal' – theological, aesthetic, devotional and sentimental. Each and all of these, I have suggested, are relevant and appropriate to the evaluation of liturgical texts.

In the contemporary *aggiornamento* of the Church, however, artistic criteria and sensibility (with its associations with the pasts and memories of communities and individuals) and – most importantly – spirituality, in its complex dimensions, have been discounted. Theological and sociological considerations have been emphasised to their exclusion.

The literature of conservative reaction to this phenomenon is as varied in quality as it is copious in quantity. Where it is often intellectually undistinguished is in the critiques of an alienated laity giving voice to their dismay and sense of dispossession, in subjective and sometimes abusive tones.

Yet it must be remembered by the theologians, liturgiologists and churchmen who scorn these outpourings that the origin of the liturgical movement in the twentieth century was a new sensitivity to the liturgical role of the laity. For liturgical authorities and, indeed, parish priests today to dismiss the conservative viewpoint of many lay people, and to refuse to acknowledge and accommodate their worshipping preferences, is an ironic development from this original motivation.

The modernisers' suggestions, furthermore, that a conservative approach to liturgical language is inevitably accompanied by weak-minded nostalgia or red-necked Toryism, are disproved by the range of criticism their reforms have produced – some of it from the most distinguished minds and spiritually perceptive Christians twentieth-century who, moreover, have a great cloud of witnesses to their convictions in the history of Christian devotion, such as John Donne:

> God loves not innovations; Old doctrines, old disciplines, old words and formes of speech in his service, God loves best.[1]

The argument, also, that the laity must be satisfied with the liturgical innovations because most of them do not protest – or do not do so audibly, simply voting with their feet – is unconvincing. Such apparent satisfaction is often merely acquiescence to the authoritarianism of the clergy – this is particularly true in Roman Catholicism – who theoretically and fashionably espouse decision-sharing with congregations, but who are, in reality, as dominant as ever in parochial life. In any case, for most of the laity under forty, a liturgy different from the evolving modern forms to which they have been accustomed since their teens or before has never been experienced as a sustained element in their worshipping lives. They are in no position to articulate a critique of the present rites in comparison with the previous dispensation. They must accept the propaganda that the *aggiornamento* has been an unquestionable benefit to them and the Church at large, that the former arrangements were unspeakable, both literally and figuratively. The growing number of young people today who are having the opportunity, through the activities of traditionalist bodies such as *Ecclesia Dei*, in Roman Catholicism, to experience the old rites and ceremonies, are discovering the falsehood of this polemic.

That the literary quality of modern liturgical composition does

1 In G.R. Potter and E.M. Simpson (eds) *Sermons* II, 4, 305.

not compare with that of Tridentine Latin or Cranmerian English is admitted by even the most fervent advocates of modern language rites. But they are prepared to tolerate 'infelicities', for they regard theological precision and clarity as all-important. Having achieved doctrinal impeccability, by their lights, often with the bonuses of ecumenical agreement and political correctness, they are not about to be thwarted by allegations of banality of vocabulary and flatness of phrasing.

However, the apprehension of spiritual truth is not only assisted by beauty of utterance, it demands it. 'Art, literature, music, culture are not external decorations, but age-long secretions in the soul of man'.[2] They enable soul to speak to soul, of the concerns of the soul.

Modern theologians and liturgiologists have confused talking about God with talking to Him. They can express, in T.S. Eliot's phrases, 'certain things about God', but they are incapable of embodying in language what it is like to '*feel* towards God'.[3] So modern services, with their literal-minded pursuit of 'participation' in worship, are ignorant of what it means, liturgically, to listen to God – and, most importantly, to wait on His presence in personal and corporate prayer. As rubricians fiddle with rules and regulations, multiplying forms and variations; as celebrants explain their already wordy liturgies as they proceed, and indulge in rambling extempore prayers of varying qualities of literacy and articulateness, they neglect the only essential rule, but the most demanding of all: 'Be still, and know that I am God'.[4] Worship, the Australian poet Les Murray has written

> does not rely on freshness or novelty to attain its effect; the familiar becomes the ever-new as we enter more deeply into it. The efficacy of the whole process depends not at all on the passionate noise of our desires and yearnings, but on the receptive quality of our stillness.[5]

'Holiness', François Mauriac has written, 'is stillness'.

That conservatives idolise the liturgical language and ceremonies that created this ambience of solemnity and reverence, of the numinous, is the most familiar misrepresentation of their position by the modernisers. It is those, on the contrary, who are obsessed with liturgical revision who have made an idol, not only out of language, but of their particular brand of it. They will not allow any other kind to speak to, and of, God in worship, in spite of the incontrovertible fact that liturgical Latin and Cranmerian English did so,

2 E.M. Forster, *Goldsworthy Lowes Dickinson*, .88.
3 'The Social Function of Poetry', *On Poetry and Poets*, 25.
4 Psalm 46:10.
5 In 'The Shape of Belief', in Gilchrist, *Rome or the Bush*, 44.

for countless multitudes, for centuries.

At its most subtle and persuasive, the conservative defence of language reaches beyond words and even liturgy itself to the silence and stillness of that pure worship which transcends human expression and passes understanding, in communion with the divine:

the unattended
Moment, the moment in and out of time,
. . . music heard so deeply
That it is not heard at all, but you are the music
While the music lasts.[6]

Those who are imprisoned by language, however – and, in particular, modern liturgical language – have become so preoccupied with it, and the need for simplification and clarity, comprehensibility and relevance, that they have lost sight of its ultimate purpose beyond what may be articulated in speech. The instruction on liturgy issued by the Vatican in 1970 warned against this outcome:

> Simplification must not go beyond certain limits. This would be to deprive the liturgy of the sacramental signs and special beauty necessary for the mystery of salvation to be really effective in the Christian community and to be rightly understood – with due instruction – under visible symbols. Liturgical reform is not synonymous with so called *desacralization* and should not be the occasion for what is called the *secularisation of the world*. Thus the liturgical rites must retain a dignified and sacred character.[7]

But the warning has not been heeded.

Conservatives are calling for the recovery of holiness in worship, for what C.S. Lewis called 'religion with a real supernaturalism'.[8] Such a religion will be recovered when theologians and liturgiologists begin to understand the truth familiar in the traditions of both Western and Eastern spirituality: that God, being infinite and transcendent, can be known only, paradoxically, in a 'cloud of unknowing', which separates Him from us. 'The experience of him', as Daphne Turner writes, 'cannot be spoken of'.

> As the normal consciousness with which language deals dies out, . . . normal language categories no longer apply. . . . Even when mystics use words, like the Jesus prayer of the Orthodox tradition or the single-word prayer of *The Cloud of Unknowing*, they seem to use them as Eastern religions use mantras: the language is being emptied of conceptual meaning and used as a focus for concentration. 'Chatter' is the enemy. . . .

6 T.S. Eliot, *Four Quartets*, 'The Dry Salvages', V.
7 Flannery (ed.) *Vatican Council II*, 211-12.
8 In William Griffin, *C.S. Lewis: A Dramatic Life*, 166.

> Meditation, the practice of inner silence, enables us to experience the thinness and theatricality of the false self, not to get involved in the chatter, and to give space for truth to emerge.[9]

The language of traditional liturgy reached beyond individual and temporal concerns to the eternal, by virtue of its poetic qualities, which were the aesthetic expression of the transcendental emphases of its doctrine. Ultimately, it reached beyond itself, as language, to evoke the mystery of faith. Perhaps the worship of which it was the linguistic vehicle placed too little emphasis on the earthly community and witness of the Body of Christ, stressing heavenly aspirations; arguably, it was to a degree deficient in its immediately didactic and forthright evangelical effectiveness. But these are secondary faults. Above all, worship must convey the sense of the presence of God to worshippers. If it fails to do that, it fails completely. Such a sense can be created by a variety of means, and in a host of circumstances. But conservatives have argued that the evidence of Christian history and spirituality has shown that the traditional languages of liturgy have (in association with music and formal ceremony, and architectural arrangements) been peculiarly and conspicuously effective in communicating the divine presence, while the character of modern language rites (with their ephemeral music, casual ceremony and contemporary decor) is such that the absence of aesthetic qualities and an imagery and symbolism redolent of the transcendence of the terrestrial is inhibiting the very spiritual process they would facilitate. As if in desert exile, the Word awaits the genuine spiritual renewal of the Churches, which the liturgical movement, to date, has failed to achieve, so that its truth might prevail in the hearts and minds of the people of God.

9 'Delight and Truth: Auden's *The Sea and the Mirror*', *Literature and Theology*, March 1989, 103.

# APPENDIX
# THE SATIRICAL CRITIQUE

Lampoon is the time-honoured weapon of controversialists. Even in Christianity, with its exhortations about loving one's enemies and preserving charity in all things, proponents of opposing viewpoints have resorted, through the centuries, to the most scurrilous satire of their antagonists. One recalls, for example, Milton's theological tracts.

In our day, critics of liturgical reform have had frequent recourse to this polemical mode which has served the dual purpose of advancing their opinions in popularist form and of providing the outlet of bitter humour for some pent-up frustrations.

A persistent and acerbic contributor to this aspect of the controversy has been Auberon Waugh, son of Evelyn, who used the Sunday section of his regular 'Diary' in *Private Eye*, the long-running right-wing English satirical magazine, for some scathing assaults on contemporary Roman Catholic parish worship:

> Half-way through church I discover to my dismay that this is Peace Sunday. We have to sit through half-an-hour of platitudes on this grisly subject.
>
> It took the Catholic Church a thousand years to wake up to the fact that people no longer use Latin as their main language. Now it will probably take another thousand years for it to discover that Pope John is dead, the sixties are over and Flower Power was always a load of rubbish. . . . I think it is time I went to see Dr Runcie [then Archbishop of Canterbury] for discussions about whether to join his lot.[1]

Not that Auberon Waugh has any time for the vernacular texts that have replaced Latin. 'Depressed . . . by the Church's retreat from spirituality . . . and disgusted by the language and form of its new services',[2] in another diary, accompanied by a cartoon (Fig. 1), he attacked a new prayer book:

> 'Lord, a healthy sexual relationship is so important in marriage that we want to thank You for ours. . . . Please help us not to forget that the sign of our Sacrament, the sexual expression of our love, makes You present in our homes'.

1 *Private Eye*, no.578, 10 February 1984, 23.

2 *Will This Do? An Autobiography*, 98.

Fig 1[3]

> Thus the new Roman Catholic prayer-book *The Treasury of the Holy Spirit* compiled by Monsignor Michael Buckley . . . in the section devoted to Prayers for a Good Sex Life. It has introductions by Cardinal Basil Vass as well as by the Roman Catholic Archbishops of Edinburgh and Armagh, by 'Killer' Runcie and, to his eternal shame, by the Bishop of London.
>
> In the week this ludicrous document appeared, Pope Ringo made a passionate plea for sexual abstinence in marriage. . . . It seems to me that the Catholic Church in England as it wheezily tries to catch up with the sex-obsessed sixties, is set on a break-away course from the zoom-ahead Pope.
>
> The late 1960s idea in Somerset is that as sexual intercourse is a Sacrament it should be joined by the whole Congregation rather than seen as a private act, as if there was something dirty about it.
>
> Whenever a couple in the parish feels the urge coming upon them, they go to church and ring a bell. Then they buckle down on the High Altar; priest and people dance around the altar, clapping their hands and making joyful noises.[3]

This prayer book, in fact, excited world-wide ridicule. Under the facetious title, 'Articles of Faith', it had been reviewed in the light-hearted 'Stay in Touch' column of *The Sydney Morning Herald*, the month before. In addition to the petition for a 'happy sexual relationship', another collect, about the 'dangers of motor vehicles', is pilloried:

> Give us a mind so set at peace with you that we may use our vehicles with a true spirit of courtesy . . . avoiding all unnecessary tensions, anxiety and desire for speed.[4]

And satire could scarcely have improved on another genuine article, also reported in the *Herald*, from a liturgy for divorcing couples ap-

[3] *Private Eye*, no. 598, 16 November 1984, 25.

[4] 17 October 1984, 18.

proved for use in the Uniting Church:

> Forgive us for the way our union has broken or drifted apart. Forgive the blind, ego-centred things which have contributed to this. . . . We affirm and believe that what is now happening is not putting asunder what you have joined together but recognising that to stay together is a false and unreal perpetuating of that which has past. Father, we are pained by this, and it should not happen, yet we affirm that it has happened and that we cannot bring that former relationship back.[5]

The Jabberwocky syntax, in an apparently unconscious parody of liturgical language, unwittingly signifies the experience of 'pain' and the subversion of traditional marriage doctrine it embodies.

The campaign of *Private Eye* against liturgical revision has been waged, however, on a much wider front than Waugh's lampoons, 'the new Mickey Mouse church of Cardinal Hume', with its 'kindergarten assemblies', being 'no more than an idle diversion for the communally minded'.[6] The anti-feminist 'Wimmin' column has exposed several factual examples of non-sexist, inclusivist revisions of Scripture and liturgy, for humorous effect, as in this example:

> John 17:1-2 – *Jesus prays for the disciples*. Having spoken these words, Jesus looked up to heaven and said, 'God my Mother and Father, the hour has come; glorify your Child that your Child may glorify you, since you have given that Child power over all flesh, to give eternal life to all whom you have given your Child'.[7]

The complication of language (rather than the simplification reputedly sought by renewing liturgiologists) is preferred in order that the odious masculine noun and personal pronoun might be avoided. And in its 'Bishop of the Month' series, 'Lucy Fer' presents diabolical character assassinations of leading prelates, such as John Bickersteth of Bath and Wells, for their liturgical peccadilloes:

> On the one hand, he supports all the silly measures brought before the General Synod, such as the Rocky Horror Service Book [*Private Eye*'s title for *The Alternative Service Book*], the Ordination of Women, and church weddings for divorcees. On the other hand, he is as snobbishly arrogant as a Victorian bishop and offends his humbler clergy by asking questions like 'Where did *you* go to school?'[8]

Eric Kemp of Chichester is similarly scorned:

> In 1974, after five years in Worcester, where he succeeded in wrecking and modernising the Sunday morning worship of

5 *The Sydney Morning Herald*, 13 June 1988, 9.
6 *Will This Do? op cit.*, 187.
7 *Private Eye*, June 1983, 10.
8 *Private Eye*, no. 580, 9 March 1984, 10.

the cathedral, he was made Bishop of Chichester. His leaving present to Worcester was a set of hideous modern vestments of fluorescent tweed.[9]

Precisely linguistic, however, is the magazine's satire of the style (and even the type-setting) of *The Alternative Service Book* (Fig. 2):

*The*
*Alternative Rocky Horror Service Book*

*No. 94 Proposed new multi-cultural multi-faith school assembly service*

***(to replace 'A Hymn and a Prayer')***

THE HEADTEACHER SHALL ENTER.

*THE GREETING*

**Headteacher:** Good morning school students. Gujerati pappadom bindhi-ghosht. Rasta, ganja, right on, man.

OR HE MAY ADD THE GREETING IN ANY OTHER ETHNIC LANGUAGE WHICH HE MAY FEEL APPROPRIATE.

**The Pupils:** Good morning M or N (HERE THEY SHALL INSERT THE FORENAME OR NICKNAME OF THE HEADTEACHER)

**Headteacher:** Do we affirm our total commitment as a school community to a multi-ethnic society?

**Pupils:** Great, right on, etc.

**Headteacher:** Do we affirm our total opposition to racism, fascism etc.?

**Pupils:** Yeah.

*THE HOMILY*

HERE THE HEADTEACHER MAY SPEAK BRIEFLY ABOUT SOME RELEVANT TOPIC OF THE DAY — e.g. the struggle of the Sikh freedom-fighters, police violence on the picket-lines, U.S. aggression in central America, or some similar theme which gives an opportunity to make simple ethical points about the world we live in.

*THE MUSICAL ELEMENT*

ALL SHALL NOW BE ENCOURAGED TO PARTICIPATE IN SOME MUSICAL EXPRESSION OF MULTI-ETHNIC COMMITMENT' E.G. THE SINGING OF 'WE SHALL OVERCOME' OR ANY TRADITIONAL GUJERATI, URDU, OR RASTAFARIAN SONGS AS MAY SEEM APPROPRIATE.

THE KIDS SHALL THEN LEAVE FOR THEIR SCHOOL TASKS, LEAVING THE HEADTEACHER TO SWEEP UP THE DOG ENDS.

Fig. 2

[9] *Private Eye*, no. 578, 10 February 1984, 10.

The revision of hymnody, too, has been the subject of satire – in *Private Eye*, where the 'Durham Hymn Book' (an allusion to the modernising Bishop Jenkins, formerly of that see) contains such up-dated versions of old standards as 'Go Away, All Ye Faithful', and in this revision of 'Immortal, Invisible, God Only Wise', by Kathleen Reeves, as sung by 'the Cathedral Choir of All Sexes at St Zeitgeist's Within the Walls', printed for satirical relief in the Episcopalian conservative journal, *The Christian Challenge*:

MODERN HYMNS FOR TODAY'S TOGETHER PEOPLE

Equivocal, mutable, tides like the sea,
Thou, God, art refrangible to our decree.
Our ancestors blinded, at last we can show
Sociology teaches all we need to know.

We've thrown out the clichés of Sin and of Grace
We have modern concepts to put in their place.
How naive our fathers (and mothers as well)
To live with such notions as 'Heaven' and 'Hell'.

Alas, poor foreparents, unable to see
That the Holy Spirit is surely a 'She'.
They wallowed in doctrines absurd, unalloyed,
Not knowing theology started with Freud.

Ah now, we're enlightened, we understand all!
No longer accepting catchwords like 'the Fall'.
Thou'rt made in our image, oh help us to see
'Tis not being 'with it' that keeps us from Thee![10]

More biting still is Reeves' 'A Wedding', a satirical account of imagined homosexual nuptials, written with the venom of Samuel Butler, and set in the Diocese of Newark, New Jersey, under the permissive rule of Bishop John Spong. Oscar W. Owl and Aubrey P. Pussycat – their surnames providing a subtext from the realm of nonsense – are married in St Insidia's Cathedral in the Diocese of Neejerk, vowing 'integrated viability in the context of affirmation for as long as is mutually relative'. The honeymoon is spent at Club Bed.

The Bishop, responding to the controversy stirred up by a 'few benighted traditionalists', is quick to validate the alliance between Owl and Pussycat:

> They are affirming not only intimacy and mutuality but also inclusiveness; there are implications for a diversity of sexual lifestyles being lived out with integrity and in Christianly

[10] *The Christian Challenge*, January/February 1987, 33.

> humanizing ways within a congregation. . . . It must be remembered that traditional marriage is really a narrow, constrictive and noninclusive idea involving only one male and one female.[11]

Reeves captures the jargon and reasoning of the radicals, both as it is already revealed in their writings and how they would hope to have it manifested in liturgy.

Then Angus Macintyre's sub-Trollopean 'Lease-a-priest' (published in *The Church Times* and *Faith and Worship* in England, and also in *Lex Orandi* in America) tells the tale of St Titus's, Slobberhouse, which has kept itself immune from liturgical renovation and, accordingly, been declared redundant – the Bishop of Slobchester gleefully anticipating revenues from its sale for 'new ecumenical centres' and salary increases for diocesan bureaucrats. Yet, St Titus's becomes the 'in place' in the diocese, to the consternation of the authorities:

> the news got about that there still existed a church where the Authorised Version of the Scriptures, the thundering cadences of Cranmer in the Book of Common Prayer, *Hymns A. & M.* (unrevised), and the great Anglican thump of the old *Cathedral Psalter* could still be heard; where you could slip in and out in decent anonymity without being called upon to embrace your neighbour, and where you could find an hour's peace on Sunday.[12]

The busy-ness of modern liturgy and the concomitant restriction on prayerfulness, its preference for incessant talk and movement by everybody over meditation and recollection, closes this catalogue with a sobering reference to a quantity as absent from modern life as from the contemporary Church. The communal kiss of peace, the cause of at least as much division in the Church as of the communality it was designed to nurture, prompted this letter to *The Times* from a layman which cleverly mixes the serious and the satirical:

> As an elderly Church of England restaurateur I have failed to come to terms with the modern-day 'sign of peace' practice of shaking hands with complete strangers in the middle of a service.
>
> Would it be possible to have a section of the church in which there is no shaking hands, just as in restaurants there is usually a section reserved for no smoking?[13]

While the episcopacy has been a favourite target of lampoon, traditionalist bishops have contributed to the satirical critique, as in

11 *The Christian Challenge*, June 1987, 8-9.

12 *Lex Orandi*, Spring 1984, 60.

13 Peter Pinkster, *The Times*, 24 September 1994, 19.

the Rt Revd Robert Mercer's transsexual fantasy of an inclusivist Lambeth conference, ' "Rockets" and "Chimmies" ' (a play on the rochets and chimeres of episcopal 'choir dress'):

> Since God is our Mother and Jesa Christa Her daughter (and we are Her bridegroom), half the bishops ride sidesaddle, dressed in lace mantillas and cascades of pretty petticoats. The female fathers and male mothers of the Anglican Communion take tea with the woman king at Buckingham Palace. Unisex is all and the neuter gender is represented by chairpersons.[14]

Cartoons, with their visual satirical impact, have also been prominent in the campaign. The Australian conservative journal *On Anglicanism* regularly features the 'Reverend Babs', a caricature of a priestess, which shows the priesthood as traduced by supposed womanish foibles (Fig. 3):[15]

Fig 3

[14] *The Christian Challenge*, April 1986, 29.
[15] 5 October 1987, 12.

Even the worldly press has contributed to this aspect of the controversy, as in Fig. 4, a cartoon from *The Bulletin*:[16]

'Most of this is just a figure of speech now!'

Fig. 4

And figure 5, from *The New Yorker*, elegantly lampoons the traditionalists, linking their secular *mores* to their conservative religious views and observances. The caption reads

> Good morning. With a touch of fall in the air, I'm happy to welcome you back from summer distribution in the Hamptons, Bay Head, Nantucket, Chatham and Northeast Harbor, and to reunite our diverse community – some in preppy garb, some in executive dress, some in the Ivy League look, and some in Wasp attire. My sermon this morning was inspired by Scripture from our 1928 Book of Common Prayer.

16 21 August 1984, 16.

Fig 5[17]

In recent times, the most publicised contribution to the liturgical debate, containing satirical elements, came from the Prince of Wales, a fervent defender of Cranmer. He brings a similar zeal to the defence of the Book of Common Prayer and the Authorised Version as he has brought to the analysis of modern architecture. In an address at the presentation of the Thomas Cranmer Schools Prize in 1989, Prince Charles begins with some satire of himself:

> I'm *not* afraid of being considered old-fashioned, which is why I am standing here at this lectern wearing a double-breasted suit and turn-ups to my trousers, ready to declaim the fact that I believe the Prayer Book is a glorious part of every English-speaker's heritage and, as such, ought to be a grade I listed edifice!

Trenchant reflections on 'the crassness of the Alternative Service Book' and epigrammatic *aperçus* – 'we commend the "beauty of holiness", yet we forget the holiness of beauty'; 'ours is the age of miraculous writing machines but not of miraculous writing'; 'how can we be lifted up by a sentence which itself needs lifting' – are complemented by satirical thrusts:

> If English is spoken in Heaven (as the spread of English as a

[17] 2 October 1989, 40.

> world language makes more likely each year) God undoubtedly employs Cranmer as his speech-writer. The angels of the lesser ministries probably use the language of the New English Bible and the Alternative Service Book for internal memos.

And he closes his address in an indictment of the whole process of liturgical revision, in quotation from Samuel Goldwyn: 'You've improved it worse'.[18]

As is true of the conservative reaction at large, the satirical critique continues to make its contribution to the evaluation and evolution of modern liturgiology. A delightful lampoon of liturgical writing appeared recently in *The Sunday Times*, in this version of the twenty-third psalm:

> The Lord and I are in a shepherd/sheep situation; and I am in a position of negative need.
>
> He prostrates me in a green-belt grazing area; He conducts me directionally parallel to non-torrential aqueous liquid.
>
> He returns to original satisfaction levels my psychological make-up: He switches me on to a positive behavioural form for maximum prestige of His identity.
>
> It should be said that notwithstanding the fact that I make ambulatory progress through the umbrageous interhill mortality slot, terror-sensations will not be instantiated within me due to para-ethical phenomena.
>
> Your pastoral walking-aid and quadruped pick-up unit introduce me into a pleasurific mood-state.
>
> You design and produce a nutrient-bearing furniture-type structure in the context of non-cooperative elements: You act out a head-related folk ritual employing vegetable extract by beverage utensil experiences in a volume crisis.
>
> It is an on-going deductible fact that your interrelational emphatical and non-vengeance capabilities will retain me as their target-focus for the duration of my non-death period; and I will possess tenant rights in the housing unit of the Lord on a permanently open-ended time basis.

Apart from its lampoons of the priority of relevance in modern Christianity – inculturation – this parody makes the important linguistic point that contemporary liturgical writing can be at least as opaque as Cranmer, for all its claims of comprehensibility; can be as afflicted with jargon as he is alleged to have been obsessed by his doctrinal views; is more often euphemistic, where he could be forthrightly frank; and – as language – is demonstrably less worthy aesthetically than the idioms and cadence of the Book of Common Prayer.

[18] 'Hearken to My Words', *Daily Telegraph*, 20 December 1989, 10.

# BIBLIOGRAPHY

*The place of publication is London unless otherwise specified.*

## PRIMARY SOURCES

### I. Prayer books and missals

Anglican

The Book of Common Prayer with the Additions and Deviations Proposed in 1928 (Oxford University Press: n.d.).
The English Missal for the Laity (W. Knott: 1958).
The Cuddesdon Office Book (Oxford University Press: 1961).
An Order for Holy Communion, Series 1 (The Church Union: n.d.).
An Order for Holy Communion, Second Series (SPCK: 1966).
An Order for Holy Communion, Series 3 (SPCK: 1971).
An Australian Prayer Book 1978 (The Standing Committee of the General Synod of the Church of England in Australia: Sydney, 1978).
The Alternative Service Book 1980 (Clowes, SPCK, Cambridge University Press: Colchester, London, Cambridge, 1980).

Roman Catholic

The Layman's Missal and Prayer Book (Burns & Oates: 1961).
Sunday Missal (Catholic Truth Society: Hong Kong, 1971).

### II. Hymn Books

The English Hymnal (Oxford University Press: 1933).
Hymns Ancient and Modern Revised (Clowes: 1950).
The Australian Hymn Book (Collins: Sydney, 1977).
Hymns for Today's Church (Hodder & Stoughton: 1982).
The New English Hymnal (The Canterbury Press: Norwich, 1986).

## III. Journals

*Anglican Catholic News* (The Anglican Catholic Church, Australia) April and November 1989.

*The Anglican Free Press* (Canada), vol. 4, No. 2, September 1987.

*The Christian Challenge* (The Foundation for Christian Theology, USA) monthly, 1985-9.

*The Evangelical Catholic* (The Evangelical and Catholic Mission, USA) monthly, 1987-9.

*Faith and Heritage* (The Prayer Book Society, England) biannual numbers appearing in Spring and Autumn, 1984-95.

*Faith and Worship* (The Prayer Book Society, England), biannual, Summer and Winter, 1980-95.

*The Latin Mass* (The Foundation for Catholic Reform, USA), bi-monthly, 1992-4.

*Lex Orandi* (The Prayer Book Society, USA), biannual, Spring and Winter, 1986.

*On Anglicanism* (The Anglican Society, Australia), 1986-8.

*The Seabury Journal* (The Foundation for Anglican Tradition, USA) monthly, 1984-6.

## IV. Other

*The Orthodox Liturgy*, English trans. (Oxford University Press: 1982).

*The Prayer Book Dictionary*, (eds) G. Harford and M. Stevenson (Pitman: 1912).

*Vatican Council II: The Conciliar and Post Conciliar Documents*, (ed.), Austin Flannery, O.P. (The Liturgical Press: Collegeville, Minn., 1975).

## SECONDARY SOURCES

Belloc, Hilaire, *Cranmer* (1931; repr. Haskell House: New York, 1973).

Bennett, Gareth, *To the Church of England*, ed. G. Rowell (Churchman: Worthing, 1988).

Blamires, Harry, *Where Do We Stand: An Examination of the Christian's Position in the Modern World* (SPCK: 1980).

Bouyer, Louis, *The Decomposition of Catholicism*, trans. C.U. Quinn (Franciscan Herald Press: Chicago, 1969).

Brook, Stella, *The Language of the Book of Common Prayer* (Deutsch: 1965).

Buchanan, C.O., *Recent Liturgical Revision in the Church of England* (Grove: Bramcote, 1973).

Cekada, Anthony, *The Problems with the Prayers of the Modern Mass* (Tan: Rockford, 1991).

Chadwick, Owen, *Michael Ramsey: A Life* (Clarendon Press: Oxford, 1990).

Churton, Toby (ed.), *Why I am Still an Anglican* (Collins: 1986).

Clarke, W.K. Lowther, *Liturgy and Worship: A Companion to the Prayer Books of the Anglican Communion* (SPCK: 1932).

Crichton, J.D., Winstone, H.E. and Ainslie, J.R. (eds) *English Catholic Worship: Liturgical Renewal in England since 1900* (Chapman: 1979).

Cryer, Neville, *Louis Evely: Once a Priest* (Mowbray: 1980).

Cuming, G.J., *A History of Anglican Liturgy*, 2nd edn. (Macmillan: 1982).

Davies, J.G. (ed.) *A Dictionary of Liturgy and Worship* (SCM: 1972).

Davies, Michael, *The New Mass* (Augustine: Chawleigh, Devon, 1977).

Davies, Michael, *The Roman Rite Destroyed* (Augustine: Chawleigh, Devon, 1978).

Day, Thomas, *Why Catholics Can't Sing* (Crossroad: New York, 1990).

Ellsworth, L.E., *Charles Lowder and the Ritualist Movement* (Darton, Longman & Todd: 1982).

Every, George, *The Mass* (Gill & Macmillan: Dublin, 1978).

Fenn, Richard K., *Liturgies and Trials: The Secularization of Religious Language* (Blackwell: Oxford, 1982).

Furlong, Monica, *Merton: A Biography* (Collins: 1980).

Gamber, Klaus, *The Reform of the Roman Liturgy* (Una Voce: San Juan Capistrano, Calif.: 1993).

Hammond, Gerald, *The Making of the English Bible* (Carcanet: Manchester, 1982).

Harrison, D.E.W. and Sansom, Michael C., *Worship in the Church of England* (SPCK: 1982).

Hebert, A.G., *Liturgy and Society* (Faber: 1935).

Jasper, R.C.D., *The Development of the Anglican Liturgy 1662-1980* (SPCK: 1989).

Johnson, Paul, *Pope John Paul II and the Catholic Restoration* (Weidenfeld & Nicolson: 1982).

Jones, Cheslyn, Wainwright, Geoffrey & Yarnold, S.J. Edward (eds), *The Study of Liturgy*, (SPCK: 1978).

Kennedy, Douglas, *In God's Country: Travels in the Bible Belt, USA* (Unwin Hyman: 1989).

Kilmister, C.A. Anthony (ed.), *When Will Ye Be Wise? The State of the Church of England* (Blond & Briggs: 1983).

McSweeney, Bill, *Roman Catholicism: The Search for Relevance* (Blackwell: Oxford, 1980).

Martin, David, *The Breaking of the Image: A Sociology of Christian Theory and Practice* (Blackwell: Oxford, 1980).

Martin, David and Mullen, Peter (eds) *No Alternative: The Prayer Book Controversy* (Blackwell: Oxford, 1981).

Moore, Caroline, *Divisive Language* (Church in Danger: East Rudham, Norfolk [n.d. *circa* 1989]).
Moore, Charles, Wilson, A.N. and Stamp, Gavin, *The Church in Crisis* (Hodder & Stoughton: 1986).
Morris, Brian (ed.), *Ritual Murder* (Carcanet: Manchester, 1980).
Nowell, Robert (ed.), *Why I am Still a Catholic* (Collins: 1982).
Oddie, William, *The Crockford's File: Gareth Bennett and the Death of the Anglican Mind* (Hamish Hamilton: 1989).
Oddie, William, *What Will Happen to God? Feminism and the Reconstruction of Christian Belief* (SPCK: 1984).
Oddie, William (ed.), *After the Deluge: Essays Towards the Desecularization of the Church* (SPCK: 1978).
Pare, Philip and Harris, Donald, *Eric Milner-White 1884-1963: A Memoir* (SPCK: 1965).
Peart-Binns, John S., *Graham Leonard, Bishop of London* (Darton, Longman & Todd: 1988).
Perham, Michael (ed.), *Towards Liturgy 2000* (SPCK/Alcuin Club: 1989).
Perman, David, *Change and the Churches: An Anatomy of Religion in Britain* (Bodley: 1977).
Phillips, C.H., *The Singing Church* (Mowbray: 1979).
Prickett, Stephen, *Words and 'The Word'* (Cambridge University Press: 1986).
Ramsey, Ian, *Words about God: The Philosophy of Religion* (Harper & Row: New York, 1971).
Robinson, Edward, *The Language of Mystery* (SCM: 1987).
Robinson, Ian, *Prayers for the New Babel* (Brynmill: Worksop, 1982).
Routley, Erik, *Church Music and the Christian Faith* (Collins: 1978).
Sheldon, Robin (ed.), *In Spirit and in Truth* (Hodder & Stoughton: 1989).
Solignac, Pierre, *The Christian Neurosis*, trans. Jane Bowden (SCM: 1982).
Speagle, H.L. (ed.), *A Way of Life* (Prayer Book Society in Australia: Melbourne, 1989).
Spurr, Barry, 'When we Worship' (privately printed for The Prayer Book Society, NSW, 1981).
Spurr, Barry, 'Ecclesiastical Apostasy' (Anglican Board of Christian Education: Adelaide, 1983) (Republished in *Faith and Worship*, Summer 1984).
Spurr, Barry, 'The Language of Liturgy' (Christ Church Press: Brunswick, Vic., 1986). (Previously published in *Lex Orandi*, Winter 1986, and republished in *The Seabury Journal*, February 1986).
Tennyson, G.B., *Victorian Devotional Poetry: The Tractarian Mode*

(Harvard University Press: Cambridge, Mass., 1981).
Thompson, Bard (ed.), *Liturgies of the Western Church* (Fortress: Philadelphia, 1961).
Underhill, Evelyn, *Worship* (Nisbet: 1936).
Waugh, Evelyn, *Letters*, ed. Mark Amory (Penguin: Harmondsworth, 1982).
Whale, John, *One Church, One Lord* (SCM: 1979).
Wiles, Maurice, *Faith and the Mystery of God* (SCM: 1982).
Wright, T.R., *Theology and Literature* (Blackwell: Oxford, 1988).

# INDEX

**U**



**V**



**W**